THE PAPAL CURSE

THE PAPAL CURSE

The Medieval Origin of the European Syndrome

LAURENT GUYÉNOT

FOREWORD BY
ALAIN DE BENOIST

ARKTOS
LONDON 2026

To Naomi,
who grew up with this book,
and made its author grow.

ISBN
978-1-918418-17-0 (Paperback)
978-1-918418-18-7 (Hardback)
978-1-918418-19-4 (Ebook)

Editing
Jafe Arnold

Layout and Cover
Tor Westman

Contents

Foreword

by Alain de Benoist

IN THIS BOOK, which explains why Europe has never been able to structure itself politically in the form of an empire, Laurent Guyénot writes that "the *empire*, and not the nation, was the ultimate and unanimous ideal of political thinkers and of peoples throughout the Middle Ages." This is definitely the key sentence. It immediately raises the question: why was this ideal never achieved? Why did this "unanimous" desire never come to fruition? To understand the question, we obviously must bear in mind what an empire is in relation to other political forms (ancient cities, city-states, nation-states, etc.) attested in European history.

When we examine its political history, we quickly see that Europe has been the place where two major models of polity, or political society, have developed, evolved, and clashed: the nation, preceded by the kingdom, and the empire. At first glance, the concept of empire is not easy to define, given the often contradictory uses to which it has been put. Therefore, the best way to understand its true nature is undoubtedly to compare it to that of the nation or nation-state.

In the current sense of the term, that is, in the *political* sense, the nation appears to be an essentially modern phenomenon. In the Middle Ages, the word "nation" (from *natio*, "birth") had an exclusively ethnic meaning, not a political one: the *nationes* of the Sorbonne were simply groups of students who spoke different languages. The political idea of nation only fully took shape in the 18th century, particularly during the French Revolution. Originally, it referred to a concept of sovereignty professed by the opponents of royal absolutism. It brought together those who shared the same political and philosophical views, namely that "the nation," and no longer the king, should embody the political unity of the country. Article 3 of the 1789 Declaration of the Rights of Man and of the Citizen proclaimed this unequivocally: "The principle of all sovereignty resides essentially in the nation."

What fundamentally distinguishes the Empire from the nation? First, the Empire is not primarily a territory, but fundamentally a principle or an idea. The political order is determined not by material factors or the possession of a geographical area, but by a spiritual or political-legal idea. It would therefore be a mistake to imagine that the Empire differs from the nation primarily in size, that it is in some way "a nation larger than the others." "The Empire is more than an enlarged state," writes Carl Schmitt. Certainly, by definition, an empire covers a large area. But that is not the essential point. In the Middle Ages, a distinction was commonly made between the concept of *auctoritas,* or moral and spiritual superiority, and that of *potestas,* or simple public political power exercised by legal means. In the Carolingian Empire, as in the later Holy Roman Empire, this distinction underlies the dissociation between the authority specific to the imperial function and the authority held by the emperor as sovereign of a particular people. Charlemagne, for example, was both emperor and king of the Lombards and Franks. Allegiance to the emperor was therefore not a matter of submission to a particular people or country. In the Austro-Hungarian Empire, loyalty to the Habsburg dynasty still took precedence over national or religious ties. Empires, Carl Schmitt further explains, are "the leading powers carrying a political idea radiating in a large determined space, from which they exclude in principle the interventions of foreign powers."

The nation, on the contrary, finds its origin in the kingdom's will to claim prerogatives of sovereignty, relating them not to a principle but to a territory. The starting point for this can be traced back to the division of the Carolingian Empire by the Treaty of Verdun. It was at this point that France and Germany began to follow separate paths. The latter remained within the imperial tradition, while the Kingdom of the Franks (*regnum Francorum*) slowly evolved toward the modern nation through the royal state. In the 16th century, the formula that the king is "emperor in his kingdom" was directly associated with the new concept of sovereignty theorized by Jean Bodin.

But the opposition between spiritual principle and territorial power is not the only one that needs to be taken into account. Another essential difference lies in the way the Empire and the nation conceive of political unity. The unity of the Empire, whose earliest theorists were Marsilius of Padua, Dante, and Nicholas of Cusa, is a composite, organic unity that transcends the boundaries of states. Insofar as it embodies a principle, the Empire envisages unity only at the level of that principle. While the nation either generates its own culture or relies on a pre-existing culture to form itself, the Empire encompasses a variety of cultures. While the nation seeks to bring the people and the state into alignment, the Empire brings together different peoples. Its general law is that of autonomy and respect for diversity. The Empire seeks to unify at a higher level without suppressing the diversity of cultures, ethnic groups, and peoples. Its main characteristic is that it aims above all to articulate differences. Sovereignty is distributed, and ethnic, cultural, religious, and customary particularities are legally recognized as long as they do not contradict common law. As in Johannes Althusius' view, the application of the principle of subsidiarity is the rule. Since nationality is not synonymous with citizenship, the political people (*demos*) is not to be confused with the ethnic people (*ethnos*), but one does not stand in the way of the other. In other words, the imperial principle aims to reconcile the one and the many, the universal and the particular.

At the height of the Roman Empire, Rome itself was first and foremost an idea, a principle, one that enabled different peoples to be brought together without converting them or erasing their identity. The principle of *imperium*, which was already at work in Republican Rome, led to the acceptance of foreign cults and diverse legal codes. Roman law (*jus*) prevailed only in relations between individuals of different peoples or in relations between cities. One could call oneself a Roman citizen (*civis romanus sum*) without renouncing one's nationality.

As a supranational institution, the medieval Reich was fundamentally pluralistic. It allowed peoples to live their own national lives and retain their particular laws. The Austro-Hungarian Empire, to name but one example, functioned very effectively for several centuries, even though minorities made up the majority of its population (60 percent of the total), including Italians and Romanians as well as Jews, Serbs, Ruthenians, Germans, Poles, Czechs, Croats, and Hungarians.

What characterizes the national kingdom, on the contrary, is its irresistible tendency toward centralization and homogenization. The nation-state's investment in space was first manifested in the delimitation of a territory over which it exercised homogeneous political sovereignty. This homogeneity can first be grasped in the domain of law: territorial unity results from the uniformity of legal norms. The 14th and 15th centuries marked a turning point in this regard. It was during this period that the state emerged victorious from its struggle against the feudal aristocracies and sealed its alliance with the bourgeoisie, while at the same time establishing a centralized legal order.

There is no doubt that monarchical absolutism paved the way for the national bourgeois revolutions. The Revolution was inevitable once Louis XIV had broken the last resistance of the nobility, and the bourgeoisie could in turn conquer its autonomy. But there is also no doubt that, in many respects, the Revolution merely continued and accentuated trends that were already at work in the Ancient Régime. This is what Tocqueville observed when he wrote: "The French Revolution created a multitude of incidental and secondary things, but it only developed the seeds of the main things which existed before it… Among the French, the central government had already taken control of local administration more than in any other country in the world. The Revolution merely made this power more proficient, more compelling, and more resourceful."

Under both monarchy and republic, the logic of the nation-state tends to eliminate anything that might stand in the way between the central state and individuals. It aims to uniformly integrate individuals under the same laws, not to bring together communities preserving their language, culture, and traditions. The power of the state is exercised over individual subjects, which is why it consistently attempts to destroy or limit the prerogatives of all intermediate forms of socialization. With the Revolution, of course, the movement accelerated. The remodeling of the territory into roughly equal departments, the fight against "provincialism," the suppression of local particularities, the offensive against regional languages and "patois," and the standardization of weights and measures, all reflect a real obsession with alignment.

It should also be added that, unlike the nation, which over the centuries has become increasingly defined by tangible borders, the Empire never presented itself as a closed entity. Its borders were by nature shifting and provisional. It was during the Revolution that the idea of France's "natural borders" came to be asserted systematically. It was also during the Revolution that the idea began to spread throughout Europe that the borders of a state must correspond to those of a language, a political authority, and a nation.

Universal in principle and purpose, the Empire was not, however, universalist in the sense commonly given to the term. Its universality never meant that it was destined to extend to the entire world. Rather, it referred to the idea of a fair order aimed at uniting peoples within a given area of civilization, on the basis of a concrete political organization, without any prospect of leveling. From this point of view, the Empire is quite distinct from a hypothetical world state or the idea that there are legal and political principles that are universally valid at all times and in all places.

In our time, when "great spaces" and "civilizational states" are once again becoming essential concepts for thinking about international relations, when the Russian Empire and NATO forces are clashing in Ukraine, when Russia is ruled by a new Tsar, Turkey by a new Sultan, and China by a new Emperor, Empire might not have said its last word.

Introduction

In 1997, Zbigniew Brzezinski and Samuel Huntington agreed that "the sustained international primacy of the United States" is the best guarantee for world peace and prosperity: "A world without U.S. primacy will be a world with more violence and disorder and less democracy and economic growth than a world where the United States continues to have more influence than any other country in shaping global affairs."[1] A quarter of a century later, the proportion of people who might agree with this statement has probably shrunk dramatically. The desolation brought by the U.S. and NATO to Yugoslavia, Afghanistan, Iraq, Libya, Syria, Ukraine, and so many other regions of the world, makes those words sound like the voice an imperial hubris that constitutes precisely the greatest danger to stability and peace in the world. What was a rather radical political opinion twenty-five years ago is now clear to all: the collective West has gone mad.

The problem is that the West cannot diagnose itself. It vaguely realizes that it is sick, but it attributes its sickness to external causes. Even the most lucid Western analysts do not get to the bottom of things. Worse, many confuse the source of the problem with the remedy. According to the theses defended in this book, the source of the problem goes back to the very childhood of European civilization,

1 Samuel Huntington, "Why International Primacy Matters," 1993, quoted in Zbigniew Brzezinski, *The Grand Chessboard: American Primacy and its Geostrategic Imperatives*, Basic Books, 1997, p. 31. To be fair, that statement is not representative of the more nuanced view developed by Huntington in 1996 in *The Clash of Civilizations*.

when its peculiar character was formed, and the most important factor in shaping that character was the papacy. Between the 9th and the 16th centuries, and most intensely between the 11th and the 13th, the Roman Church launched Western Christendom on a path of fragmentation and chronic instability, messianic exaltation, and addiction to holy wars. Simply stated, the papacy influenced the infant soul of Europe like no other force did, for better or for worse.

This book is about the worse. But, to be fair, a word about the better part is in order. In my book *La Mort féerique* ("The Fairy Death"), I occasionally complained that we know so much about the way churchmen thought during the Middle Ages, but so little about the way laymen thought, although laymen represented more than ninety percent of the population. That is because clerics were, almost by definition, the only people who could write. And so our primary sources about the European Middle Ages are overwhelmingly clerical. We tend to see the Middle Ages through the eyes of medieval popes, bishops and monks. We can complain about it, but we must thank the Church for having any source at all. It is hard to imagine a civilization without a written language. So let us admit it: the Church nursed Western European civilization during its convalescence after the fall of the Western Roman Empire.

The Roman Church, however, went through various transformations. The most profound took place in the second half of the 11th century. The Gregorian Reform was, according to Marc Bloch, "an extraordinarily powerful movement from which, without exaggeration, may be dated the definite formation of Latin Christianity."[2] Robert Moore described it as the "first European revolution" — "revolution" meaning a radical, global and irreversible transformation of society, with a permanent impact on the collective psyche. What the popes accomplished in less than two centuries was to create "an entirely different world — a world pervaded and increasingly molded by the

---

2 Marc Bloch, *Feudal Society*, vol. 1: *The Growth of Ties of Dependence*, Routledge, 1962, p. 107.

well-drilled piety and obedience associated with the traditional vision of 'the age of faith,' or of medieval Christianity."[3]

The present book is about the influence of the papacy on European society from the 11th century onward. Before then, popes had a very limited, mostly regional influence. Aviad Kleinberg even wrote that, "Until the twelfth century, when the pope's status as the ultimate religious authority in matters of teaching and jurisdiction took hold, there was not any actual entity that could be called 'the church.'"[4] Until then, the Church had been different things in different places. In most places outside central Italy, the pope had no influence on the lives of Christians.

The papacy of the early second millennium, which launched the Crusades and the Inquisition, created something different from the Church that had sustained Europe in the first millennium. The Orthodox understand this change as a betrayal, and no one has better expressed that view than Fyodor Dostoevsky, when he wrote that Roman Catholicism "has proclaimed a new Christ, not like the former one, but one who has been seduced by the third temptation of the devil — the temptation of the kingdoms of the world: 'All these things will I give thee if thou wilt fall down and worship me!'" By "Roman Catholicism" is not meant Western popular piety, but the powerful transnational state known as the Roman Curia. Writing a few years after Pope Pius X proclaimed the dogma of "papal infallibility," Dostoevsky paraphrased the pope's demonic claim in this way: "So you thought that I was satisfied with the mere title of King of the Papal State? Know that I have always considered myself potentate of the whole world and over all earthly kings, and not only the spiritual, but their mundane, genuine master, sovereign and emperor. It is I who am king over all kings, and sovereign over all sovereigns, and to

3 Robert I. Moore, *The First European Revolution, c. 970–1215*, Basil Blackwell, 2000, p. 174.

4 Aviad Kleinberg, *Flesh Made Word: Saints' Stories and the Western Imagination*, Belknap Press, 2008, p. 50.

me alone on earth belong the destinies, the ages and the bounds of time."[5] As we shall see, Dostoevsky was not exaggerating. Gregory VII (1073–85), who gave his name to the "Gregorian Reform," postulated in his *Dictatus papae* that "the pope alone can use the imperial insignia," and that "all princes are to kiss the feet of the pope alone."

Today, the West has long been de-Christianized, but its mindset has remained marked by these formative years. The West never got over the trauma of the second-millennium papacy. In fact, there is a striking resemblance between the new assertion that the primacy of the United States is necessary for the welfare of the world and the old assertion that "it is absolutely necessary for the salvation of every human creature to be subject to the Roman pontiff" (Pope Boniface VIII, *Unam sanctam*, 1302). There is also a certain resemblance in the means employed to impose this primacy and to overcome resistance. These resemblances are not accidental; they are the result of a direct filiation.

In this book, I analyze the deep and lasting impact of the medieval papacy on the character of the West in four complementary theses.

In the first and longest chapter, "Failed Empire," I establish that the most obvious problem of Europe, its inability to form a legitimate, unified political body, and its resultant chronic state of civil war, is a legacy of the struggle of medieval popes against the only power capable of achieving this unity: the central continental "Roman Empire" of the German kings.

In Chapter II, "Fools' Crusade," I explain that the popes' holy wars in the Middle East and elsewhere distracted Europe from its organic political growth, and that they still determine the way the West sees the rest of the world and its role in it. The West has remained, to this day, the civilization of the Crusades.

5 Feodor Dostoievsky, *The Diary of a Writer*, Charles Scribner's Sons, 1919, "March 1876," p. 255.

In Chapter III, "New Romes," I argue that the West suffers from the repression of its guilt in the fall of the Byzantine Empire, and of its immense cultural debt to it. The erasure of Byzantine civilization from Western historiography has generated a geopolitical bias among Westerners that makes them incapable of understanding the Middle East, Asia, and Russia.

In Chapter IV, "Weird West," I show that the deadly virus of individualism has been injected into the West by a doctrine of salvation which places the individual man alone in front of the individual God, makes the faithful a subject rather than a member of the Church, and wages war against blood solidarities and ancestor veneration.

This book does not pretend to give a balanced view of the role of the papacy in European Medieval history. I do not deny that the formidable structure of the Roman Church had positive effects. But that is not the subject of this book. Its goal is to show that the "Western syndrome," whose symptoms are getting more pronounced with each passing year, dates back to a civilizational trajectory driven by the medieval papacy.

I

Failed Empire: The Origin of the European Disunion

EUROPE WAS A civilization. From Charlemagne until the 16th century, European civilization was "Christendom." It had Rome as its capital, and Latin as its language. But that unity was, in theory, purely religious. Rome was the seat of the papacy, and Latin the language of the Church, known only to a tiny minority. Europe therefore had a religious unity, but it had no political unity. Unlike all other civilizations, Europe never matured into a unified political body. In other words, Europe has never been an empire in any form. After the failure of the Carolingian Empire, too brief and too obscure for us to distinguish the reality from the legend, Europe progressively crystallized into a mosaic of independent and rival states. The outlines of these national states, which would become "nation-states" in the 19th century, were formed in the 13th century.

In addition to their common religion, the principalities of Europe were united throughout the Middle Ages by their sovereigns' blood ties, resulting from a diplomacy of marriage. But this community of faith and blood did not prevent the European states from being separate political entities, jealous of their sovereignty and always eager to extend their borders. In the absence of an overarching imperial authority, this rivalry engendered an almost permanent state of war. Europe is an ever-smoldering battlefield. Historian and political scientist Charles Tilly has calculated that between 1500 and 1800, European polities were at war for 80–90 percent of the time, and that matters were even worse during the preceding 500 years. England alone was at war for about half of the time from 1100 to 1900.[1]

If we think of Europe as one single civilization, then we have to think of its deadly wars as civil wars. German historian Ernst Nolte did just that for the two global conflicts of the 20th century, which he saw as one long "European Civil War."[2] Neither common religion nor family ties prevented European civilization from tearing itself apart with unheard-of hatred and violence. Remember that on the eve of the First World War, King George V, Kaiser Wilhelm II and Tsar Nicolas II were first cousins and all defenders of the Christian faith. On the eve of WWI, for both the old aristocracy and the new moneyed elites, "Europe was a single entity and national borders mattered but little to them," as Hans Vogel writes.[3] Yet there was no higher authority to arbitrate their quarrels and prevent the bloodshed they caused.

In the interwar period, the European ideal of unity in diversity (the "concert of nations") leaned toward greater uniformity, with the model of the "United States of Europe" penned by the Austrian Richard Coudenhove-Kalergi (*Pan-Europa*, 1923), by which he meant the abolition of borders from the Atlantic to the Black Sea. It never got traction. After WWII came the "European construction" with the aim of making European wars impossible or at least improbable. But the European Union was founded on a purely economic basis, starting in 1951 with the European Coal and Steel Community. This may have made war less likely, but a free market alone cannot engender political unity. Instead, it stripped the nations of their sovereignties

1 Charles Tilly, *Cities and the Rise of States in Europe, A.D. 1000 to 1800*, Westview Press, 1994.

2 Ernst Nolte, *Der Europäische Bürgerkrieg 1917–1945. Nationalismus und Bolschewismus*, Herbig, 2000.

3 Hans Vogel, *How Europe Became American*, Arktos, 2024, p. 76.

and handed them not to a legitimate supranational state, but to a monster of bureaucratic corruption and incompetence that makes every European hate Europe. Realistically, only a victory of the Third Reich in WWII could have led to the political unity of Europe, since Great Britain was only interested in keeping the continent divided. After WWII, the European project was an anachronism, because European civilization was already dead, with no vital energy left to resist being colonized by the new, dynamic, self-confident American empire. Ironically, English has become Europe's *de facto* international language, even though England has never been fully integrated into Europe. The supremacy of English is only a manifestation of America's cultural colonialism.

The European Union is not supported by any "civilizational consciousness." Many people still feel organically and spiritually connected to their nation, sensing, as Ernest Renan once said, that "a nation is a soul, a spiritual principle" (*Qu'est-ce qu'une nation?* 1882). But no one feels such a connection to Europe, because Europe is not perceived as a spiritual being endowed with an individuality, a will, and a destiny of its own. There has never been a great European narrative to unite in shared pride all the peoples crammed in the European peninsula. Each country has its little *roman national*, ignored or contradicted by those of its neighbors. This point was well put by Christopher Dawson in *The Making of Europe*. Although European civilization is "a concrete social organism," he writes:

> modern history has usually been written from the nationalist point of view. Some of the greatest of the nineteenth-century historians were also apostles of the cult of nationalism, and their histories are often manuals of nationalist propaganda. … In the course of the nineteenth century this movement permeated the popular consciousness and determined the ordinary man's conception of history. It has filtered down from the university to the elementary school, and from the scholar to the journalist and the novelist. And the result is that each nation claims for itself a cultural unity and self-sufficiency that it does not possess. Each regards its share in the

> European tradition as an original achievement that owes nothing to the rest, and takes no heed of the common foundation in which its own individual tradition is rooted. And it is no mere academic error. It has undermined and vitiated the whole international life of modern Europe.

Writing in 1932, Dawson added: "Yet if our civilization is to survive it is essential that it should develop a common European consciousness and a sense of its historic and organic unity."[4] Not only has that hope not been realized, but today it sounds like empty rhetoric.

There certainly exist some shared myths in European culture. Charlemagne is one example, but the French and the Germans each have their own version of him (he is Karl der Grosse for the Germans). The partition of his empire in 843 is interpreted not as a failure, but as the birth of France, Italy, and Germany. And every monarch after him who pursued the dream of re-creating a European Empire is judged as a reactionary only delaying the inevitable emergence of the sovereign nation-states.

The other big European myth is that of the Crusade. But the Crusades illustrate precisely the inability of Europeans to unite on a project for Europe. By the Crusades, the popes sent Europeans to conquer a city in a distant part of the world that was already coveted by two other civilizations (the Byzantine and the Islamic). Europeans were told that Jerusalem was the spiritual cradle of their civilization. There could not be a more anti-European project. The Crusades, in fact, only exported national rivalries into the Middle East. Sure, they make a good story, but it is really a great lie, since their only lasting results were the fragmentation of Eastern Christendom and the reunification of the Islamic world, ultimately into a new, powerful empire that would chip away parts of Europe towards the end of the Middle Ages (more on the Crusades in Chapter II).

---

4 Christopher Dawson, *The Making of Europe: An Introduction to the History of European Unity*, Meridian, 1956, pp. 19–21.

The Middle Ages, anyway, are the beginning and the end of the European grand narrative. After that, the average Frenchman knows almost nothing about the history of Germany, because he is taught the history of France and a little world history, but never the history of Europe. Basically, for most people, the notion of a "European civilization" calls to mind the Middle Ages and nothing else. And that's logical. Europe was a brilliant civilization during the central Middle Ages (11th–13th centuries). But because this medieval civilization did not embody itself politically into an empire, it fragmented into several micro-civilizations, each playing its own imperial game against the others. And so we had, in the 19th century, a French Empire, a British Empire, and a German Empire, all trying to outdo each other. They were colonial empires: having failed to create a European Empire, European powers exported their rivalries in predatory conquests on every other continent. Great Britain, in particular, created a worldwide "empire on which the sun never sets." Ultimately, European peoples colonized the New World and gave birth to the United States of America, an empire born in genocide and the most brutal slave trade, fated to bring the plague back on its genitors.

In the 20th century, Europe felt so little like an organism that when the USSR tore off its eastern part, Western Europeans felt no pain, as Milan Kundera lamented in his memorable 1983 essay, "A Kidnapped West": "The disappearance of the cultural home of Central Europe was certainly one of the greatest events of the century for all of Western civilization. … How could it possibly have gone unnoticed and unnamed? The answer is simple: Europe hasn't noticed the disappearance of its cultural home because Europe no longer perceives its unity as a cultural unity."[5] In reality, the problem was not about cultural unity. Only political unity could have kept Europe together, for there can be no political will without political unity.

5 Milan Kundera, "The Tragedy of Central Europe," *New York Review of Books*, April 26, 1984.

The Emperor and the Pope

In the 21st century, wrote Samuel Huntington in 1996, "The world will be ordered on the basis of civilizations or not at all." In this emerging "civilization-based world order," "countries group themselves around the lead or core states of their civilization."[6] Thirty years later, this idea has gained wide acceptance. A multipolar world is indeed being born, despite U.S. efforts to kill it in the womb.

How will Europe fit in that world? Europe is a civilization, but it has no "core state." It has always resisted having one. The European Union was actually founded after World War II on the explicit rejection of the notion of a core state. Because Europe wants to be a multipolarity by itself, it cannot be a pole in global multipolarity. And so, according to Christopher Coker, author of *The Rise of the Civilizational State*, "Europeans cannot become a civilizational state. The fault lines across Europe have settled the question."[7] Europe is a failed civilizational state. It is incapable of playing a part in the new emerging multipolar world order, because it is not a unified "pole" with a civilizational field of its own, let alone with a voice of its own. As for European nations separately, they are not players in this game. The notion of their "sovereignty" may have had some meaning as long as they were parceling domination over other continents, but it is now an empty slogan. This is the conclusion of the French sociologist and demographer Emmanuel Todd in *The Defeat of the West* (2024). Questioning the axiom of the "nation-state" which has dominated geopolitical discourse since the second half of the 19th century (implicit in the very charter of the United "Nations"), Todd proposes "a post-Euclidean interpretation of world geopolitics," based not on

---

6 Samuel P. Huntington, *The Clash of Civilizations and the Remaking of World Order,* Simon & Schuster, 1996, pp. 156, 20.

7 Christopher Coker, *The Rise of the Civilizational State,* Polity, 2019. Interview for the French magazine *Éléments,* April-May 2023, p. 78.

nation-states, but on their disappearance. In this new competition, the European disunion is the forgone loser.[8]

The big question therefore remains: Why has Europe never reached the maturity of an imperial state, which would have made its kingdoms, duchies, and counties parts of a great unified organism, with a will and a voice of its own—and, today, the possibility of an independent destiny? It is not for lack of an ambition for this unity. Europe has longed to be an empire, but it has not succeeded. Sovereigns, intellectuals, and peoples have aspired to this ideal, synonymous in their eyes with peace and prosperity. This is well documented by Robert Folz in *The Concept of Empire in Western Europe from the Fifth to the Fourteenth Century*: the empire, and not the nation, was the ultimate and unanimous ideal of political thinkers and of peoples throughout the Middle Ages.[9] This aspiration should not be understood anachronistically, however. As Ernst Kantorowicz explains in his outstanding biography of Frederick II Hohenstaufen: "The ideal World-Empire of the Middle Ages did not involve the subjection of all peoples under the dominion of one. It stood for the community of all kings and princes, of all the lands and peoples of Christendom, under one Roman Emperor who should belong to no nation, and who, standing outside all nations, should rule all from his throne in the one Eternal City."[10] One of the reasons Frederick stood as the most brilliant incarnation of this ideal was his international background, culture, and vision.

Even after his death and the extermination of his progeny by the pope's henchmen, the dream lived on. The Empire was a metaphysical being, the very image of God, as Dante Alighieri argued around 1310 with this beautiful thought: "the human race is most like unto

8 Emmanuel Todd, *La Défaite de l'Occident,* Gallimard, 2024, pp. 24–25.

9 Robert Folz, *The Concept of Empire in Western Europe from the Fifth to the Fourteenth Century,* Edward Arnold, 1969.

10 Ernst Kantorowicz, *Frederick the Second (1194–1250)* (1931) Frederick Ungar Publishing, 1957, p. 385.

God when it is most one, for the principle of unity dwells in Him alone. … the human race is most one when all are united together, a state which is manifestly impossible unless humanity as a whole becomes subject to one Prince, and consequently comes most into accordance with that divine intention…" (*De Monarchia* I,8).[11]

If Europe longed to be an empire, then what curse prevented it from becoming one? Caspar Hirschi has attempted to answer that question in *The Origins of Nationalism*. His explanation is that the competition between several powers for imperial supremacy was never won by any, but froze into a chronic state of conflict between rival imperial ambitions, a permanent clash of nations: "an imperialist political culture, dictated by the ideal of a single universal power inherited from Roman Antiquity, coexisted within a fragmented territorial structure, where each of the major powers was of similar strength (Empire, Papacy, France, England and later Aragon). In the realm of Roman Christianity, this led to an intense and endless competition for supremacy; all major kingdoms aimed for universal dominion, yet prevented each other from achieving it." National states were the unintentional result of this failure, and nationalism is nothing but "a political discourse constructed by chronically failing would-be-empires stuck in a battle to keep each other at bay."[12]

But this explanation only pushes the question further back: what mechanism prevented one power from winning the competition for empire? After all, virtually all empires were born from such competition. Only Western Europe failed to reach this stage, remaining a civilization without a central state, like a body without a head—or worse, with multiple heads biting at each other. What happened? Or rather, what didn't happen? Hirschi's thesis lacks an explanation of the inhibiting factor that prevented the unification of Europe. But

11 *De Monarchia of Dante Alighieri*, trans. Aurelia Henry, Boston, 1904, pp. 26–27.

12 Caspar Hirschi, *The Origins of Nationalism: An Alternative History from Ancient Rome to Early Modern Germany*, Cambridge UP, 2012, pp. 14, 2.

there is also an error in his perception of the European dynamic. The competition for the empire was not, as he writes, between "Empire, Papacy, France, England and later Aragon." Until the middle of the 11th century, only the Germans' so-called Roman Empire claimed imperial sovereignty. Then one single other independent power started to compete with it for political supremacy: the papacy. From then on, every pope strove to put the emperor under his supervision on the one hand, and to consolidate the competing states on the other, while preventing any of them from becoming dominant. Quite plainly, the pope wanted to force all European powers under his suzerainty.

For more than two centuries, the competition between emperor and pope dominated European politics, from the chancelleries to the battlefields. The whole of Europe was drawn into that struggle. No other factor is comparable in importance in the High Middle Ages. In the 13th century, the papacy got the upper hand. "The Roman Curia," wrote Michael Mitterauer, "was the most elaborate administrative apparatus in medieval Europe; no secular administration could come anywhere near it." It was truly the "first Western state." Its cultural and political domination was felt in the four corners of Europe.[13] Yet it was defeated at the start of the next century by the French king, who had taken advantage of the struggle between Rome and the German empire to build his own centralized state. Ultimately, neither the emperor nor the pope were able to reign over Europe. It was only in the 14th century, when the Holy Roman Empire had been reduced to one European state among others, that France, Spain, and England, began to manifest imperial inclinations of their own and entered a competition that could only lead, from that time on, to a stalemate, and a permanently divided Europe.

It can therefore be said that the papacy, by clipping the German empire's wings and reducing it to the rank of one European state among many, created this unstable equilibrium that Europe has

13 Michael Mitterauer, *Why Europe?: The Medieval Origins of Its Special Path*, University of Chicago Press, 2010, p. 150.

become. The political action of the popes from the time of the Gregorian Reform in the 11th century is the single reason why Europe could not lay the foundations of its political unity. The popes deliberately and persistently prevented the expansion of the Germanic empire, which styled itself the "Roman Empire" and was, for geographical as well as historical reasons — and perhaps anthropological reasons as well — the only political power capable of unifying Europe. In the process, the papacy consolidated other emerging states, all the while playing one against the other to prevent any of them from prevailing. For example, after supporting Philip Augustus against Otto IV and John Lackland at the Battle of Bouvines in 1214, the pope took the side of John against Philip and forbade the latter to land in England.

The popes' "balance-of-power policy" was a means and not an end. Their ultimate goal was to create not a "Europe of nations," but a papal empire. Their project had been first conceived by a group of intellectuals whose most prominent figure was the Cluniac monk Hildebrand, who became pope under the name of Gregory VII in 1073. The outlines of his program are contained in the twenty-seven propositions of his famous *Dictatus Papae*, in which we read: "2. Only the Bishop of Rome is by law called universal. 3. He alone can depose or reinstate bishops. … 8. He alone may use the imperial insignia. 9. The Pope is the only man whose feet shall be kissed by all princes. … 12. He may depose Emperors. … 19. He must not be judged by anyone. … 22. The Roman church has never erred, nor, as witness Scripture, will ever do so."

This goal remained unchanged for two centuries. One hundred and thirty years after Gregory VII, Innocent III declared that he sat "above kings on the throne of God's glory" because "The Lord gave to Peter not only the lordship over the universal Church, but also over the whole world." The means employed to turn those words into reality show that they were not mere rhetoric. To subdue the sovereigns who resisted his suzerainty, the pope brandished two swords:

by the "spiritual sword," he could excommunicate his enemy, which amounted to canceling any loyalty sworn to him; and by the "temporal sword," he could mobilize armies against him. Innocent III's record includes the excommunication of one emperor, seven kings, and countless lords. "It was his ambition," wrote Thomas Tout in *The Empire and the Papacy*, "to bind as many as he could of the kings of Europe to the Papacy by ties of political vassalage."[14] And so he appeared to his contemporary Gervase of Tilbury as the *verus imperator*, the true emperor above the nominal one. His influence over princely and public opinion was unparalleled. Innocent III's modern biographer Jane Sayers writes: "The chancery was used as a propaganda machine perhaps as never before. ... At least some 6,000 letters are likely to have been issued during Innocent III's reign. ... Letters exhorted, corrected and broadcast excommunications. They found their way into all parts of Europe and all were trumpets of power."[15]

And yet, contrary to the empire of the German kings, whose growth seemed to obey an organic necessity, the imperial project of the Vatican had no chance of lasting success, because it had no historical, rational, legal, or scriptural legitimacy. Its main justification was a forgery: the Donation of Constantine, by which the popes fraudulently declared themselves owners of the Western *Imperium* under the fake signature of Roman Emperor Constantine the Great (to be discussed further below).

The Endless European Civil War

The first setback was a famous slap inflicted on Boniface VII in 1303, after he had told Philip IV of France: "Those who persuade you that you have no superiors and that you are not subject to the supreme hierarch of the Church are deceiving you and are outside the fold of the Good Shepherd" (bull *Ausculta fili,* December 5, 1301). Boniface

14 T. F. Tout, *The Empire and the Papacy (918–1273)*, 1903, p. 325.

15 Jane Sayers, *Innocent III, Leader of Europe,* Pearson, 1993, pp. 99–100.

had overplayed his hand by declaring, *ego sum Caesar, ego imperator.* Philip had him judged posthumously for heresy, sodomy, and sorcery, and moved the papacy to Avignon. In the next century, Bohemia attempted to break away from the papacy. German princes then responded to Luther's call *To the Christian Nobility of the German Nation* (1520). England took advantage of the movement to nationalize her own church, while France ultimately decided to be the faithful "eldest daughter of the Church," French "Gallicanism" remaining a half-measure compared to Anglicanism.

In England, as in Germany, the Protestant Reformation was primarily a movement of national emancipation from the papacy, comparable to a struggle for decolonization. The papacy was denounced as a foreign and exploitative power. In his *Letter Concerning Toleration* published anonymously in Holland in 1689, the Englishman John Locke simply called for a ban on Catholicism on the following grounds: "That Church can have no right to be tolerated by the magistrate which is constituted upon such a basis that all those who enter into it do thereby ipso facto deliver themselves up to the protection and service of another prince. For by this means the magistrate would give way to the settling of a foreign jurisdiction in his own country and suffer his own people to be listed, as it were, for soldiers against his own Government." The accusation was in no way rhetorical: to the extent that the pope governed a state in the Italian peninsula, he was indeed, for any other state, a foreign monarch, and his bishops foreign agents.

From the moment that, for lack of a secular empire, independent national states were formed in Europe, the days of the papacy as a supra-national power were numbered. The papal empire failed, but its lasting achievement is to have stood in the way of the only empire that could have succeeded, leaving Europe divided by both national interests and religious creeds.

Is that disunion a failure? One could, after all, see in the European order of nation-states some great progress. Two questions must be distinguished. Was the political unity of Europe even possible, absent the opposition of the papacy? And was it desirable? The first question can be answered by an objective assessment of the historical forces leading in that direction. That implies renouncing the teleological perspective developed by 19th-century nationalist historians such as the Prussian Leopold von Ranke, whose task, as Peter H. Wilson writes in *Heart of Europe*, was "to record their national story" by constructing "linear narratives based around the centralization of political power or their people's emancipation from foreign domination." From this perspective, Ranke interpreted the history of the Holy Roman Empire, which was abolished in 1806, as a story of failed nation-building.[16] In this chapter, I make the opposite argument that the formation of the national states is a story of failed empire-building.

The answer to the second question—was Europe's imperial unity desirable?—depends on the point of view. The nationalist will say that it is fortunate that Europe was not an empire, for then nations would not have existed—at least not as sovereign polities. With an empire, there would perhaps have been a Europe of regions, perhaps a Europe of nationalities, but certainly not a Europe of nations as nationalists imagine it. Therefore, as Walter Scheidel sees it in *Escape from Rome*, polycentrism, or "the competitive fragmentation of power," and "the enduring absence of hegemonic empire on a subcontinental scale," was "the single most important precondition for modern economic growth, industrialization, and global Western dominance much later on."[17] Eric Jones has made the same argument in *The European Miracle*. To prove that multiple, competing states are more innovative than empires, he cites the examples of the city-states in ancient Greece and the city-states in Renaissance Italy, which

16 Peter H. Wilson, *Heart of Europe: A History of the Holy Roman Empire*, Belknap Press, 2020, pp. 2–3, 8.

17 Walter Scheidel, *Escape from Rome: The Failure of Empire and the Road to Prosperity*, Princeton UP, 2019.

have been unusually dynamic in art, politics, and military technology.[18] However, as Jack Goldstone retorts: "For 200 years, from AD 750 to 950, most of the Muslim world was unified under the rule of the Abbasid Caliphate, with its magnificent capital Baghdad. There, the caliphs, or rulers, had assembled not only great wealth and outstanding craftspeople, but also the foremost scholars of the Muslim world."[19] Competition cannot, therefore, be seen as the necessary condition for innovation.

Competition certainly can be a factor in some fields. In *Why the West Rules — For Now,* Ian Morris takes the example of oversea navigation and the discovery of the New World: "no one now disputes that when Europe's great age of maritime discovery was just beginning, Chinese navigation was far more advanced and Chinese sailors already knew the coasts of India, Arabia, East Africa, and perhaps Australia. When the eunuch admiral Zheng He sailed from Nanjing for Sri Lanka in 1405, he led nearly three hundred vessels. ... By contrast, when Christopher Columbus sailed from Cadiz in 1492, he led just ninety men in three ships." The key difference is that Zheng's was an imperial expedition, and for some reason, in the 1430s, the Chinese emperor banned oceanic voyages, ending the great age of Chinese exploration. "In fragmented Europe, by contrast, monarch after monarch could reject Columbus's crazy proposal, but he could always find someone else to ask." Morris adds, "We might speculate that if Zheng had had as many options as Columbus, Hernán Cortés might have met a Chinese governor in Mexico in 1519, not the doomed Montezuma."[20]

---

18 Eric Jones, *The European Miracle: Environments, Economies and Geopolitics in the History of Europe and Asia,* Cambridge UP, 2003.

19 Jack Goldstone, *Why Europe?: The Rise of the West in World History, 1500–1850,* McGraw Hill, 2009, p. 141.

20 Ian Morris, *Why the West Rules — For Now: The Patterns of History and What They Reveal About the Future,* Farrar, Straus & Giroux, 2010, pp. 28–30.

A similar argument has been made about armaments by William McNeill in *The Pursuit of Power*. The Chinese were far advanced in armaments. They had gunpowder since about 1000 and guns by 1300. But Chinese emperors felt no incentive to industrialize these innovations. In the West, the constant state of war between states greatly stimulated the development of military technology. The commercialization and the industrialization of war began in the 11th century, whereafter "Technological and organizational innovation continued, allowing Europeans to outstrip other peoples of the earth more and more emphatically until the globe-girdling imperialism of the 19th century became as cheap and easy for Europeans as it was catastrophic to Asians, Africans, and the peoples of Oceania."[21]

One may ask, therefore: What did the rest of the world gain from the West's naval and military supremacy, regardless of whether or not it resulted from the competitive fragmentation orchestrated by the papacy? One could also ask: What good did it do for the West itself? The above-quoted British historian Thomas Tout wrote : "The conflict of Papacy and Empire ... made possible the growth of the great national states of the 13th century, from which the ultimate salvation of Europe was to come."[22] Tout was writing before World War I, so his optimism can be excused. But still, what "ultimate salvation of Europe" was he talking about? That of a Europe set on fire and drowned in bloodshed during the Hundred Years' War (1337–1453), the Italian Wars (1494–1559), then the Thirty Years' War (1618–48), followed by the Seven Years' War (1756–63), which may be counted as the first world war on account of its extension into America and India?

The long and bloody Hundred Years' War, which consisted for a large part in the destruction of civilian life, is classically regarded as

21 William H. McNeill, *The Pursuit of Power: Technology, Armed Forces, and Society since A.D. 1000*, University of Chicago Press, 1982, p. 143.

22 Tout, *The Empire and the Papacy, op. cit.*, pp. 2, 6.

the matrix of English and French national identities.[23] Significantly, its end coincided with the fall of Constantinople to the Turks. Enea Silvio Piccolomini, who would become pope five years later, lamented: "Christianity has no longer a head: neither Pope nor Emperor is adequately esteemed or obeyed; they are treated as fictitious names and painted figures." There was no hope that European rulers would join forces to repel the Turks, for every country thought only either of protecting itself from its neighbors, or taking revenge against them, while "the Germans are greatly divided and have nothing to unify them."[24] Europe was torn by so many overlapping wars that it is hard to keep track of them. Who but the Poles and the Lithuanians know today of the Polish-Lithuanian-Teutonic War and of the Battle of Grunwald (1410), one of the largest in medieval Europe?

In 1536, during the Italian Wars which pitted François I against Emperor Charles V, the French king allied himself with the Ottomans, who had already conquered part of Europe and besieged Vienna, with this justification: "I cannot deny that I very much want to see the Turk powerful and ready for war, not for his own sake, for he is an infidel and the rest of us are Christians, but to erode the power of the Emperor and involve him in crippling expense." The English king Henry VIII, for his part, regretted that joining forces against the Turks was out of the question, "so long as such treachery prevails among the Christian powers that their sole thought is to destroy one another." In 1559, the French political philosopher Louis Le Roy pleaded with Christian rulers to end hostilities, lamenting that "Europe is soaked in her own blood … as though in answer to Mohammedan prayers."[25]

---

23 Colette Beaune, *Naissance de la nation France*, Gallimard, 1985; George Minois, *La Guerre de Cent Ans. Naissance de deux nations*, Perrin, 2010, p. 12.

24 John Hale, *The Civilization of Europe in the Renaissance*, Fontana Press, 1994, pp. 102–103.

25 *Ibid.*, pp. 40, 132, 6.

In the next century, the Thirty Years' War was fueled by Cardinal Richelieu, who financed and armed the Protestants (Lutherans as well as Calvinists) in order to ruin the empire of the Catholic Habsburgs. By uniting Spain and the Holy Roman Empire, the Habsburgs had created the largest political European entity ever. It had to be destroyed, Richelieu wrote in his memoirs, "for the good of the Church and Christianity, because the universal monarchy, to which the King of Spain aspires, is very harmful to Christianity, to the Church and to the pope."[26]

The Thirty Years' War was the birth pang of a Europe that no longer had anything Christian about it. "In the space of three decades," writes Arnaud Blin, "the medieval idea of a unified Christian Europe gave way to a political chessboard governed by a new mechanism of international relations based on the balance of power and the amoralism of realpolitik."[27] "Unity in diversity" became the ideal of most European political philosophers after the Peace of Westphalia (1648) which put an end to Germany's imperial pretensions. Edward Gibbon, Montesquieu, Voltaire, David Hume, and Friedrich Schiller would all share in that ideal. Hume in particular, in his *Political Discourses* (1758), celebrated European fragmentation as the spur of natural emulation between neighbors.

But the hypocrisy of France soon became obvious: no sooner had it ruined imperial Germany under Louis XIII than it dreamed itself as the new imperial power under Louis XIV. Hence the alarm sounded in 1667 by a servant of the House of Austria, François-Paul de Lisola, in a book denouncing the French's "design of universal monarchy."[28]

26 Quoted in Arnaud Blin, *1648, La Paix de Westphalie, ou la naissance de l'Europe politique moderne,* Éditions Complexe, 2006, pp. 70–71.

27 *Ibid.*, pp. 5–6.

28 Bruno Arcidiacono, *Cinq types de paix. Une histoire des plans de pacification perpétuelle (XVIIe–XXe siècles),* Graduate Institute Publications, 2015, pp. 1–74.

War had become the permanent condition of Europe, its very life. As John Hale notes in *The Civilization of Europe in the Renaissance*: "By the early seventeenth century James I of England earned mockery as 'the wisest fool in Christendom' partly because of his belief that rulers could learn to live in amity in spite of differences in their religious creeds and historical claims and grudges."[29]

Large states have an inherent tendency to expand, and Europe's largest states, far from being satisfied with a balance of power, engaged in implacable competition. What the Peace of Westphalia inaugurated is perfectly captured by Montesquieu exactly a century later in *L'Esprit des Lois* (1748):

> A new disease has broken out in Europe: it has infected our rulers and caused them to maintain armies which are out of all proportion. It has its recurrences and soon becomes contagious; inevitably, because as soon as one state increased the number of its troops, as they are called, the others at once increase theirs, so that the general ruin is all that comes out of it. Every monarch keeps permanently on foot armies which are as large as would be needed if his people were in imminent danger of extermination; and this struggle of all against all is called peace.[30]

It is from this sad observation that, fifty years later, in his *Towards Perpetual Peace* (1795), Kant came up with his project of a "league of republican nations." He hoped for a peace in Europe that would be more than a temporary cessation of hostilities, which was the only thing possible as long as nations only obeyed the "state of nature." Kant therefore wanted to make nations obey some international law of his own making. Two and a half centuries after his treatise, which is considered the cornerstone of the "international relations theory," the outcome is disappointing, to say the least.

---

29 Hale, *The Civilization of Europe in the Renaissance, op. cit*, p. 102.

30 *L'Esprit des Lois*, XIII,17, quoted in Bertrand de Jouvenel, *On Power: Its Nature and the History of Its Growth*, Beacon Press, 1962, p. 383.

In between the two world wars of the 20th century, Marcus Elie Ravage wrote in *The Malady of Europe* that each European state seemed to be less concerned with its own people than with its relation with other states:

> Its pivotal department is its foreign office. ... And, judged by its foreign relations, the European state is essentially a predatory organization... [In every European country] a small invisible clique in frock-coats and top-hats can, when they choose—and for reasons that the masses of the people do not understand and do not even as much as know—send the barefooted illiterate peasant and the spectacled university student to their death. The mental state of the European peoples has produced a vicious circle in their inter-relations. Wars have assumed a serial character. They interlock like links in a chain. One quarrel leads to another in the nature of the thing, by a sort of fatality. Wars in Europe are, in the nature of its history and political organization, inevitable. Whether they should be let loose to-day or to-morrow lies purely with the prospective antagonists.[31]

The Westphalian system never worked because European states circumvented it by entering into military alliances, which in turn had the effect of globalizing their local conflicts. To speak only of the Second World War, it was the Anglo-Polish agreement of 1939 that pushed Poland to reject compromise with Hitler on the Danzig question, which in turn motivated the German-Soviet pact and the invasion of Poland, which forced England to declare war on Germany, which forced France to join the war on the side of Great Britain because of a military alliance; and it was the tripartite pact that forced Germany to unite with Japan and declare war on the U.S. in December 1941. Thus, the system of military alliances transformed a local territorial conflict into a world war. This demonstration could be repeated for virtually all European armed conflicts from the 17th century onwards.

Failing to achieve political unity, European states were turned into military monsters. Bertrand de Jouvenel analyzed this development

31 Marcus Elie Ravage, *The Malady of Europe*, Macmillan, 1923, pp. 49–65.

in his memorable essay *On Power*, written in the aftermath of the Second World War: "if we arrange in chronological order the various wars which have for nearly a thousand years ravaged our Western World, one thing must strike us forcibly: that with each one there has been a steady rise in the coefficient of society's participation in it, and that the total war of today is only the logical end of an uninterrupted advance towards it, of the increasing growth of war."[32] Europe exported industrial wars and weapons of mass destruction to the rest of the world. As Samuel Huntington remarked: "The West won the world not by the superiority of its ideas or values or religion, but rather by its superiority in applying organized violence. Westerners often forget this fact, non-Westerners never do."[33] Non-Western countries had no choice but to join the arms-race in the 19th century. Japan is a case in point: from the 16th to the mid-19th century, Japan rejected Western influence, but this isolationism came to an end with the forcible opening of Japan by Commodore Perry in 1854, which left Japan with no choice but to fully Westernize and modernize its army in the Meiji era. China's isolation was likewise brought to an end by Western arms during the Opium Wars of 1839–42, a lesson that the Chinese are not ready to forget.

Armies were paid by taxes and wars were financed by debts to the point that, by the Napoleonic Wars, Europe had become enslaved to war-profiteering bankers. Assuming European nations could ever free themselves from this financial parasitism, would they ever be able to live peacefully while being sovereign? No, and for a very simple reason: the world is now made up of empires, and no nation can compete with empires. Without political unity, Europe will always be kept in the subservience of one empire or another. Today, Europe is a vassal of the United States through NATO. What about tomorrow?

---

32 Bertrand de Jouvenel, *On Power, op. cit.*, p. 3.

33 Huntington, *The Clash of Civilizations, op. cit.*, p. 51.

The idealist can dream of national sovereignty for France or any other European nation, but the realist understands that, as things stand, in order to free itself from the grip of the American empire, Europe has no alternative but to ally itself with the Russian imperial power—for the Russian Federation is indeed an empire. The realist does not give up on Europe, but he wagers that the multipolar world order that Russia is now promoting will be much more favorable to the maturing of Europe than constant American bullying. The realist also recognizes that, despite so many odds, Germany has once more emerged as the natural leader of Europe. One can debate the reasons why this is so, but one cannot deny it. Nothing good will happen to Europe if Germany does not resist NATO's racket and form a lasting alliance with Russia—an alliance that Bismarck had made the cornerstone of his foreign policy. Alas, the pathetic lack of German reaction after the Nord Stream pipelines sabotage on 26 September 2022—with some German leaders even blaming it on Russia—leaves little hope for the near future.

In the wake of these preliminary remarks, I will endeavor to prove my theory, namely, that the policy of the papacy during the Middle Ages was the main cause for Europe's failure to gain political unity, and therefore that the papacy's policy ultimately served as the root cause of Europe's complete subjugation by Washington through NATO. In this chapter, the papacy will be considered solely as a political power. Only later will we come to discuss Christianity as a belief system or religious practice. The papacy and the religion of Christ, albeit connected, are ultimately two distinct realities.

Theoderic and Charlemagne's Empires

Although the present work is mainly concerned with the history of Western Europe from the dawn of the second millennium AD, it is nevertheless important to know how the stage had been set over the preceding five centuries. Medieval European civilization emerged from the ruins of the Western Roman Empire. According to the most common interpretation, the destruction of the Empire and of Roman civilization was caused by the barbarian invasions. But there is a major problem with that interpretation: all historians agree that none of the Germanic invaders wanted to destroy the Empire. As Belgian historian Henri Pirenne stated almost a century ago, "There was nothing to provoke the Germans against the Empire: no religious motives, no racial hatred, and still less any sort of political consideration. Far from hating the Empire, they admired it. All they wanted was to settle down in the Empire and enjoy its advantages."[34] Although they looted their way across Roman territory and often battled against Roman legions, their aim was to have a land of their own and cultivate it under the *Pax Romana.* And there was nothing their kings coveted more than an official Roman title of consul or general. The Franks and the Goths ultimately came to rule over most of Italy, Gaul, and Spain, but they maintained Roman culture and law and sought to be legitimately integrated into the imperial structure.

The fall of the Western Roman Empire is traditionally dated to 476, when the German military commander Odoacer deposed the child emperor Romulus Augustus. But what Odoacer really did was send to Constantinople the imperial *ornamenta* (the symbols of the emperor's authority) along with an embassy to inform Emperor Zeno that he recognized him as sole emperor over East and West. Some historians therefore argue, quite logically, that 476 marked not the "fall of the Roman Empire," but rather its reunification.[35]

In 488, Zeno decided to oust Odoacer and sent the Ostrogothic king Theoderic to take possession of Italy. Theoderic had been raised in Constantinople, where he was sent at eight years old as a hostage, being the nephew of the king of the Goths settled in Pannonia

34 Henri Pirenne, *Mohammed and Charlemagne*, 1954 [(French edition 1939], Dover Publication, 2012, pp. 21–22.

35 Karl Ferdinand Werner, *Naissance de la noblesse. L'essor des élites politiques en Europe,* Arthème Fayard/Pluriel, 2010, p. 45.

(royal hostages were a common and efficient guarantee for the respect of treaties in the ancient world). In 471, Theoderic succeeded his uncle as king of the Pannonian Goths, and served in military campaigns against Rome's enemies at the head of his Ostrogoth warriors. In 475, Zeno made him high military commander (*magister militum*), and in 484, granted him the supreme honor of the consulship. Theoderic completed the conquest of the Italian peninsula and Sicily in 493. According to Jonathan Arnold, author of *Theoderic and the Roman Imperial Restoration*, "within less than a decade of his triumph over Odoacer, Theoderic would be hailed as a new Trajan and Valentinian … and would begin a series of massive renovation projects hailed by contemporary Italo-Romans as 'surpassing ancient wonders.'" A source known as the *Anonymus Valesianus* claims that, following an embassy of Rome's Senate to Constantinople in 497, Emperor Anastasius returned to Theoderic "all the *ornamenta* of the palace which Odoacer had sent to Constantinople."[36] The Western Empire was back.

In 511, Theoderic controlled most of the Roman West north of the Mediterranean, directly over Italy and indirectly over the South of Gaul, as regent for his Visigothic son-in-law, Eutharic. The king of Burgundy was also his son-in-law, and the king of the Vandals in Carthage was his brother-in-law, making Theoderic the most powerful man in all of Western Europe, with his influence extending into Central Europe. Theoderic's Italy, Arnold writes, "was a true Roman Empire that presented itself as such and exceeded the expectations of many of its Roman inhabitants; and it would have persisted in its Roman identity, had it not been for the unforeseeable intervention of the east Roman state."[37]

Peter Heather takes the same revisionist approach as Arnold in *The Restoration of Rome*, published the same year. According to

36 Quoted in Jonathan J. Arnold, *Theoderic and the Roman Imperial Restoration*, Cambridge UP, 2014, p. 70.

37 Arnold, *Theoderic and the Roman Imperial Restoration*, *op. cit.*, pp. 58, 7–8.

Heather, "from 498 onwards, Theoderic was ruling with all the rights and perquisites of a Western emperor, clothed in some of the appropriate vestments, and living in a palace [in his capital Ravenna] which was not only styled on that of Constantinople, but decorated as such." The writings of Italo-Romans living under Theoderic's rule indicate that "*ius* and *civilitas* presided in Theoderic's palace, *ius* designating the fundamentals of Roman law, *civilitas*, ... the state of higher civilization that written law generated."[38] In *The Inheritance of Rome*, Chris Wickham objects that Theoderic did not fit the universal function of Roman Emperor because he still considered himself the king of a particular ethnos.[39] But being king of the Franks would not stop Charlemagne from being crowned emperor by the pope. Still later, the Holy Roman Emperor was also king of the Germans, without anyone objecting. Therefore, if Theoderic had been granted full recognition of his imperial title by the Eastern Emperor, that very well would have been a novelty, but one that became the norm three centuries later anyway, without the transnational dimension of the empire being diminished by the royal crown of the emperor.

The reason why European historiography has denied Theoderic what it granted Charlemagne without reservation is that history is written by the victor, who, in the first case, was Emperor Justinian, the destroyer of the Ostrogothic kingdom after Theoderic's death. If, with Arnold and Heather, we consider Theoderic as the restorer of Roman imperial authority in the West, then the real fall of the Western Roman Empire was caused by Justinian's Gothic War (535–554) waged under the pretext of the Goths' "Arian" heresy. Justinian's general Belisarius devastated northern Italy for twenty years, turning Rome into "a rural town dependent on agricultural produce close at hand, within the Aurelia Walls or just outside," according to

38 Peter Heather, *The Restoration of Rome: Barbarian Popes & Imperial Pretenders*, Oxford UP, 2014, pp. 93, 80.

39 Chris Wickham, *The Inheritance of Rome: A History of Europe from 400 to 1000*, Penguin Books, 2010, pp. 139–145.

Peter Heather.[40] That made Italy easy prey for the Lombards, who in 568 swept out of the Middle Danube region. Since the Persians had taken advantage of the Romans' western wars to regain territory in the East, the Byzantines could not mount an effective resistance to the Lombards, and they barely managed to retain control of Ravenna, while Rome was largely left to itself. The election of the prefect of Rome, Gregorius Anicius, as Pope Gregory I (590–604) marks the beginning of the medieval papacy as a political entity in its own right, one that ruled Rome in relative independence.

Meanwhile, the Franks, led by Clovis, had united northern Gaul and part of Germania (with royal centers from Paris and Orléans, through Reims and Metz, to Cologne). The Franks converted to Nicene Christianity, which, according to Heather, "must be understood in a broader diplomatic context: Clovis's decision to seek East Roman assistance as he challenged Theoderic in the west."[41] As the Christological controversy turned into a geopolitical issue, the bishop of Rome became an agent of the enemy in Theoderic's eyes. In 507, Clovis attacked the Visigoths of Aquitaine and drove them out of Gaul. According to Gregory of Tours, our only source of those events (*Historia Francorum* II,28), he received from Anastasius the title of consul and a purple tunic in 508. Theoderic reacted by occupying Visigothic Spain, nominally ruling for Alaric's son Amalaric (511–31). Theoderic was able to contain Frankish expansion, but it picked up in earnest after his death in 526. Clovis's sons took over the Burgundian kingdom in 534. Then the Ostrogothic kingdom disappeared during Justinian's Gothic War.

In the middle of the 7th century, the Arab conquest of Syria and North Africa destroyed the relative unity of the Mediterranean world. Sea trade between East and West receded, and port activity in the West declined. Northern Europe was less affected, because its

---

40 Heather, *The Restoration of Rome, op. cit.*, p. 143.

41 Peter Heather, *Christendom: The Triumph of a Religion*, Knopf, 2023, p. 193.

agrarian economy was less dependent on Mediterranean trade. The Austrasian Franks even benefitted from an increase of sea and river trade in the North. Europe's center of gravity moved north.

Rome became further estranged from Constantinople. The breaking point was reached in 722, when Emperor Leo III announced important tax increases to compensate for the loss of Egypt and Syria to the Arabs, and, shortly afterwards, began his iconoclastic campaign. The citizens of Rome, led by Pope Gregory II, refused to pay and entered into open revolt. The exarch of Ravenna, the chief imperial representative in the entire Italian peninsula, approached Rome with everything he could muster, but was forced to retreat. "At this moment, more than in any other," Peter Heather writes, "the independent Republic of St. Peter was born: the direct progenitor of the papal states which would finally be dismantled in the nineteenth century by a combination of the greater and lesser Napoleons."[42]

Rome, however, still needed the protection of an imperial power. After Ravenna fell to the Lombards in 751, the pope appealed to the Frankish king Pepin the Short. For historians, the year 752 marks the end the "Byzantine papacy" and the beginning of what might be called the "Frankish papacy." In 774, Pepin's son Charlemagne beat the Lombards and declared himself king of both the Franks and the Lombards. With Italy and the united Frankish kingdom, he was now reigning on a territory that was almost equivalent in size to the old Western Roman Empire. Seizing the pretext that the Eastern Empire was headed by a woman (Empress Irene of Athens), Charlemagne declared the throne vacant and arranged for Pope Leo III to crown him Emperor in Rome on Christmas Eve 800, in exchange for escorting him back to Rome from where he had been expelled under accusations of adultery and perjury. The agreement between Charlemagne and Leo III included the former's confirmation that his father Pepin had donated the city of Rome and a vast territory around

42 *Ibid.*, p. 342.

it—although the authenticity of this "Donation of Pepin" is ever in doubt. The alliance between emperor and pope also gave the Roman Church immense weight in the state affairs. As Christopher Dawson underscored, the Carolingian Empire "possessed no trained bureaucracy or class of lawyers and was consequently far more dependent on the assistance of ecclesiastics in the task of civil administration than was the Byzantine State." Thus "the clergy took a leading part in the secular administration of the Empire." Practically, the personnel of the government and of the Church were the same.[43]

Bishop Hincmar of Reims's retelling of the semi-legendary account of Clovis' coronation in his *Life of Saint Remigius*, written under Charlemagne's grandson Charles the Bald, is worth quoting as a classic expression of how the Church tied its destiny to Frankish power, with a taste for Old Testament references. Hincmar presents Remigius as speaking to Clovis "the language of the ancient Moses to the ancient People of God":

> Learn, my son, that the kingdom of the Franks is predestined by God to defend the Roman Church, which is the only true Church of Christ. This kingdom will one day be great among all kingdoms. It will embrace all the boundaries of the Roman Empire. It will subject all peoples to its scepter. It will last until the end of time. It will be victorious and prosperous as long as it remains faithful to the Roman faith. But it will be severely punished whenever it is unfaithful to its vocation.[44]

What we have here is a political theology drawn from Deuteronomy and the Books of Kings which subjects royal power to priestly power. The anointing of the king with the sacred oil from the holy ampoule, which Hincmar also introduced into the legend, and which would become the high point of the rite of coronation of every French

43 Christopher Dawson, *Medieval Essays*, Catholic University of America Press, 1954, p. 69.

44 Camille Pascal, *Ainsi Dieu choisit la France. La véritable histoire de la fille aînée de l'Église*, Presses de la Renaissance, 2016.

king, is directly borrowed from the anointment of David by Samuel that made "the spirit of Yahweh seize on David" (1 Samuel 16:13). In his letter to Leo III (*circa* 795), Charlemagne compared himself to Joshua fighting against the Amalekites, while: "It is up to you, most holy Father, raising your hands to God with Moses, to help with your prayers for the success of our arms" (reference to Exodus 17:11).[45] Christopher Dawson wrote in *The Making of Europe*, that the Carolingian imperial ideal "was based on the teaching of the Bible and St. Augustine rather than on the classical tradition of imperial Rome. … Charles was the new David and the second Josias, and as the latter had restored the law of God, so too Charles was the lawgiver of the Church and held the two swords of spiritual and temporal authority."[46] This biblical political theology would remain a characteristic of Western Christendom.

Despite the Church's expectation, the Carolingian Empire was, according to Dawson, "a Roman Empire without the Roman law and without the Roman legions, without the City and without the Senate. It was a shapeless and unorganised mass with no urban nerve centres and no circulation of economic life."[47] In other words, in terms of *Romanitas*, Charlemagne's empire was way below Theoderic's. That's probably why it didn't last more than half a century. Philippe Wolff points out another weakness: "[Charlemagne] tried in his own way—the heavy handed way—to play the part of a Christian emperor as it had been envisaged since Constantine, but he was unable to divest himself of the Frankish custom of dividing up his inheritance, and distributed his possessions among his sons as if he were dealing with a family estate rather than the *res publica*." Although by chance Louis the Pious inherited the whole, he repeated the mistake. "The ensuing squabbles and divisions were one cause of the

45 Heather, *Christendom, op. cit.*, p. 362.

46 Dawson, *The Making of Europe, op. cit.*, pp. 189–190.

47 Dawson, *Medieval Essays, op. cit.*, p. 218.

Carolingian decline."[48] In other words, the Carolingians were always more Frankish kings than Roman Emperors. Ferdinand Gregorovius wrote in his *History of the City of Rome* in eight volumes (1872): "The appearance of the Great Charles may be compared to a flash of lightning, which, piercing the night, illuminated the earth for a moment, only to leave darkness behind."[49] Charlemagne's oversized place in our historiography is the result of the cult that was created around him by Otto III, who miraculously "discovered" his tomb in the year 1000, and later by Frederick Barbarossa, who had him canonized in Aachen in 1165.

The Donation of Constantine

One of the most important legacies of the Carolingian era is the "Donation of Constantine," forged in some unknown scriptorium between 750 and 850. Known in a shorter version as the *Constitutum Constantini*, it can be regarded as the "Constitution" given by the popes to Western Europe, under the fake signature of Constantine the Great. From the 11th century, it probably had more political influence than any other written document in human history. By this document, Emperor Constantine the Great, out of gratitude for having been cured of leprosy by the water of baptism, ceded "to Sylvester the universal pontiff and to all his successors until the end of the world" all the imperial insignia — namely the diadem, tiara, shoulder band, purple mantle, crimson tunic, scepter, spear, standard and banner — "and all the advantage of our high imperial position, and the glory of our power." Constantine also ceded to Pope Sylvester "both our [Lateran] palace and the city of Rome and all the provinces, localities and cities of Italy or the Western regions." And in order to leave the pope full power over the West, Constantine allegedly

48 Philippe Wolff, *The Awakening of Europe*, Penguin, 1968, p. 18.

49 Ferdinand Gregorovius, *History of the City of Rome in the Middle Ages*, vol. 3, George Bell & Sons, 1895, p. 68.

decided to withdraw to Byzantium—"for, where the supremacy of priests and the head of the Christian religion has been established by a heavenly ruler, it is not fitting that there an earthly ruler should have jurisdiction." On the basis of this fraud, for more than half a millennium, the popes would claim to have received full imperial authority and the right to bestow it on the man of their choosing, or to take it away from him if he fell short of their expectation. The forger of the Donation was not content with asserting that the pope holds temporal supremacy over the entire West. He also gave him spiritual supremacy over the entire world, meaning over both Eastern and Western Christianity: "[the bishop of Rome] shall govern the four patriarchates of Alexandria, Antioch, Jerusalem and Constantinople, as well as all the Churches of God throughout the entire world. And the pontiff who will now preside over the destiny of the most holy Roman Church will be the highest, the head of all priests in the whole world, and all things will be regulated according to his decisions."

One does not need to be a philologist to detect the fraud in the Donation of Constantine: how, for example, can Constantine mention the patriarchate of Constantinople when it does not yet exist? And yet, it was not until 1440 that the fraud was demonstrated and admitted in Western scholarly circles. This should have undermined the pope's claim at universal supremacy, but since it occurred on the eve of the fall of Constantinople, soon reduced to silence for eternity, nothing changed in the discourse and attitude of the papacy. No apology was ever offered by the Vatican for this outrageous lie.

In fact, there had been protests from the 11th century, when the popes started making intensive use of the Donation. In the year 1001, in response to a request from Pope Sylvester II to "restore" to the Holy See eight counties of Italy, Emperor Otto III denounced "the negligence and incompetence" of the popes, as well as "the lies invented by them, by means of which the cardinal-deacon John ... drew up in letters of gold the 'privilege' which he mendaciously caused to be back-dated very far in time and placed under the name of the great Constantine."[50] In the middle of the 12th century, the Italian priest Arnaud de Brescia saw in the Donation a heretical legend inspired by the Antichrist. He was burned as a heretic. At the beginning of the 13th century, the poet Walther von der Vogelweide did not dispute the origin of the Donation but saw it as a great misfortune, a reversal of the natural order of the world. The angels in heaven, he wrote, cried out "Alas!" three times when the Donation was signed.[51] Frederick II Hohenstaufen had his lawyers declare it unlawful, for Constantine had no right to make this donation. Innocent IV responded that, all things belonging to Christ, whom the pope represented on earth, the Donation was only a "restitution" anyway. Dante Alighieri wrote in *Inferno,* Canto XIX: "Ah, Constantine, how much evil was born, / Not from your conversion, but from that donation / That the first wealthy pope received from you." In the second part of the 14th century, when the authenticity of the Donation became more openly questioned, the cleric Pierre Jame d'Aurillac stated that the question was irrelevant, since the Donation, whether genuine or not, was obviously in accordance with God's will.[52]

The Donation of Constantine is included in a collection of a hundred other false decrees and synodal acts known today as the False Decretals, or the Pseudo-Isidorian Decretals. The main purpose of these forged decrees was to invent precedents for the exercise of the sovereign authority of the Bishop of Rome over the universal Church on the one hand, and over all Western secular sovereigns on the other. These forgeries were incorporated in the 12th century into the *Decretum* of Gratian which would become the basis of all canon law. In addition to the Pseudo-Isidorian Decretals and the false Donation

50 Quoted in Robert Folz, *The Concept of Empire in Western Europe from the Fifth to the Fourteenth Century*, Edward Arnold, 1969, p. 187.

51 Johannes Fried, *"Donation of Constantine" and "Constitutum Constantini,"* De Gruyter, 2007, p. 7.

52 Domenico Maffei, "The forged donation of Constantine in medieval and early modern legal thought," *Fundamina*, n° 3, 1997, pp. 1–23.

of Constantine, the papal jurists designed the "false symmachians," fictitious legal precedents meant to immunize the pope against judgment.

The Ottonian Empire

Let us come back to the 10th century, when a new Roman Empire was emerging in Saxony. Otto the Great was the son of Henry the Fowler, Duke of Saxony, who in 911 was elected king by a coalition of princes wishing to federate their five duchies (Lotharingia, Saxony, Franconia, Swabia, Bavaria) in order to repel the attacks of the Danes, Slavs, and Hungarians. The name "German" having little use at the time, Henry took the title "king of the Romans." His son Otto I was in turn elected king of the Romans in 936, and took in addition the title of king of Italy through his marriage to the widow of the previous king, followed by military conquest. Then he was crowned "Emperor of the Romans" by a grateful Pope John XII in Rome in 962. This established a safeguard for the Eastern frontiers of Christendom on the one hand, and the unity of Germany and Italy on the other, which thus constituted the two pillars of the new "Roman Empire."

Yet the actual unity of Italy and Germany was always hampered by the barrier of the Alps standing in between, and by their different political traditions: Germany was still a loose confederation of poorly urbanized duchies, while Italy was more a collection of ancient city-states, sometimes joined in leagues. The emperors, residing in Germany, would have the greatest difficulty in gaining and keeping the loyalty of the rich Italian cities, whose separatist tendencies would be exploited by the popes.

By the *Privilegium Ottonianum,* probably derived from the Donation of Constantine, Otto granted the pope a long list of domains, including "the city of Rome with its duchy" and "the entire exarchate of Ravenna." This may or may not have been a confirmation of an earlier donation by Pepin the Short or Charlemagne. The two Papal States created by this grant cut the Italian peninsula in two. A quick look at the map of Italy is enough to understand that, once they had appropriated this *Patrimonium Petri*, the popes would be obsessed by the fear of seeing it caught "like a nut within a giant imperial nutcracker,"[53] and would have the constant priority of preventing any sovereign from reigning over both southern Italy and northern Italy. Therefore, even before inquiring as to why Europe never achieved political unity, we know why Italy, the historic heart of the Roman Empire and the richest region of Europe throughout the Middle Ages, never achieved its own political unity: the unity of Italy could never be achieved without the disappearance of the Papal States, which would not happen until 1859.

Machiavelli made this point very clear in his *Discourses on Livy* (I,12):

> by the Church our country is kept divided. … The Church, therefore, never being powerful enough herself to take possession of the entire country, while, at the same time, preventing any one else from doing so, has made it impossible to bring Italy under one head; and has been the cause of her [Italy] always living subject to many princes or rulers, by whom she has been brought to such division and weakness as to have become a prey, not to Barbarian kings only, but to any who have thought fit to attack her. For this, I say, we Italians have none to thank but the Church.

Machiavelli hoped that the Florentine Medici family (Cosimo the Elder and his grandson Lorenzo the Magnificent) who at one point controlled the papacy (Giovanni de' Medici was Pope Leo X from 1513 to 1521), would take the lead in the movement of national redemption. He wrote *The Prince* and dedicated it to Lorenzo with that in mind, and titled its last chapter: "An Exhortation to Deliver Italy from the Barbarians."[54] The opportunity was missed, and the unification

53 Jane Sayers, *Innocent III, Leader of Europe,* Pearson, 1993, p. 79.

54 James Burnham, *The Machiavellians: Defenders of Freedom,* John Day Co., 1943, pp. 33–38.

and independence of Italy had to wait until 1861. The fragmentation of Italy by the popes' will is like a reduced image of the fragmentation of Europe by the same.

Bearing the Italian case in mind, let us go back to the Ottonian dynasty. Following Otto the Great, his son Otto II and grandson Otto III were in turn elected kings of the Romans and then crowned emperors, respectively in 973 and 996. The Ottos thus established the tradition of having the German princes elect their king, who by right becomes the candidate for the title of emperor until his coronation by the pope. In general, the reigning king obtained the agreement of the princes for the future election of his son, but the German kingship remained elective in principle.

The Ottos' imperial authority was well accepted in Europe and beyond. In 973, Otto the Great was at the zenith of his prestige, confirmed by emissaries from Denmark, Poland, Bohemia, Greece, Bulgaria, Hungary, and Italy flocking to the imperial castle of Quedlinburg to pay homage to the greatest ruler of the West. While claiming the imperial *auctoritas* for the West, the Ottos recognized and courted the powerful Byzantine emperors of the Macedonian dynasty. Otto I negotiated the marriage of his son Otto II with Princess Theophano, niece of the Byzantine Emperor John Tzimisces. Otto III, born of this marriage, grew up under the influence of his mother and her Byzantine retinue. He himself obtained the hand of a niece of Emperor Basil II, but when she landed in Bari in 1002, it was only to learn that Otto III had died. He was only 21 years old.

Beyond the restoration of the twofold Roman Empire, the aim of the Ottonian-Byzantine alliance was the retrieval of southern Italy and Sicily, which were still officially Byzantine but partly occupied by the Saracens. Otto III had made plans to mobilize a large army against them. He would then have established his capital in Rome. His death made way for the Normans who settled permanently in southern Italy and Sicily, as vassals of the pope in what would be called the Kingdom of Sicily or the Kingdom of Naples. As they would in England half a century later, the Normans became proxies in the popes' strategy of keeping Saxon ambitions at bay and keeping southern Italy out of imperial reach.

The Ottos modeled their imperial policy on the Byzantine concept of the *Oikoumene*, the community of Christian peoples under the leadership of the Emperor. They favored the emergence of relatively autonomous Christian kingdoms, the Emperor becoming the godfather of kings who received their crowns from him. In the East, the Ottonians undertook the Christianization of the Slavs beyond the Oder (Poland and Bohemia) and the Hungarians. Bohemia would eventually become an integral part of the empire, retaining the status of a duchy. The kingdom of Poland did not fully integrate into the empire, but remained anchored to the Latin Catholic Church. In Hungary, King Géza baptized his son Stephen, to whom Otto III granted the royal crown on Christmas Day of the year 1000.

In the West, the Ottos took control of Lotharingia (the future Lorraine, including Alsace). Otto I entrusted this duchy to his younger brother Brunon, also archbishop of Cologne. He married his sister Hedwig to the Frankish Duke Hugues the Great. When the latter died in 954, his son Hugues Capet was placed under the tutelage of Brunon of Cologne. He was crowned king of the Franks in 987 by Archbishop Adalberon of Reims, also a member of the Ottonian family, with the support of Gerbert of Aurillac, tutor of Otto III and future Pope Sylvester II. Thus, the Capetian monarchy was born in the shadow of the Ottonian Empire, and was intended to remain part of what was called "the Ottonian order." The Ottos, as dukes of Saxony, were also relatives of the Saxons of England since the marriage of Otto I with Edith of England, which made him the brother-in-law of king Æthelstan, the first monarch to reign over most of England.

In their religious policy, the Ottonian dynasty sought to reproduce the Byzantine system which placed the Church under the protection of the Emperor, giving him the right to depose a patriarch deemed unworthy. In 963, Otto I crossed the Alps to depose Pope

John XII and appoint Leo VIII in his place. He further required that the people of Rome take an oath that "they would not elect or ordain any pope except with the consent of Lord Otto or his son."[55] Otto III installed his cousin Bruno of Carinthia as Pope Gregory V, who in return crowned him emperor in 996. Upon Bruno's death, he placed his tutor and friend Gerbert of Aurillac, who took the name Sylvester II, thus giving Otto III the standing of a new Constantine.

What fundamentally distinguished the Ottonian Empire from the Byzantine Empire is that Constantinople possessed an elite of literate laymen for its administration and bureaucracy, whereas this would not be the case in Europe for several centuries. The Germanic emperors were entirely dependent for their administration on the networks of archbishops and bishops, whose appointment they needed to control. Archbishops were the chancellors of the empire. As such, they also served as a counterweight to the dukes. Bishoprics thus tended to become fiefdoms, especially since bishops had temporal resources consisting mainly in cultivated lands. It was therefore not uncommon for bishops to be chosen from among members of the royal family. One of Otto I's brothers was archbishop of Cologne, as already mentioned, and one of his bastard sons, William, was archbishop of Mainz.

In conclusion, the three Ottos laid the foundations for a lasting imperial structure that was respected by most of Europe's princes. It was, in everyone's eyes, the Western Roman Empire *redivivus.* When the young but charismatic Otto III was crowned emperor in Rome, he declared himself more Roman than the Romans. While competing with the Byzantine Emperor for control of certain territories, the Ottos believed they had restored the bipartite unity of the Roman Empire, synonymous with Christendom. Otto III wanted to make Rome his capital and aimed at reconstituting the ancient

55 Francis Rapp, *Le Saint Empire romain germanique, d'Otton le Grand à Charles Quint*, Seuil, 2003, p. 56.

Roman Empire as a supranational structure bringing together all the Christian polities of the Latin West.[56]

The Salian Dynasty and the Investiture Contest

Having died childless, Otto III's crown was entrusted to the grandson of Otto I's brother, Henry II (1002–24). Then the male branch of the house of Saxony died out, and the German princes elected Conrad of Franconia, the founder of the Salian dynasty. Over ten years of reign, Conrad II extended the influence of the empire. In 1033, he secured for himself the kingdom of Burgundy, which had earlier absorbed the kingdom of Arles. He thus wore the three crowns of Germany, Italy and Burgundy, a triad that formed the basis of a political edifice of which the empire was the crowning glory. Conrad II was succeeded by his son Henry III (1039–56), who consolidated the attachment of Poland, Bohemia, and Hungary to the empire and tightened ties with the Kingdom of France by marrying Agnes of Poitou.

The system of the "imperial Church" was then firmly in place. However, the emperors' control over the papacy was always insecure, since the papacy, amounting to lordship over Rome and the papal duchies, was coveted by various aristocratic families. From 1012 to 1045, the counts of Tusculum monopolized the throne of St. Peter. In 1046, Henry III deposed three rival popes and appointed the bishop of Bamberg (Clement II) in their place. On the latter's death ten months later, he appointed the archbishop of Toul, Bruno von Egisheim-Dagsburg, who took the name of Leo IX. The latter was a moderate reformer from the school of Cluny, and he proved to be a good example of a pope made by an emperor yet highly regarded by ecclesiastical historians. "For the short five years of his pontificate, he threw himself with all his heart into a policy of reformation," writes Thomas Tout; "the special characteristic of his pontificate was his constant journeying through all Italy, France, and Germany. During

56 Henry Bogdan, *Histoire de l'Allemagne*, 1999, Tempus/Perrin, 2003, p. 74.

these travels, Leo was indefatigable in holding synods, attending ecclesiastical ceremonies, consecrating churches, and transferring the relics of martyrs."[57]

Church historians highlight Leo IX's unfailing dedication to purifying the Church of simony (the acquisition of clerical titles through money), which was universally considered a form of corruption. Henry III supported Leo's reform. But Leo surrounded himself with more radical reformers imbued with the Cluniac monastic spirit, such as Hildebrand and Humbert de Moyenmoutier. In his *Adversus simoniacos*, written in 1057, Humbert equated secular investiture to simony. This was an extremist interpretation. Until then, as Jacques Van Wijendaele explains, "investiture by lay people was a common practice accepted throughout Christianity. Reformers as demanding as Pierre Damien saw no harm in it as long as it happened for free without the candidate paying for his nomination, which would amount to simony."[58]

The death of Henry III in 1056 left as heir a five-year-old son who, although already elected king of the Romans in 1054, had been placed under the regency of his mother. The papacy took advantage of Henry IV's minority to sever its ties of dependency on temporal power. The reforming party had their candidate Stephen IX named without imperial agreement, which constituted a first declaration of papal independence. His successor Nicholas II laid down new rules for the election of the pope: seven cardinals (Italian bishops) should choose the new candidate, then seek his confirmation by the rest of the Roman clergy. In practice, this strengthened the influence of the aristocratic families of Rome and generated an unprecedented mixture of nepotism and simony. In the 13th century, Innocent III would

57 Tout, *The Empire and the Papacy, op. cit.*, pp. 101–102.

58 Jacques Van Wijendaele, *Propagande et polémique au Moyen Âge*, Bréal, 2008, p. 98.

make four of his relatives cardinals and enrich the Conti family, while Boniface VIII would make the fortune of his own Caetani clan.[59]

In 1073, it was the Cluniac monk Hildebrand who, after having worked in the shadow of four other popes, took power under the name of Gregory VII. The decree promulgated by Gregory VII at a synod in Rome in 1075, which prohibited the appointment of a bishop or an abbot by secular rulers, marks the beginning of the Investiture Contest: "If an emperor, a king, a duke, a count, or any other lay person presume to give investiture of any ecclesiastical dignity, let him be excommunicated."[60] Emperor Henry IV, who was then twenty-six, resisted being dispossessed of his customary rights. When he intervened in the election of the archbishop of Milan, Gregory VII reminded him that his orders were as binding as those of God. Henry IV replied with a brutal letter, calling "brother Hildebrand" a "false monk," a fornicator, and a sower of discord. He enjoyed the support of most of the German episcopate, who met at Worms on January 24, 1076 to declare Gregory VII a usurper. Sigebert of Gembloux, a highly regarded Benedictine scholar, accused Gregory of trying to degrade the sacraments under the guise of fighting against simony.[61] Some enemies of the pope accused him of having assassinated the four popes he had served before usurping their throne. Cardinal Bennon said Gregory was sent to earth by Satan to "ruin the name of Christ."[62] There is also no shortage of criticism against the enrichment of the papacy, which became a formidable financial power under Gregory VII. It was claimed that "Gregory VII owed his fortune to the support of the Roman *monetarii* or *nummularrii* (bankers-changers)," according to historians Sandro Carocci and Marco Vendittelli. The irony, for a supposedly anti-simoniac

59 Sandro Carocci and Marco Vendittelli, "Société et économie," in André Vauchez, ed., *Rome au Moyen Âge*, Cerf, 2021, pp. 127–188.

60 Tout, *The Empire and the Papacy, op. cit.*, p. 127.

61 Entry for the year 1074 in his *Chronica*, bcs.fltr.ucl.ac.be/ENC2/08.html.

62 Sylvain Gouguenheim, *La Réforme grégorienne*, Temps Présent, 2017, p. 181.

movement, is that Roman politics revolved around a system of organized corruption, by which "great largesse were granted to the pope, the cardinals and the members of the pontifical curia to obtain sentences, concessions and favors of a legal, political and administrative nature."[63]

What is important to understand is that the Investiture Contest was not just a conflict between the emperor and the pope, but a conflict within the Church, particularly between the traditionalist bishops, who considered themselves servants of the imperial order, and the supporters of the revolutionary ideology of papal supreme monarchy, who were linked to the extended network of interconnected abbeys that developed from Cluny.

In order to overpower Henry IV, Gregory VII employed the magic weapon he had forged for himself: he declared Henry IV excommunicated and his vassals freed from their oath of loyalty, for, as he put it, "I have received from God the power to bind and to loose in Heaven and on earth."[64] It was a formidable, supernatural weapon. In a political order based on personal loyalties, where lords derived their authority from the homage paid to them, cancelling the binding power of the vassals' oaths undermined the political order. Several German princes threatened to elect a new king if Henry was not released from excommunication within a year. Henry IV decided to yield: he crossed the Alps in the middle of winter and implored, as a penitent, the forgiveness of Gregory VII, who had him wait three days and three nights, barefoot in the snow, in front of the castle of Canossa. Such is, at least, the famous story told by the monk Lambert of Hersfeld, a fervent supporter of the pope and enemy of the emperor. That story is now considered a piece of papal propaganda written to illustrate how the vicar of Christ holds the power to crush a German king into the dust, and then raise him up again by grace

63 Carocci and Vendittelli, "Société et économie," *op. cit.*

64 Tout, *The Empire and the Papacy*, *op. cit.*, p. 129.

from his deepest abasement. Indeed, one of the considerable advantages the pope wielded over the emperor was an extensive network of ecclesiastical writers, copyists, and propagandists of all kinds. All in all, Canossa was a milestone in the showdown between pope and emperor.

Henry IV obtained the lifting of the excommunication, but the truce was short-lived. In March 1080, the pope excommunicated him again and recognized the king elected by the rebellious German princes, the Duke of Swabia Rudolf of Rheinfelden. Gregory cast a spell on Henry: "May this same Henry with his accomplices lose all his strength in battles"; and he promised Rudolf's supporters "absolution of all their sins and blessing in this life and in the future life."[65] When Rudolph died prematurely, the pope asked the princes to find "a king suitable for the honor of Holy Church" and to have him swear before his legate the following formula:

> From this hour onwards I shall be the vassal in good faith of the blessed apostle Peter and of his vicar who now lives in the flesh, Pope Gregory; and whatever the pope commends me with the words 'in true obedience' I shall faithfully comply with, as a Christian ought … I shall, with Christ's help, pay to God and St Peter all due honour and service; and on the day when I shall first come into the pope's presence, I shall become St Peter's knight and his by an act of homage.[66]

This was too much for the German princes, who rallied around Henry IV. The German archbishops officially deposed Gregory VII and elected as new pope Guibert of Parma, bishop of Ravenna, who took the name Clement III. With the support of the majority of the German episcopate, Henry marched on Rome. The pope, entrenched in Castel Sant'Angelo, called on his Norman vassals in Sicily for help; they rescued him, but they plundered Rome and set it on

65 Van Wijendaele, *Propagande et polémique, op. cit.*, pp. 47–48.

66 I. S. Robinson, *The Papacy, 1073–1198: Continuity and Innovation,* Cambridge UP, 1990, p. 411.

fire. In March 1084, Henry IV was the master of the city and could be crowned emperor by Clement III. Gregory VII died in isolation in Salerno in May 1085. A rumor reported by Sigebert de Gembloux, evocative of the general sentiment in the imperial Church, claims that Gregory confessed on his deathbed to having acted at the instigation of the devil to arouse hatred and anger among humankind.[67]

The Cluniac-Gregorian party nevertheless remained strong and the struggle resumed when the Frenchman Eudes of Châtillon, former abbot of Cluny, was elected pope under the name of Urban II, with the same ideas and the same energy as Gregory VII. Urban II confirmed the excommunication of Henry IV, and determined to drive him out of Italy.

The Investiture Contest ended with the Concordat of Worms signed on September 23, 1122 by Emperor Henry V, son of Henry IV. The emperor waived any right to appoint a bishop, but the pope recognized that the prelates were vassals of the emperor with regard to their domains, and granted him the right to be present or represented during their elections, as well as to intervene in case of discord. In his book *On the Medieval Origins of the Modern State*, Joseph Strayer sees the victory of the papacy as the turning point from which Europe evolved into a multi-state rather than an imperial structure: "By asserting its unique character, the Church unwittingly sharpened concepts about the nature of secular authority." Moreover, "the Investiture Conflict weakened the Empire more than any other secular political organization. Other rulers settled their disputes with the reformers independently and on better terms than did the emperor. … Each kingdom or principality had to be treated as a separate entity; the foundations for a multi-state system had been laid."[68]

---

67 Mireille Chazan, *L'Empire et l'histoire universelle de Sigebert de Gembloux à Jean de Saint-Victor (XIIe–XIVe siècle)*, Champion, 1999, p. 143.

68 Joseph Reese Strayer, *On the Medieval Origins of the Modern State*, Princeton UP, 1973, pp. 22–23.

The Concordat of Worms was by no means a mortal blow to the empire, however, as it left the emperor room for maneuver. Moreover, as the administrative structures of the empire consolidated, the role of churchmen could be compensated by a secular elite. Nevertheless, the Investiture Contest was a major battlefront in a war for the supreme political power over Europe. The Gregorian Reform, named after Gregory VII, was, according to Robert I. Moore's classic book, "the first European revolution."[69] It was a coup of vast proportion and long-term execution, led by a monkish conspiracy, to make the pope the *verus imperator*. Indeed, as Arnold Toynbee wrote: "Hildebrand and his successors succeeded in creating the master-institution of Western Christendom. They won for Papal Rome an empire which had a greater hold on the human heart than the Empire of the Antonines, and which on the mere material plane embraced vast tracts of Western Europe beyond the Rhine and the Danube where the legions of Augustus and Marcus Aurelius had never set foot."[70]

The Two Swords and Political Augustinianism

Most Catholics have no idea about Catholic political doctrine. They don't even know there is one, although it has had far more concrete consequences than the Catholic doctrine of faith which, while it may save them in the other life, has no direct impact on this one. The political doctrine of the Church is generally known as the "theory of the two swords." It distinguishes between the spiritual sword and the temporal sword, but states that both swords must be under the control of the same person. The spiritual sword is drawn *by* the Church (i.e. by the pope) and the temporal sword is drawn *for* the Church

---

69 Robert I. Moore, *The First European Revolution, c. 970–1215*, Basil Blackwell, 2000.

70 Arnold Toynbee, *A Study of History*, Vol. 1: *Abridgement of Volumes I–VI*, new edition, Oxford UP, 1987, p. 403.

(i.e. by order of the pope). Boniface VIII dogmatized the idea in his bull *Unam Sanctam* in 1302:

> We are informed by the texts of the gospels that in this Church and in its power are two swords; namely, the spiritual and the temporal. … both are in the power of the Church. … the latter is to be exercised on behalf of the Church; and truly, the former is to be exercised by the Church. The former is of the priest; the latter is by the hand of kings and soldiers, but at the will and sufferance of the priest. … Hence we must recognize the more clearly that spiritual power surpasses in dignity and in nobility any temporal power whatever, as spiritual things surpass the temporal. … For with truth as our witness, it belongs to spiritual power to establish the terrestrial power and to pass judgment if it has not been good. … Therefore, if the terrestrial power err, it will be judged by the spiritual power; but if a minor spiritual power err, it will be judged by a superior spiritual power; but if the highest power of all err, it can be judged only by God, and not by man.[71]

The two-sword metaphor was first used by Bernard of Clairvaux in the context of the Crusades. Bernard, one of the most influential men of his time, extolled the unique authority of Saint Peter and his successors, who are entrusted with "the government of the whole world" (*On Consideration* II,8). This was no novelty, and added nothing substantial to the political doctrine written down by Gregory VII in his *Dictatus Papae*, according to which "all princes shall kiss the feet of the Pope alone." The two-sword doctrine has also been called "political Augustinianism," because it is loosely based on the writings of Saint Augustine, and especially on his best-seller, *The City of God* (early 5th century). There is indeed a certain correspondence between Augustine's "two cities" and the "two swords." Augustine is the most influential of the Latin Fathers (he is mostly ignored in the Greek Orthodox tradition), and *The City of God* has almost the status of a

71 Pope Boniface VIII, "Unam Sanctam: One God, One Faith, One Spiritual Authority," *Papal Encyclicals Online* [https://www.papalencyclicals.net/Bon08/B8unam.htm].

sacred book in the West. That is why Augustine's political theory has always been a major center of interest in Catholic erudition.[72]

Political Augustinianism has been defined in 1934 by the French priest Henri-Xavier Arquillière as "the tendency to absorb the natural order into the religious order, the right of the state into the right of the Church."[73] It opposes Aristotle's principle of a "natural law of the state," which implies that every state has the right to exist, independently of the Church. This right, in the Aristotelian tradition, is based on the very nature of man, who is created as a social being and can only develop his abilities through life in society. Since God constituted him in this way from the beginning, He at the same time wanted the essential conditions for social life: the authority of the leader and the obedience of the subordinates.

The first Christians held to that principle, trusting Saint Paul: "Let very person be subject to the governing authorities. For there is no authority except from God, and those that exist have been instituted by God" (Romans 13:1). The Eastern Church admitted this theory, and very logically since Constantine the Great, the first Byzantine emperor, obviously did not derive his power from the Church: on the contrary, the Church only existed by his protection. "In Byzantium," Arquillière writes, "the imperial coronation was never more than an accessory ceremony. When the emperor was elected by the Senate—often after being acclaimed by the army of the people of Constantinople—he immediately came into possession of all his powers. The coronation liturgy, which sometimes took place a year later, added nothing."[74]

The leaders of the Gregorian Reform emphasized, on the contrary, that emperors and all sovereigns could not receive their

72 Michael J.S. Bruno, *Political Augustinianism: Modern Interpretations of Augustine's Political Thought,* Fortress Press, 2014.

73 Henri-Xavier Arquillière, *L'Augustinisme politique, essai sur la formation des théories politiques au Moyen Age,* 1934, Vrin, 1972, p. 55.

74 *Ibid.*, pp. 112–113.

authority directly from God, but only from the Church. The 11th-century reform movement is the most complete expression of political Augustinianism, claiming that the state only existed as an organ of the Church and that its fundamental purpose was to cooperate in the salvation of souls.[75] Humbert de Moyenmoutier, one of the pioneers of this movement, wrote in 1057: "the priesthood is analogous to the soul and the kingship to the body. … It follows from this that, just as the soul excels the body and commands it, so too the priestly dignity excels the royal or, we may say, the heavenly dignity excels the earthly."[76]

Gregory VII claimed to have received from Christ, as heir to Saint Peter, the power "to withdraw and to concede to anyone whomsoever, according to his merits, empires, kingdoms, principalities, duchies, marches, counties and the property of all men." Not only did kingship have no legitimacy by itself, but it needed to be redeemed by the Church because it originally came from the devil: "Who does not know that kings and dukes are descended from those who, in disregard of God, through arrogance, plunder, treachery, murder, finally through almost all crimes, prompted by the prince of this world, the devil, strove to dominate their equals, that is, [their fellow] men, in blind greed and intolerable presumption. … Human pride has created the power of kings; God's mercy has created the power of bishops. The Pope is the master of emperors."[77]

Whether we call it the two-sword theory or political Augustinianism, the political doctrine of the Roman Church has not changed. Around 1265, fifty years after the death of Innocent III, in a treatise dedicated to King Hugh II of Cyprus (a vassal to the pope), Thomas Aquinas boils it down to the idea that "the ministry of this

75 Folz, *The Concept of Empire in Western Europe, op. cit.*, p. 80.

76 Malcolm Barber, *The Two Cities: Medieval Europe 1050–1320*, Routledge, 1992, p. 88.

77 Robinson, *The Papacy 1073–1198, op. cit.*, p. 296, 399; Tout, *The Empire and the Papacy, op. cit.*, p. 126.

kingdom" (that is, the government of this world) "has been entrusted not to earthly kings but to priests, and most of all to the chief priest, the successor of St. Peter, Vicar of Christ, the Roman Pontiff. To him all the kings of the Christian People are to be subject as to our Lord Jesus" (*De Regno*, I,14).

There is a paradox, not to say a colossal hypocrisy, in the very principle of the hierarchical superiority of the pope over all sovereigns. For while claiming to be above material interests, the pope has direct temporal sovereignty over the Papal States (the Patrimony of Saint Peter), which makes him a competitor in the geopolitical game—but a competitor playing with different rules and superhuman means that only he possesses.

The Pope as the Kings' Overlord

We have seen that the popes' political strategy was determined first of all by the need to protect their own duchies in central Italy, which entailed ensuring that northern and southern Italy would never fall into the same hands. But the popes were not satisfied with these duchies. From the middle of the 11th century they began a policy of transforming as many kingdoms as possible into vassal states, which were obliged to pay an annual tribute in gold or silver.

It began in 1059 with the Treaty of Melfi, by which Pope Nicholas II invested the Norman adventurer Robert of Hauteville, known as Guiscard (i.e. "the cunning one"), with the titles of duke of Apulia and of Calabria (southern Italy), and, if he could conquer it from the Saracens, the station of count of Sicily—all as a vassal of the pope. In 1059, Robert stripped the Greek monasteries and churches in favor of Latin establishments. In the early 1070s, the Byzantine Emperor Michael VII attempted to turn Robert around by offering him an alliance sealed by the marriage of his son to Robert's daughter. But Michael was deposed by his rival Nikephoros Botaneiates, who denounced the contract. Frustrated, Robert appealed to Pope Gregory

VII, who excommunicated the "usurper" as well as his successor, Alexios Komnenos. In 1081, Robert invaded the Balkans with sixteen thousand men and the papal blessing, inflicted a crushing defeat on Alexios's army, and marched on Constantinople. But before he reached the city, he was called back by the pope, who was besieged by the German emperor Henry IV, as recounted earlier.

When Robert's nephew was crowned king of Sicily in 1130, under the name Roger II, "the famous alliance between the Normans and the Papacy was consummated," writes Thomas Tout, "which by uniting the strongest military power in Italy to the papal policy, enabled the Holy See to wield the temporal with almost as much effect as the spiritual sword. Thus the Papacy assumed a feudal suzerainty over southern Italy which outlasted the Middle Ages."[78]

This was just the beginning. In 1073, Landolph VI, Prince of Benevento, submitted himself as a vassal to Pope Gregory VII, and on his death, the principality of Benevento passed under the direct rule of the Holy See. Countess Matilda, who supported Gregory VII against Henry IV (the castle of Canossa was her residence) also donated Tuscany to the papacy. Gregory then expanded his fiefs beyond Italy. Five Spanish princes agreed to become his vassals. The racket used by the pope to force certain princes to accept his suzerainty is well illustrated by a threatening letter he wrote in 1080 to the prince of Sardinia, Orzocorre: "We do not wish to hide from you the fact that your country has been sought from us by many peoples: we have been promised great tributes if we would allow it to be invaded; such that they wish to leave one half of the whole land for our own use and to hold the other half in fealty from us. Although this was repeatedly demanded of us — not only by Normans, Tuscans and Lombards, but also by certain people from beyond the Alps — we determined never to give our assent to anyone in this matter, until we had sent our legate to you and discovered your opinion." In another

78 Tout, *The Empire and the Papacy, op. cit.*, p. 115.

case, Gregory suggested to King Sweyn II of Denmark to invade "a certain very wealthy province by the sea, which is held by base and ignoble heretics, and we desire that one of your sons be made duke and prince and defender of Christianity in that province"— on the condition, of course, that Sweyn accepted holding it as a fief from the pope. Gregory VII supported the conquest of England by William of Normandy in 1066 and, after the latter's victory over Harold Godwinson, he asked William to "return loyalty" to him, reminding him "how effective I have been in your affairs," but complaining that his reputation had suffered from it: "I was branded with infamy by some of the brethren, who complained that in conferring such a favor, I had devoted my energies to perpetrating so many murders." Indeed, Gregory's geostrategic intrigues were not to everyone's taste. The anti-Gregorian polemicist Wenrich of Trier satirized them in a letter of 1081: "There is no lack of men who seized kingdoms by tyrannical violence, whose paths to the throne lay through blood, who set a gory diadem upon their heads. All these are called the friends of the lord Pope; all are honored by his blessings and saluted by him as victorious princes."[79]

The correspondence of Gregory VII demonstrates intense diplomatic activity. The recipients of his more than 400 surviving letters include virtually all the rulers of Western Europe, as well as the Byzantine Empire, Rus', Serbia, Hungary, and even North Africa. This correspondence, studied by Robert Bartlett, makes perfectly clear the pope's determination to become the suzerain of all kings, and, in some cases, to claim full ownership of their kingdoms. The kingdom of Hungary, he affirmed, "was long ago handed over to the holy Roman Church as its property." And the kingdom of Spain "was

---

79 All quotes in this paragraph are from Robinson, *The Papacy 1073–1198*, *op. cit.*, pp. 303–317.

handed over to Saint Peter and the holy Roman Church as its rightful property."[80]

Gregory VII's successors carried on his aggressive policy of vassalizing kings with as much efficiency. In 1139, Alfonso I of Portugal had no choice but to declare himself a vassal of the Roman pontiff Innocent II. When his son Sancho neglected to pay the annual tribute, Innocent III reminded him, and the ensuing conflict, including threats of excommunication, resulted in Sancho's submission, making Portugal "a true protectorate where Innocent III, the protector, exercised the high religious, judicial and political magistracy," as Achille Luchaire explains in his biography of Innocent III. Peter of Aragon went to Rome in 1204 to hand over his crown to Innocent III and receive it back from his hand, making Aragon a fief of the pope. After Peter's death, Innocent took guardianship of his son, appointed his advisors, and formed his government. In the end, as John of Salisbury wrote, "kinglets of Spain and Portugal, chiefs of the Magyar and Slavic tribes, all resigned themselves, after flashes of revolt, to submitting to the domination of the great spiritual authority which, since Gregory VII, had endeavored to place the whole of Europe under his high sovereignty and even in his direct vassalage."[81]

In 1155, with the *Laudabiliter* bull, the English Pope Adrian IV gave Ireland as a "hereditary possession" to the king of England, Henry II, "for all islands are said to belong to the Roman church by ancient right, according to the Donation of Constantine, who richly endowed it."[82] The Church of Ireland had been founded on a very ancient monastic tradition and resisted papal supervision. The Anglo-Norman conquest of Ireland was the start of 800 years of

---

80 Robert Bartlett, *The Making of Europe: Conquest, Colonization and Cultural Change (950–1350)*, Penguin Books, 1994, pp. 248–249.

81 Achille Luchaire, *Innocent III. Les Royautés vassales du Saint-Siège*, Hachette, 1908, pp. 6, 39, 74.

82 According to John of Salisbury, quoted in Robinson, *The Papacy 1073–1198*, *op. cit.*, p. 311.

colonization, for which the Irish would be notoriously ungrateful. Adrian's bull reflects the hegemonic greed of the papacy, complete with an hypocritical candor about the salvation brought to peoples by war. Adrian congratulated Henry for his willingness

> to spread abroad the glorious name of Christ on earth, and thus store up for yourself in heaven the reward for eternal bliss, while striving as a true Catholic prince should, to enlarge the boundaries of the Church, to reveal the truth of the Christian faith to peoples still untaught and barbarous, and to root out the weeds of vice from the Lord's field. … That Ireland, and indeed all islands on which Christ, the sun of justice, has shed His rays, and which have received the teaching of the Christian faith, belong to the jurisdiction of blessed St. Peter and the holy Roman Church is a fact beyond doubt, and one which your nobility recognizes.

Twice the pope reminded King Henry that his blessing was conditioned on Henry's willingness "to pay St. Peter the annual tax of one penny from each household."[83] But Henry II did not see it that way. In 1157, he declared himself a vassal of the German emperor and, through the Constitutions of Clarendon, asserted his authority over the clerics of his kingdom. However, taking advantage of the crisis triggered by the murder of Archbishop Thomas Becket (1170), Pope Alexander III forced Henry to revoke these Constitutions and to declare to him by letter: "The kingdom of England is under your jurisdiction; I do not recognize, in feudal law, any other suzerain than you."[84] When Henry's son, John Lackland, wanted to cancel this enfeoffment and refused to pay the required tribute, Innocent III excommunicated him, placed an interdict on his kingdom, and tasked Philip Augustus of France with deposing him and replacing him with his own son, the future Louis VIII. King John chose to save both his

83 Translation from Sebastian Lidbetter, "Hadrian IV (1154–1159) and the 'Bull' Laudabiliter: A Historiographical Review," MA thesis, Wilfrid Laurier University, 2019.

84 Luchaire, *Innocent III, op. cit.*, p. 99.

soul and his kingdom; he paid an annual tribute of 1,000 marks to the "Lord Pope" and wrote to him in a *confiteor*:

> We want it to be known to you all, through this charter bearing our seal, that since we have committed many offenses against God and our mother the holy Church, since, as a result, divine mercy fails us, and since we can only offer to God and the Church the satisfaction due to them by humbling ourselves and our kingdoms, … by our good and spontaneous will and by the common council of our barons, we freely confer and concede to God and to his holy apostles Peter and Paul and to the holy Roman Church our mother and to the lord Pope Innocent and to his Catholic successors, the whole kingdom of England and the kingdom of Ireland, with all their rights and allegiances, for the remission of all our sins and those of our race, both for the living and for the deceased; and henceforth, receiving and holding these kingdoms of God and of the Roman Church as vassal, … we have made and sworn loyalty to the lord Pope Innocent and his Catholic successors and to the Roman Church, and we will pay liege homage in his presence, if we can find ourselves before him; and we obligate our legitimate successors and heirs in perpetuity.[85]

It was undoubtedly Innocent III (1198–1216) who pushed the pontifical policy of the vassalization of European kingdoms to its limit. "During his eighteen years as pope," writes Malcolm Barber, "Innocent made and unmade rulers; presided over, at one time or another, as vassal states, the kingdoms of Sicily, Iberia, and England, as well as possibly Hungary, Poland and Bulgaria."[86] Innocent III was the first pope to wear the three-crown tiara (Paul VI, 1963–1978, was the last), symbolizing his triple authority as "father of kings, regent of the world, and vicar of Jesus-Christ."

The imperial policy of the popes is both the most important and the least known political fact of the classical Middle Ages. One of its applications, to be examined in the next chapter, was the prerogative

85 Bernard Cottret, *Histoire de l'Angleterre, De Guillaume le Conquérant à nos jours,* Texto/Tallandier, 2019, pp. 60–61.

86 Barber, *The Two Cities, op. cit.*, p. 105.

of the popes to raise armies of "crusaders" in all the kingdoms, duchies, and counties of Europe. In doing so, the papacy claimed the magical power to wash away the sins of anyone willing to go and shed the blood of the infidels.

How deeply papal imperialism affected medieval society can be deduced from the fact that the gesture of clasped hands, which in feudal ceremonial expressed the vassal's homage to his overlord, and which standard iconography show kings adopting in relationship to the pope—as in the 13th-century image of Charlemagne's coronation by Leo III (reproduced on the present book's cover)—became the natural attitude of prayer for Catholics.

The Hohenstaufen Dynasty

Let us now pick up the thread of the epic war between popes and emperors where we left off. Upon the death of Henry V in 1125, the Salian dynasty came to an end. Then began a period of rivalry between two powerful families: the Hohenstaufen from Swabia, and the Welfs from Saxony and Bavaria. In 1138, Conrad III was the first King of the Romans from the Hohenstaufen family. When he died in 1152, the throne passed to his thirty-year-old nephew, Frederick, nicknamed Barbarossa; his Welf ancestry through his mother worked in his favor. With him, the pope believed he had found a faithful ally. In exchange for the imperial crown, Barbarossa subdued the city of Rome, which had revolted against the pope, and undertook to fight for the complete expulsion of the Byzantines from Italy.

The prestige of Frederick Barbarossa was immense, and his *imperium* was recognized even by the kings of France and England. We have a letter from Henry II of England, who reigned over what some modern historians confusingly call the "Plantagenet Empire," written to Frederick in 1157: "We lay before you our kingdom and whatever is anywhere subject to our sway, and entrust it to your power, that all things may be administered in accordance with your nod and that in all respects your imperial will be done. Let there be, therefore, between us and our peoples an undivided unity of affection and peace, safe commercial intercourse, so that to you, who excels us in worth, may fall the right to command (*imperandi auctoritas*), while we shall not lack the will to obey (*voluntas obsequendi*)."[87]

As one might expect, the Hohenstaufen dynasty was in almost constant conflict with the popes, who encroached on their imperial prerogatives. Barbarossa was the first to attach the adjective *Sacrum* to his *Romanum Imperium,* to signify that it drew its legitimacy directly from God and not from the Church. An incident that occurred during a great diet convened by Barbarossa in Besançon in 1157 illustrates the bone of contention. The papal envoy, Roland Bandinelli of Siena, came to remind the emperor that he had received his imperial title from the pope. Barbarossa, relying on Roman law, replied by circulating the following statement: "since, through election by the princes, the kingdom and the empire are ours from God alone, Who at the time of the passion of His Son Christ subjected the world to dominion by the two swords, and since the apostle Peter taught the world this doctrine: 'Fear God, honor the king,' whosoever says that we received the imperial crown as a fief [*pro beneficio*] from the lord pope contradicts the divine ordinance and the doctrine of Peter, and is guilty of a lie."[88]

When Bandinelli himself became Pope Alexander III, Frederick refused to recognize him and supported a rival pope. Alexander III excommunicated him and stirred a rebellion among the cities of northern Italy. At that time, the cities were organized into independent communes associated in leagues. The Lombard League, led by Milan, was formed in 1168 with the support of the pope to resist the emperor. Over the course of his career, Barbarossa led four military expeditions to subjugate them, razing Milan in 1162, but ultimately

87 Otto of Freising, *The Deeds of Frederick Barbarossa,* III, xi, quoted in Folz, *The Concept of Empire in Western Europe, op. cit.,* p. 196.

88 Tout, *The Empire and the Papacy, op. cit.,* p. 254.

failed. In Venice in 1177—one hundred years after Canossa—he humbled himself before Pope Alexander III and recognized the autonomy of the Lombard cities (some of which would later side with him).

Ten years later, Pope Urban III was about to excommunicate Frederick Barbarossa again when news reached Europe of the fall of the Kingdom of Jerusalem. Urban died and was replaced by Gregory VIII, who called for a new crusade (the third). Frederick left in 1189, before Philip II of France and Richard I of England, perhaps hoping to use this opportunity to forge an alliance with the *basileus* in Constantinople. But after some military successes against Saladin, he died.

Frederick had previously arranged the marriage of his son Henry, the future emperor Henry VI, to Constance of Hauteville, daughter of the Norman king of Sicily Roger II. When William II of Sicily died childless in 1189, his inheritance was claimed by his aunt Constance, which made the son of Henry VI and Constance, the future Frederick II, the king of Sicily (the Kingdom of Sicily comprised the southern part of the Italian peninsula). This is how the Hohenstaufen family would realize the dream of Otto III and the nightmare of the pope: the union of southern Italy with Germany. As soon as he was invested, Henry VI's priority was to put down the rebellion of the Norman barons of Sicily, who were supporting another pretender to the throne. But he also had to confront the young Pope Innocent III, who pursued with unparalleled energy the theocratic project of the papacy.

At the death of Henry VI in 1197, the struggle between the supporters of the Welfs and those of the Hohenstaufen resumed. Henry VI had his son Frederick elected before his death, but he was only three years old at the time. It was therefore Henry VI's younger brother, Philip of Swabia, who was elected by a diet of nobles gathered in Mainz (1198). But the supporters of the Welfs gathered in Frankfurt the following year and elected a certain Otto IV of

Brunswick. Pope Innocent III, who feared the unification of Italy under the same dynasty, sided with Otto and excommunicated Philip, after having made the former promise never to attempt to reunite Sicily with the Empire. A nearly ten-year war ensued between the two factions, which would echo for two more centuries in the Italian civil war between Guelphs and Ghibellines, whose names are derived from the Italian forms of Welf and Weiblingen (the Hohenstaufen stronghold).

Otto was crowned emperor by Innocent III in 1209. He immediately betrayed his promise not to covet southern Italy and launched his army on the kingdom of Sicily. Innocent III promptly excommunicated him and convinced the nobles of Germany to elect a new king. Philip of Swabia having died in the meantime, their choice fell upon his nephew, the son of Henry VI Hohenstaufen, Frederick, who was now sixteen years old and in full possession of his title of king of Sicily. The pope had no choice but to support him against Otto IV, but his support was lent on the condition that Frederick committed to swear allegiance to him, to protect the papal principalities, and to renounce Sicily in favor of his son Henry, born of his recent marriage to Constance of Aragon. Frederick acquiesced and, during his coronation as king of the Romans at Aachen in 1215, he additionally promised to lead a crusade to retake Jerusalem. Here is how Ernst Kantorowicz explains this unexpected initiative that took the pope by surprise: "It was an almost inspired masterstroke of diplomacy that prompted the young King to set himself at the head of the crusading movement. Unwittingly he thus took the leadership and direction of the Crusade out of the hands of the papal Imperator and took up again the noblest task of an Emperor — by common consent the imperial prerogative — to lead the knights of Christendom to the Holy Land."[89]

89 Kantorowicz, *Frederick the Second, op. cit.*, p. 73.

Abandoned by the pope, Otto IV allied himself with the king of England, John Lackland, while Philip Augustus of France supported Frederick II. The defeat of Otto at the battle of Bouvines on July 27, 1214 ensured Frederick II the rallying of the majority of the German princes. He spent eight years traveling through Germany to pacify the kingdom and consolidate his authority, then returned to his kingdom of Sicily while leaving the government of Germany to his son Henry. This was contrary to the oath he had sworn to Innocent III, but the new Pope Honorius III was accommodating and crowned him emperor in 1220, while urging him to fulfill his crusading vows. Frederick pledged to leave in 1225 at the latest.

The project took a peculiar turn in 1225 when, having become a widower, Frederick married the daughter of the exiled king of Jerusalem, John of Brienne, and immediately, to his father-in-law's surprise, asserted himself as the new king of Jerusalem. In 1227, however, Frederick had still not left for the Holy Land, held back as he was by troubles in Italy and then by an epidemic that broke out just when he was about to sail from Brindisi. The new Pope Gregory IX, a relative and disciple of Innocent III, used this as a pretext to excommunicate Frederick, henceforth prohibiting him from going on a crusade. After a stormy negotiation between the two men, the pope called Frederick "a monster out of the sea, whose mouth opens only to blaspheme God." On November 17, 1227, he published the official excommunication and declared that "any city which offered him hospitality would automatically be placed under ban."[90]

Frederick nevertheless embarked toward the Holy Land on June 28, 1228, assuming—wrongly—that the excommunication would fall by itself. It would be a crusade without bloodshed: Frederick obtained from Sultan Al-Kamil the restitution of Jerusalem, as well as Bethlehem and Nazareth, thanks to his diplomatic skill and his friendship with the ambassador of the sultan, Emir Fakhr al-Din.

---

90 Jacques Benoist-Méchin, *Frédéric de Hohenstaufen ou le rêve excommunié (1194–1250)*, Perrin, 2008, p. 236.

Frederick crowned himself king of Jerusalem before sailing back West.

This peaceful crusade was not to the taste of the pope, who accused Frederick of having made a pact with the infidel. In fact, while the excommunicated Frederick was negotiating the restitution of the Holy Places, Gregory IX launched his own crusade against him, and stirred the rebellion of the Lombard cities. The pope even circulated the rumor of Frederick's death to justify his military campaign against Sicily. At the very moment when Frederick was about to deliver Jerusalem, the pope's troops penetrated deep into Sicily, seizing several large cities and sowing terror in their path.[91]

But Frederick's prestige upon his return from the Holy Land was immense and forced the pope to lift the excommunication. This inaugurated a period of ten years during which Frederick would leave his indelible imprint in fields as diverse as architecture, science, law, and poetry. He is credited with the construction of more than 200 castles, some of spectacular originality, like the octagonal Castel del Monte in southeast Italy. Frederick made the Kingdom of Sicily a beacon of scholarship and science with the creation of a university in Naples and a medical school in Salerno, both emancipated from canonical prohibitions and the compulsory use of Latin. He wrote for the kingdom a code of laws, the *Liber Augustalis*, stating in its preamble that: "Necessity, no less than the inspiration of Divine Providence, created the rulers of the peoples."[92] The scientific and experimental methods encouraged by Frederick made Pope Gregory IX fulminate, and he excommunicated him again in 1239, declaring: "We say it, we repeat it, we are ready to prove it: this king of pestilence openly asserts that man should only believe what can be demonstrated by experience

91 Pierre Boulle, *L'Étrange croisade de l'empereur Frédéric II*, Flammarion, 1968, p. 187.

92 Kantorowicz, *Frederick the Second, op. cit.*, p. 243.

and reason."[93] Frederick was a man of the Renaissance long before the Renaissance.

Frederick did not forget Germany and, after dethroning his son for rebellion, he solemnly restored "Public Peace" during a great diet in Mainz in 1235 (the edict was published in German, a first in history). This period saw the expansion of the Empire to the East, with the help of the Teutonic Order, whose Grand Master Hermann von Salza was his most faithful friend. Within two decades, the Teutonic Knights conquered Prussia and Livonia, founded such cities as Thorn, Kulm, and Elbing, and attracted German settlers. German influence also spread in Bohemia, Hungary, and Poland, where German colonists were welcomed. In 1236, Frederick mobilized a large army to subdue the Lombard cities that the pope continually incited against him. He received the support of Henry III of England (Frederick, again a widower, had married his sister) as well as Louis IX of France.

The pope tried, in vain, to turn Louis against the emperor by flattering him in his bull *Dei Filius* of October 21, 1239, much quoted ever since by French Catholic nationalists: "Just as in times past God preferred the tribe of Judah to those of the other sons of Jacob and granted it special blessings, so He chose France, in preference to all other nations on earth, for the protection of the Catholic faith and the defense of religious freedom. For this reason, France is the kingdom of God itself, and the enemies of France are the enemies of Christ."[94]

Raised in Apulia, southern Italy, Frederick did not share the hostility of the Latins against the Byzantines, and even supported the resistance of the latter who, from Epirus and Nicaea, sought to reconquer Constantinople from the Franks who had taken it in 1204. "In 1238, in the midst of Gregory's efforts to recruit a crusade against

93 Benoist-Méchin, *Frédéric de Hohenstaufen, op. cit.*, p. 361.

94 Camille Pascal, *Ainsi Dieu choisit la France. La véritable histoire de la fille aînée de l'Église,* Presses de la Renaissance, 2016.

the Greeks, Frederick marked a new alliance with John Vatatzes, emperor of Nicaea, which culminated in the marriage between John and Frederick's daughter, Constance/Anna, in the early 1240s."[95]

The efforts deployed by Gregory IX to harm Frederick II (including assassination attempts) were matched only by the next pope, Innocent IV, who took up the ideas of his namesake on the pope's *plenitudo potestatis*. In July 1245, at the Council of Lyon, Innocent IV confirmed the excommunication of Frederick and wanted to dispossess him. On this occasion, the king of France Louis IX protested on the grounds of the natural law of the state, a direct challenge to papal political theory: "we solemnly oppose any measure of deposition. As powerful and respected as he is, the Pope does not have the right to depose a king. Every monarch is on his throne by virtue of Divine Right, and Divine Right is superior to the Apostolic Right which the Pope holds as heir to Saint Peter. We therefore formally oppose Pope Innocent's deposition of Emperor Frederick, because this act, which generates endless disorder, would have the main effect of shaking the Christian community to its very foundations."[96]

In a manifesto that smelled strongly of heresy to the pope, Frederick called on all the princes of Europe to a general revolt against the papacy's abuses and corruption: "God is our witness that our intention has always been to force churchmen to follow in the footsteps of the Primitive Church, to live an apostolic life, and to be humble like Jesus Christ. In our days the Church has become worldly. We therefore propose to do a work of charity in taking away from such men the treasures with which they are filled for their eternal damnation. … Help us to put down these proud prelates, that we may give mother Church more worthy guides to direct her."[97]

---

95 George Demacopoulos, *Colonizing Christianity: Greek and Latin Religious Identity in the Era of the Fourth Crusade*, Fordham UP, 2019, pp. 95–96.

96 Benoist-Méchin, *Frédéric de Hohenstaufen*, *op. cit.*, p. 465.

97 Tout, *The Empire and the Papacy*, *op. cit.*, p. 389.

Frederick died in 1250 at the age of 55. His son Conrad, born from Yolande of Brienne, left Germany for Sicily, but died two years later at the age of 26. His half-brother Manfred declared himself regent of the Kingdom of Sicily on behalf of Conrad's son, Conradin, who was only two years old. But the pope gave the kingdom to Charles of Anjou, an ambitious, cruel, and unscrupulous character, very different from his brother Louis IX. Charles landed in Sicily in January 1266 with a powerful army of mercenaries and overcame Manfred, who was killed in battle (the pope had his remains dug up and thrown into the Garigliano). Charles captured the young Conradin and had him beheaded, an act that shocked the world. Manfred's widow was also captured and thrown in prison, where she died after five years. The eyes of her three male children were gouged out and they were locked up in the basement of Castel del Monte, where they also died soon after.[98]

Epilogue

Fighting against the formidable power of four popes and excommunicated three times, Frederick II had nevertheless endowed the Holy Roman Empire with unprecedented influence and prestige. He was transforming Europe and building bridges between the Christian and Islamic civilizations. Despite all the efforts of the papacy to vilify him as the Antichrist, Frederick II, "the child of Apulia," was a "wonder of the world" (*stupor mundi*) and the herald of a new age. His death and the systematic extermination of his descendants broke the momentum and changed the destiny of the world. But his memory, somehow merging with that of his grandfather, Barbarossa, became immortal, giving rise to the German legend of the Sleeping Emperor who will one day emerge from his mountain to revive the Empire and provide the world with a long era of peace. Francis Rapp said it well:

98 Benoist-Méchin, *Frédéric de Hohenstaufen, op. cit.*, p. 539.

> Charged with this messianic hope, the imperial idea kept all its vitality despite the miseries that afflicted the Empire in reality. This expectation of a bright future comforted the Germans who were saddened by the spectacle of the present. When they remembered the past, they found reasons to be proud, of a pride mixed with bitterness, because if the century of the Hohenstaufen symbolized in their eyes the Empire in full force, this glory had the heartrending light of the sunset, since the apogee was immediately followed by the fall, the ruin that the pope had wanted.[99]

After the death of Frederick II in 1250, the imperial seat remained vacant for more than sixty years, as popes refused to crown a successor. It was not until 1310 that a German king, Henry VII of Luxembourg, came to Rome to be crowned emperor. Meanwhile, the Holy Roman Empire, as it continued to be called, had been deprived of all its Italian conquests, while the Capetians had captured its western provinces, Alsace and Burgundy. The weakening of imperial power had plunged the Germanic duchies themselves into feudal wars.

After the defeat of the Hohenstaufen dynasty, the idea of the emperor as universal monarch reflecting the divine monarchy was still upheld by Dante Alighieri in *De Monarchia*, but then slowly receded into mythology. A conception of the world without an emperor emerged, where kings alone ensured the defense of the Church and the peace and salvation of their respective peoples. The Church was left, for some time, as the only vision of unity for Western Europe.[100] The popes' victory seemed overwhelming. The 13th-century Papacy was a formidable institution, without parallel in history: an almost successful case of imperial government by monk-priests, with an elected king-priest who declared himself suzerain of all the sovereigns of Europe, from whom he demanded homage, tribute, and armed service. A king of kings. Ultimately, however, the popes failed in their imperial coup, because they could not escape the paradox that their own authority was dependent on the prestige and the

99 Rapp, *Le Saint Empire romain germanique, op. cit.*, p. 218.

100 Chazan, *L'Empire et l'histoire universelle, op. cit.*, p. 703.

protection of the emperor. The popes could not totally usurp the imperial majesty, and by weakening it, they sawed off the branch on which they were sitting. The shrinking of the empire and the emergence of national states led inevitably to questioning and ultimately rejecting the pope's hegemonic pretense, which now appeared misplaced. The empire of the popes could not succeed, but its legacy has endured: European disunion. The papacy tried to usurp the empire by the forgery of the Donation of Constantine, but could never be more than "the ghost of the deceased Roman Empire, sitting crowned upon the grave thereof" (Thomas Hobbes, *Leviathan*, chapter 47).

France, which had taken advantage of the struggle between popes and emperors, emerged as the greatest European power. Hence, in the early 14th century, Philip IV the Fair was the first to ungratefully emancipate himself from papal suzerainty. His conflict with Boniface VIII is comparable in intensity to that between Emperor Henry IV and Pope Gregory VII, but this time it turned to the advantage of the king. Philip put the papacy under his control by moving it to Avignon, and the next seven popes would all be French, as would most of their cardinals. Philip was so confident that, in 1308, following the assassination of Emperor Albert I of Habsburg, he sought the imperial crown for his brother, Charles of Valois.

This irreversible defeat of the papal project launched two and a half centuries earlier made possible the development of the monarchical states along secular lines. Thus it has been said that, by desacralizing royalty, the Gregorian Reform paved the way for the modern, secular state. The Empire, however, continued to haunt Europe, like a ghost looking for a new body. On the occasion of the death of Emperor Albert of Habsburg in 1308, the French scholar Pierre Dubois wrote a memorandum to his King Philip IV, urging him to be proclaimed Emperor by Pope Clement V. In the eyes of the French, the papacy still seemed necessary for the Empire, and this may be the reason why Philip kidnapped it rather than destroyed it. But a good century later, Henry VIII felt strong enough to break with the papacy and organize the transfer of Church property for the benefit of the gentry (France would do the same during the Revolution, but for the benefit of the bourgeoisie).

France and Spain remained Catholic and competed for the Empire. The Italian Wars which pitted Francis I against Charles V, both eager to take away the pope's temporal sword but not his spiritual sword. With the sack of Rome in 1527, the "eternal city" was pillaged for nearly a year by the mercenary troops of Charles V, who resigned in disgust. Most archives were destroyed or lost. Visiting the city in 1581, Michel de Montaigne wrote in his journal: "those who said that at least the ruins of Rome could be seen there were saying too much; for the ruins of such a formidable edifice would bring more honor and reverence to its memory; it was nothing but its sepulcher."[101] This sepulcher of Rome was also that of the medieval ideal of the Empire; from Otto I to Frederick II, each and every "Roman Emperor" had wanted to make Rome the capital of his empire, but had faced the fierce resistance of the popes, who invoked the false Donation of Constantine to prohibit the emperor from residing there. Without Rome as its capital, the medieval Roman Empire could never be fully embodied.

The idea, however, continued to float around, looking for a suitable vehicle. Some British thinkers turned to it during the reign of Queen Elizabeth I (1558–1603). The polymath and "cosmopolitical philosopher" John Dee tried, with mixed success, to advise the Queen on her imperial role. In his *Memorials Pertaining to the Perfect Art of Navigation* (1576), he argued that Britain could establish a "Cosmopolitical Government" and surpass "any other particular Monarchy that ever was on Earth since Man's Creation."[102]

Two centuries later, the imperial fever would take hold of Napoleon. The Napoleonic odyssey proves two things: first, that the

101 Michel de Montaigne, *Journal de Voyage*, Folio/Gallimard, 1983, p. 200.

102 Jafe Arnold, "Esoteric Imperialism: The Solomonic-Theurgic Mystique of John Dee's British Empire," *Endeavour* 43 (2019), pp. 17–24.

Idea of Empire was still vibrant in Europe at the beginning of the 19th century, and second, that the Empire was never for France to have (it is significant that Napoleon was not born French, which confirms that the French Empire was not a French idea). The French Empire failed, despite spilling an enormous quantity of blood: at Leipzig in 1813, the largest battle ever fought in history to date left one hundred thousand dead soldiers. "During four days," Hans Vogel writes, "half a million soldiers from all over Europe did their utmost maneuvering trying to kill each other. In this vast battle, Napoleon's military backbone was forever broken and Germany was liberated from the French occupation under which it was reeling."[103] In order to prevent France from upsetting the European balance of power once again, the Congress of Vienna (1815) came up with the "Holy Alliance" between Russia, Prussia, and Austria.

French occupation and the dissolution of the remnant of the Holy Roman Empire stimulated a German national reaction and revived the memory of the greatness of medieval imperial Germany. In 1815, the poet Friedrich Rückert composed his ballad "Barbarossa," and Wagner later cried out: "When will you come back, Frederick, splendid Siegfried?"[104] A new pan-Germanism was emerging. The Westphalian order would soon have to deal with the rise of a Germany reunited around Prussia, hearing again the call of her imperial destiny. Meanwhile, Great Britain had developed a clear and simple European strategy that rested on two pillars, as Hans Vogel explains in *How Europe Became American:* "One was the 'freedom of the seas,' which was just a neutral way of saying that those seas were in fact controlled by the Royal Navy, the most powerful in the world. The other was always to support the second-most powerful state on the continent, to make sure that the most powerful one would not establish dominance over the entire continent." Based on

103 Vogel, *How Europe Became American*, *op. cit.*, p. 88.

104 Pierre Racine, *Frédéric Barberousse, 1152–1190*, Perrin, 2009, pp. 11–12.

the "Heartland" theory of Halford Mackinder, a geographer by training, England made it a rule to sabotage any alliance between Russia and Germany, both of whom had every reason to make such alliance, "since in economic terms, Russia and Germany were perfectly complementary," with Russia providing the wheat and raw materials that Germany needed to make the industrial goods that Russia needed in return.[105] The Industrial Revolution had given England a considerable advantage, but by the beginning of the 20th century, Germany had more than caught up with her. The British Lord Archibald Rosebery wrote in *The Times*: "I am afraid of Germany. Why am I afraid of the Germans? Because I admire and esteem them so much. They are an industrious nation; they are, above all, a systematic nation; they are a scientific nation, and whatever they take up, whether it be the arts of peace or the arts of war, they push them forward to the utmost possible perfection with that industry, that system, that science which is part of their character. Are we gaining on the Germans? I believe, on the contrary, we are losing ground."[106]

Hence the First World War. It would not bring an end to Germany, which rose again, bruised, amputated and embittered, but still confident in her destiny. It is no coincidence that the best biography of Frederick II was published in Germany in 1927. Ernst Kantorowicz's book made a great impression on Hitler and Göring, who gifted a copy to Mussolini. In 1938, Carl Jung responded to the American journalist Hubert Knickerbocker who asked his psychiatric opinion on the "Hitler case": "He is the loud-speaker which magnifies the inaudible whispers of the German soul until they can be heard by the German's conscious ear. He is the first man to tell every German what he has been thinking and feeling all along in his unconscious about German fate ... Hitler's power is not political; it is magic."[107]

---

105 Vogel, *How Europe Became American*, *op. cit.*, pp. 66, 71.

106 Lord Rosebery at Colchester, *The Times*, quoted in exergue of E. E. Williams, *Made in Germany*, London, 1896.

107 H. R. Knickerbocker, *Is Tomorrow Hitler's?*, New York, 1941.

It would take Churchill and one more world war to break Germany (and ruin the British Empire in the process).[108] In 1948, Europe's future looked dim. Francis Parker Yockey wrote in his grand book *Imperium: The Philosophy of History and Politics*:

> The present chaos—1948—is directly traceable to the attempt to prevent the integration of Europe. As a result, Europe is in a swamp, and extra-European forces dispose of former European nations as their colonies. ... Either Europe will become totally integrated, or it will pass entirely out of history, its peoples will be dispersed, its efforts and brains will be at the disposal forever of extra-European forces. ... I condemn here at the outset the miserable plans of retarded souls to 'unite' Europe as an economic area for purposes of exploitation by and defense of the Imperialism of extra-European forces. ... Not trade and banking, not importing and exporting, but Heroism alone can liberate that integrated soul of Europe which lies under the financial trickery of retarders, the petty-stateism of party-politicians, and the occupying armies of extra-European forces.

Fortunately, Germany was spared the dreadful "Morgenthau Plan" that aimed at turning the country into a purely agricultural land, and soon resurrected from its ashes, albeit as a vassal to an American empire. In 1952, Spanish diplomat and Oxford professor Salvador de Madariaga wrote in his *Portrait of Europe*:

> Germany is the core of Europe. She stands at the center of her body, at the apex of her mind, in the innermost chambers of her conscious and unconscious being, the source of her most glorious music. Philosophy, science, history, technology are unthinkable without Germany. If Germany falls, Europe falls. If Germany goes mad, Europe goes mad. The moral health of the German people is one of the chief conditions for the moral health, indeed for the very existence of Europe.[109]

---

108 How Churchill liquidated the British Empire's jewels in the process of winning WWII is best told by David Irving in *Churchill's War*, vol. 2: *Triumph in Adversity*, Focal Point, 2002.

109 Salvador de Madariaga, *Portrait of Europe* (1952), University of Alabama Press, 1967, p. 107.

11

Fools' Crusade: Jerusalem at the Heart of Europe

AT THE END of the 11th century, the popes instilled in the ruling caste one particularly revolutionary idea: the Crusade. It was a revelation, a new road to salvation, as well as a paradoxical attempt to unify Europe around Jerusalem. It brought the best and the worst out of the warrior class, it was embraced by the kings (the Third Crusade was "the Crusade of the Kings") as well as by the masses (there was even a "Children's Crusade" in 1212), and it gave the pope unprecedented spiritual and political domination. The Crusade was the quintessence, or the central paradigm, of the European Middle Ages, and it became a core element in Europe's identity and sense of mission.

The Crusades were the popes' wars. But more than that, they were the popes' obsession. And because the Papacy had by then more spiritual influence on Europe than any other institution, the popes' obsession became Europe's obsession. Consider what Jane Sayers writes in her sympathetic biography of Innocent III, who in 1215 convened the biggest international conference ever, where every prince from Paris to Constantinople was either present or represented: "He preached more crusades than any other pope and contributed more to the crusading movement than anyone since Pope Urban II. A large part of the pope's correspondence is concerned from the earliest years of the pontificate with the necessity of financing and undertaking a new crusade. Innocent, it has been said, was haunted by the crusading idea."[1]

In this chapter, I intend to show that the Crusades were such a potent experience that their influence on Western civilization outlasted the fall of papal autocracy and is still felt today. My purpose is not to repeat the history of the Crusades, but to explain their essence and derive therefrom some insight into the inherited character of the West. The focus will be on what the Crusades did to the West, rather than what they did to the East, although that is also part of the subject.

Dressed in new clothes, the Crusade remains a core principle of the Western elite's worldview. It is the West's defining Big Idea: redeeming the world—and itself—through wars in the name of lofty principles. Democracy and Human Rights have replaced Christ, but the West, under the leadership of the U.S., is still the Civilization of the Crusade. It was not innocently that, upon coming back from church service on the Sunday following September 11, 2001, George W. Bush made this televised declaration, broadcast throughout the world: "This crusade, this war on terrorism, is going to take a while." To Middle-Eastern ears, that sounded like the omen of a long series of attacks by fanatical barbarians, who would disguise their dark designs as noble causes. The Crusade is still relevant today because it became part of the West's DNA a thousand years ago.

The Impact of the Crusades

In a study published in 2006 on recent developments in the historiography of the Crusades, Norman Housley writes that everyone agrees today that "the crusades played a central rather than a peripheral role in the development of medieval Europe." "There can be no doubt," he adds, "that crusading was one of the features of medieval life that gave Catholic Europe its remarkable rate of growth.

1 Jane Sayers, *Innocent III, Leader of Europe*, Pearson, 1993, p. 181.

This established an inherent dynamism that characterized the central Middle Ages."[2] More than anything else, of course, as Michael Mitterauer insists, "The crusading movement produced a radical change in Western Christendom's attitude toward war, marking a turning point in the history of Western thinking." It also set the pattern for European expansionism, which "is a fundamental feature of Europe's special path." The Crusade is a purely Western idea, Mitterauer emphasizes: "The Byzantine Empire did not mobilize any Crusades. Just the opposite: it fell victim to a Crusade itself in 1204. Among the many variously configured Christian groups in the medieval world, the Crusade was an institution restricted to the Western Church. … the Crusade was the pope's war. … Without the pope, there was no Crusade."[3]

In Constantinople, when Emperor Nicephorus II Phocas (963–969) proposed an imperial decree stating that all soldiers killed in fighting the Muslims have died a martyr's death, the Patriarch of Constantinople rejected it. He refused to sanction a declaration that meant recruiting warriors in exchange for the promise of paradise if killed. That is why there was never any crusade from the Byzantine Empire.[4] The notion of holy war declared by ecclesiastical authority has always been repugnant to the Eastern Church. All military expeditions were placed under the authority of the *basileus*, never of the patriarch. The idea that churchmen may fight, as was the case among the crusaders, it horrified the Byzantines. As Jonathan Harris wrote, "the Byzantines had a pronounced reluctance to go to war. Unlike western Europe where prowess in battle was a mark of status and distinction, the Byzantines seem to have regarded war as, at best, a distasteful necessity."[5] "The Byzantines were not a warlike people,"

---

2 Norman Housley, *Contesting the Crusades,* Blackwell, 2006, pp. 144, 154–155.

3 Michael Mitterauer, *Why Europe?, op. cit.*, 2010, pp. 153, 194, 196.

4 *Ibid.*, p. 196.

5 Jonathan Harris, *Byzantium and the Crusades*, 2nd ed., Bloomsbury Academic, 2014, p. 13.

Kaldellis also insists, for "[m]oney, silk, and titles were the empire's preferred instruments of governance and foreign policy, over swords and armies."[6]

One remarkable aspect of the Crusades is their sudden and spectacular appearance. "It was not the culmination of an evolution, but the almost spontaneous outpouring of a prodigious power of collective animation," wrote French historian Paul Alphandéry.[7] We can pinpoint the day (27 November 1095) when the call fell like the Holy Spirit on bishops and abbots, whereafter it was spread to the lay population of France and Germany by an army of itinerant preachers.

The First Crusade (1095–97) was a success, and it was celebrated by countless heroic tales, which can be regarded as the earliest mass propaganda. The First Crusade became for Westerners what the Trojan War was for the ancient Greeks.[8] Christopher Tyerman writes:

> The scale and rapid production of histories of the First Crusade by eyewitnesses and others eager to interpret the startling events didactically finds no parallel in medieval historiography. Within a dozen years of Jerusalem's capture, at least four full eyewitness accounts, three major western histories and part of the great Lorraine version by Albert of Aachen were being circulated along with a bevy of other accounts, more or less derivative, imaginative or polemic. While originating in monasteries and cathedrals, these texts reflected and excited secular interests, for example in local heroes or national pride. Most of the histories sculpted stirring tales of faith, bravery, suffering, danger, tenacity and triumph. The theologians distilled the message of God's immanence and Christian duty; the no less artful eyewitnesses provided accessible tales of miracles and butchery. One of the very earliest, the *Gesta Francorum,* included elaborate scenes with stereotype exotic Orientals declaiming extravagant, bombastic nonsense

6 Anthony Kaldellis, *Streams of Gold, Rivers of Blood: The Rise and Fall of Byzantium, 955 A.D. to the First Crusade,* Oxford UP, 2019, p. xxvii.

7 Paul Alphandéry and Alphonse Dupront, *La Chrétienté et l'idée de croisade,* Albin Michel, 1995, p. 13.

8 As noted by Oswald Spengler, *The Decline of the West,* vol. 1, Legend Books, 2024, pp. 12, 34.

much in the style of the verse *chanson de geste*. Naturalistic representation, especially of the enemy, did not feature.[9]

The impact of these tales was such that, when the Second Crusade was preached in 1145, the response was again overwhelming. "I opened my mouth, I spoke, and at once the Crusaders have multiplied to infinity," Bernard of Clairvaux wrote to the pope, with some exaggeration and perhaps some vanity. "Villages and towns are now deserted. You will scarcely find one man for every seven women. Everywhere you see widows whose husbands are still alive."[10] Bernard had an undeniable talent of persuasion. Here is one of his rhetorical arguments from his pamphlet *In Praise of the New Knighthood*:

> the knights of Christ may safely fight the battles of their Lord, fearing neither sin if they smite the enemy, nor danger at their own death; since to inflict death or to die for Christ is no sin, but rather, an abundant claim to glory. In the first case one gains for Christ, and in the second one gains Christ himself. The Lord freely accepts the death of the foe who has offended him, and yet more freely gives himself for the consolation of his fallen knight. … The knight of Christ, I say, may strike with confidence and die yet more confidently, for he serves Christ when he strikes, and serves himself when he falls. … Should he be killed himself, we know that he has not perished, but has come safely into port. When he inflicts death it is to Christ's profit, and when he suffers death, it is for his own gain.[11]

In other words: blessed if you kill, blessed if you die.

Although it was a papal idea from the beginning, the Crusade grew deep roots in the minds and hearts of the knightly class and colonized every region of lay culture. Some vernacular accounts of

---

9 Christopher Tyerman, *God's War: A New History of the Crusades*, Penguin, 2006, p. 244.

10 Steven Runciman, *A History of the Crusades*, vol. 2: *The Kingdom of Jerusalem and the Frankish East, 1100–1187*, Cambridge UP, 1951, p. 253.

11 "Medieval Sourcebook: St. Bernard of Clairvaux (1090–11–53): In Praise of the New Knighthood," Fordham University [sourcebooks.web.fordham.edu/source/Bernard-praiseofnewknighthood.asp].

the First Crusade, such as the immensely popular versified *Chanson d'Antioche*, competed with the genre of apocryphal gospels in their lavish use of prophecies, visions, miracles, angels and demons, and other signs of divine Providence. Both genres actually merged in the international bestsellers of the Grail corpus: Chrétien de Troyes's seminal romance *Le Conte du Graal*, written around 1180, was woven around esoteric icons of the Crusade: the grail containing the host (i.e. the body of Christ) is a symbol of the Holy Sepulchre, while the "bleeding lance" is rather transparently the Holy Lance that pierced Christ's side, whose spearhead was miraculously discovered in Antioch by the besieged crusaders.[12] It is no overstatement that implicit evocations of the Crusade are present in almost all medieval lay literature, from the earliest *chansons de geste* to the latest Arthurian romances.

Through the Crusades, Northwest Europe made a place for itself in history. "Before their inception," writes Steven Runciman in his unsurpassed *History of the Crusades*, "the centre or our civilisation was placed in Byzantium and in the lands of the Arab caliphate. Before they faded out the hegemony in civilisation had passed to Western Europe."[13] In other words, Western Europe became a civilization in its own right through the Crusade.

The end of the Crusades is traditionally dated to 1291, when the city of Acre, the last Latin stronghold in Syria, fell to the Mamluks, leaving no possible landing site for new expeditions. Strictly speaking, therefore, the Crusades lasted two centuries. Modern historians have conventionally numbered them from one to eight, but in reality, there was an uninterrupted flow of military expeditions to the Middle East of various sizes and origins. For example, at least six separate campaigns were launched between the First and the Second Crusade,

12 Laurent Guyénot, *La Lance qui saigne. Hypertextes et métatextes du 'Conte du Graal,'* Champion, 2010.

13 Steven Runciman, *A History of the Crusades*, vol. 1: *The First Crusade and the Foundation of the Kingdom of Jerusalem*, Cambridge UP, 1994, p. xi.

which are not counted as full-fledged crusades but as reinforcements to the Latin states carved out during the First Crusade. The Crusades to the Levant can therefore be considered one single war lasting two centuries, the longest in human history.

During the same period, some Crusades were launched in other directions. Just after the Fourth Crusade, Innocent III called for a crusade against all "heretics" (i.e., Christians who rejected the pope's authority) in the South of France, offering the county of Toulouse to anyone who would seize it under the banner of the pope. Then, in 1222, Pope Honorius III called for a crusade to the North, using the Swedes and the Teutonic Order to bring Rus' to her knees. "We command," he wrote, "that these Russians should be forced to observe the rites of the Latins where they have followed those of the Greeks, in separation from the head, that is, the Roman Church."[14] The attempt failed because Alexander Nevsky, prince of Novgorod, came to an understanding with the Mongols and repelled the Catholic horde (1240–42). Indirectly, therefore, the Crusades also defined the fate of Russia, which remained under the yoke of the Golden Horde until 1476, when Tsar Ivan III refused to pay tribute to the Khan.

Many more wars would continue to be waged under papal banner until the late 16th century, all with the full theological arsenal of the Crusades. In the 15th century alone, no less than seven papal bulls for crusades were promulgated.[15] As Christopher Tyerman sees it:

> Crusading did not decline after 1291. It changed, as it had over the previous two centuries since the First Crusade. … the crusade mentality, transmitted through long habit, current liturgy and constant renewal in fresh appeals for alms, tax, purchase of indulgences and, occasionally, armed service, framed a way of regarding the world. This mentality, widely dispersed through society, allowed the expression of faith and identity

14 Robert Bartlett, *The Making of Europe: Conquest, Colonization and Cultural Change (950–1350)*, Penguin, 1994, p. 255.

15 Jérôme Baschet, *La Civilisation féodale. De l'an mil à la colonisation de l'Amérique*, Flammarion, 2006, p. 373.

> through social rituals and religious institutions without the necessity of individual political or military action. The relative scarcity of *crucesignati* [crusaders] was masked by cultural ubiquity. Independent of fighting and wars, crusading evolved as a state of mind; a means of Grace; a metaphor and mechanism for redemption; a test of human frailty, Divine Judgement and the corruption of society. Crusading became something to be believed in rather than something to do.[16]

The Crusade mystique became entrenched in the European mind, and in the French national narrative in particular, for the Crusade was a French specialty. The First Crusade was preached in France to a French assembly by a French pope — who took this opportunity to excommunicate a French king. It became "the acts of God through the Franks" (*Gesta Dei per Francos*), in the title of Guibert of Nogent's chronicle. French became the main language in the kingdom of Jerusalem, forming later the *lingua franca* of mediterranean trade. And French kings (Louis VII and Louis IX) participated the most in the Crusades to the Levant. "By 1300," Tyerman writes, "crusading had been claimed almost as a national prerogative, an enterprise in which the king of France held the major shareholding."[17] Based on this role and on the earlier legend of Clovis's baptism, monarchical France flattered herself as "the eldest daughter of the Church" with a special messianic mission. That sense of mission was inherited by the French Republic after 1789. Although they repudiated Catholic and monarchical institutions, the revolutionaries repackaged the national messianism that had become so essential to French identity. France was now chosen to enlighten the world with the new Trinity: *Liberté, Égalité, Fraternité*. In a speech printed in April 1791, Robespierre thanked the "eternal Providence" that called on the French, "alone since the origin of the world, to restore on earth the empire of Justice and Liberty."[18]

---

16 Tyerman, *God's War, op. cit.*, p. 825.

17 *Ibid.*, pp. 276–277, 909.

18 Auguste Valmorel, *Œuvres de Robespierre*, 1867 (fr.wikisource.org), p. 71.

Redemption by War and Money

The Crusade introduced a new way of individual salvation: penitential warfare. God, speaking through his vicar on earth, now granted full remission of sins (hence a place in Heaven) to whoever would swear to travel to the Holy Land and kill infidels or be killed by them. According to the historian Orderic Vitalis, writing around 1135, "the pope urged all who could bear arms to fight against the enemies of God, and on God's authority he absolved all the penitent from all their sins from the hour they took the Lord's cross."[19] Judging from the six partial versions of Pope Urban II's sermon preserved in chronicles, it is unclear if he presented things in so explicit terms when calling for the First Crusade in November 1095. He may have simply decreed penance, as reported by Bishop Lambert of Arras, a direct witness: "Whoever for devotion alone, not to gain honor or money, goes to Jerusalem to liberate the Church of God can substitute this journey for all penance."[20] And he may have added, as reported by Fulcher of Chartres: "All who die on the way, whether by land or by sea, or in battle against the pagans, shall have immediate remission of sins. This I grant them through the power of God with which I am invested." He probably was the first to give a radically new interpretation of Matthew 10:38, as reported by Robert the Monk: "Whoever does not take up their cross and follow me is not worthy of me" — a formula that best illustrates the militarization of the Gospel.[21]

Whatever were the exact words of Urban II, full and immediate remission of all confessed sins for all *cruce signati* (those marked with a cross sown on their clothes) was clearly the culmination of

19 Jonathan Riley-Smith, *The First Crusade and the Idea of Crusading*, University of Philadelphia Press, 1986, p. 28.

20 Louise and Jonathan Riley-Smith, ed. & trans., *The Crusades: Ideas and Reality, 1095–1274*, Edward Arnold, 1981, p. 37.

21 "Medieval Sourcebook: Urban II (1088–1099): Speech at Council of Clermont, 1095," *op. cit.*

the development of Crusade theology over the years, largely thanks to apologists like Innocent II, Saint Bernard of Clairvaux, and the great canonist Gratian.[22] In 1187, in the letter *Audita tremendi* which launched the Third Crusade, Pope Gregory VIII declared: "to those who with contrite hearts and humbled spirits undertake the labor of this journey and die in penitence for their sins and with right faith, we promise full indulgence of their faults and eternal life; whether surviving or dying they shall know that through the mercy of God and the authority of the apostles Peter and Paul and our authority they will have relaxation of the satisfaction imposed for all their sins, of which they have made proper confession."[23] Note that only confessed sins can be forgiven (annual oral confession was to become mandatory for Roman Catholics at the 1215 Lateran Council).

The Crusade was a new religion of salvation. Guibert of Nogent, an enthusiastic chronicler of the First Crusade, remarked that if knights could previously only attain salvation by giving up their way of life and becoming monks, then now "God has instituted in our time holy wars, so that the order of knights and the crowd running in their wake … might find a new way of gaining salvation." The Crusade, declared a 14th-century grand master of the Knights Hospitallers, became "the nearest route to Paradise." The Welsh priest Adam of Usk went further in his *Chronicon* (early 15th century): "Any man who will not set off at once / for the land where God lived and died, / any man who will not take the Holy Land's cross / will have but little chance of going to heaven."[24] The Crusade represented an extraordinary religious innovation. While the Roman Church had sought to repress private wars by the movement of the Peace of God in the 10th century, it now declared that the only authorized war was in the Holy Land. The Church which had decreed that even

22 Riley-Smith, *The First Crusade and the Idea of Crusading, op. cit.*, p. 1.

23 Jonathan Riley-Smith, *What were the Crusades?*, 3rd ed., Ignatius Press, 2002, p. 62.

24 Tyerman, *God's War, op. cit.*, pp. 827, 756.

tournaments — "execrable fairs" according to Saint Bernard — were a mortal sin, and that finding death there sent you directly to Hell, invented Holy War which propels each soldier who dies there directly to Paradise.

Blood vengeance, a supreme value of barbarian and feudal ethics, also found its Christian redemption in the Crusade. Certain preachers of the First Crusade, and perhaps Urban II himself, integrated this idea into their sermons: the outrage done to the tomb of Christ had to be avenged. For Raymond of Aguilers, the First Crusade, in which he participated, was "the enterprise which aimed to avenge our Lord Jesus Christ, on those who had unworthily seized the native land of the Lord and his apostles."[25] Some crusaders adopted the very unevangelical war cry of *Vengez Jésus*![26] The idea of avenging the profanation of Christ's tomb irresistibly gave rise to the idea of avenging his death; for this, there was no need to go to the East, remarked the Burgundian monk Raoul Glaber, "while we have the Jews right here, before our eyes."[27]

Killing or being killed in the Crusade would earn you some treasures in heaven, but material gain was not excluded for the survivors. According to Archbishop Baldric of Dol, Urban II had stated: "The possessions of the enemy, too, will be yours, since you will make spoil of their treasures and return victorious to your own; or empurpled with your own blood, you will have gained everlasting glory."[28] Yet, the pursuit of material gain was never the major incentive of the crusaders. Most of those who joined did so with the conviction of saving

---

25 Raymond d'Aguilers, *Histoire des Francs qui prirent Jérusalem. Chronique de la première croisade,* Les Perséides, 2004, p. 140.

26 Laurent Guyénot, *La Lance qui saigne,* Champion, 2010, p. 198.

27 Dominique Barthélemy, *Chevaliers et miracles. La violence et le sacré dans la société féodale,* Armand Colin, 2004, p. 269.

28 "Medieval Sourcebook: Urban II (1088–1099): Speech at Council of Clermont, 1095, Six Versions of the Speech," Fordham University [sourcebooks.fordham.edu/source/urban2-5vers.asp].

their souls. As strange as it may seem to us today, they believed that the pope knew what he was talking about when he distributed remissions of sins (called "indulgences") in exchange for military service. They trusted that this imaginary crypto-currency was legal tender in the Otherworld. Historians have given up trying to explain the "idea of the Crusade" as a mere religious pretext for greed. "In the light of the evidence," writes Jonathan Riley-Smith in *The First Crusade and the Idea of Crusading*, "it is hard to believe that most crusaders were motivated by crude materialism. Given their knowledge and expectations and the economic climate in which they lived, the disposal of assets to invest in the fairly remote possibility of settlement in the East would have been a stupid gamble. It makes much more sense to suppose, in so far as one can generalize about them, that they were moved by an idealism which must have inspired not only them but their families."[29] If the crusaders were looking for personal gain, it was more in terms of social credit. From the 12th century, as Christopher Tyerman explains, "crusading acted as a mechanism of social advancement, … a means of entry to the ranks of the knightly and respectables for parvenus, a ticket of admission into the secular social elite."[30] What this means is simply that the Crusade was part of the dominant value system.

The vow of "taking the cross" was binding, and failure to act upon it could cause excommunication, tantamount to a sentence to hell. Fortunately for those who had ceded to peer pressure but then found excuses for themselves, the Crusade indulgence was extended to those who, instead of going themselves after taking the vow, sent another in their place or gave money to finance the military campaign: this dispensation in return for a money payment was called the "redemption of vow." From the pontificate of Alexander III (1159–1181), Tyerman explains, "vow redemption helped alter radically the

29 Riley-Smith, *The First Crusade*, *op. cit.*, p. 47.

30 Tyerman, *God's War*, *op. cit.*, p. 885.

funding of crusading, the manner in which the cross was preached, the methods of recruitment and planning, and even the reputation of the exercise itself as the system became vulnerable to charges of 'crosses for cash.'" Indulgences became "part of a general penitential system, increasingly commercial as redemption of vows or even the performance of any particular meritorious act gave way to simple sale and payment." It was under Clement VI (1342–1352) that we encounter in perfected form "the doctrine of a Treasury of Merits, a sort of divine bank account laid up by God to be drawn on by the penitent faithful."[31]

Thus, the gospel of salvation by war slowly evolved into the gospel of salvation by money. According to Norman Housley, the marketing of indulgences "was certainly a major constituent of the trend which conflated the devotional emphasis on works with the substantial volume of specie that could be released in an increasingly commercial society."[32] Alongside this official racket came the black market: in the years 1226–1228, scandals broke out in Germany and Italy when impostor preachers accepted the redemption of Crusade vows for more or less large sums, one of whom managed to pass himself off as the pope and, for nearly six weeks, relieved a crowd of would-be crusaders and pilgrims of their vows.[33]

The trade in indulgences did not start with the Crusade, but originated further upstream, from a legal and fiscal conception of sin specific to Latin theology since Saint Augustine, which insisted on the notions of "debt" and "redemption" (from the Latin *redimere*, "buying back"). The bookkeeping of sins and remissions, codified in the "penitentiaries" (manuals for the use of confessors), is a trend that grew from the Gregorian Reform, led by jurist or banker popes like Hildebrand (Gregory VII). The idea that the Church could forgive

31 *Ibid.*, pp. 481, 888.

32 Housley, *Contesting the Crusades, op. cit.*, p. 148.

33 Alphandéry and Dupront, *La Chrétienté et l'idée de croisade, op. cit.*, p. 419.

spiritual debts in exchange for services lends itself particularly well to the military service of the crusaders. Around 1230, the Parisian theologian Guillaume of Auvergne explained the use of indulgences by comparing them to a soldier's salary:

> If a king or prince is going to war he gives his commanders the power to seek out and recruit honorable warriors and give them good wages. Therefore, because the king of kings, the ruler of rulers, Christ, has been waging wars from the time when the Church took up war, not just spiritual wars, I say, but also literal or corporeal or material, … he necessarily granted his commanders, that is the prelates, the power to seek out material warriors and to recruit them and give them proper wages. … And what is it to remit their enjoined penances if not to give them a share in the wages? For whereas the wages of sin is death, as it says in Romans 6, thus the wages for the greatest and most noble portion of such warriors will be the eternal wages.[34]

The selling of indulgences would ultimately ruin the Catholic Church's credibility. Such became the object of Martin Luther's central charge against the papacy in his perfectly reasonable *Ninety-five Theses,* as well as one of his justifications for calling the pope, in his *Smalcald Articles,* "the real Antichrist who has raised himself over and set himself against Christ." Indeed, it is hard to deny that, by some Luciferian hubris, the popes undermined their own status and the unity of European Christendom by plunging Europe into religious wars.

The institutional monetization of salvation is obviously linked to the increasing role of banking in the Crusade business. Crusades were costly expeditions involving mortgages and loans on a hitherto unknown scale. The Order of the Temple of Solomon, founded at the beginning of the 12th century by nine monk-soldiers from the city of Troyes and placed under the direct authority of the pope, specialized in banking and insurance activity. The Templars developed the use of

34 Ane L. Bysted, *The Crusade Indulgence: Spiritual Reward and the Theology of the Crusades, c. 1095–1216*, Brill, 2015, p. 2.

bills of exchange, and their commanderies served as safes for kings, popes, and wealthy individuals. They transported funds and also acted as bailiffs to recover debts or consign assets that were the subject of disputes; finally, they played the role of notaries by distributing the inheritances entrusted to them. In the mid-13th century, by seizing the property of their debtors upon their death, the Templars appropriated a considerable part of French territory and formed a state within the state. Inevitably, they became usurers, but they managed to circumvent the ban on usury by "reciprocal gifts."[35] The Crusades were also instrumental in the development of a tax legislation and bureaucracy, first in England, where the "Saladin tithe," created to finance the Third Crusade (1189–92), was the first tax levied on the revenues and properties of the entire population.

Making Jerusalem the Capital of Europe

It has been said that the Crusades were "the first unifying event in Europe." French historian Francois Guizot stated in his lectures at the Sorbonne in 1828: "The first character of the crusades is their universality; all Europe concurred in them; they were the first European event. Before the crusades, Europe had never been moved by the same sentiment, or acted in a common cause; till then, in fact, Europe did not exist. The crusades made manifest the existence of Christian Europe."[36] The crusades "so stirred and united Europe that we may count them as the beginning of modern history," wrote Halford Mackinder in his seminal 1904 article on "The Geographical Pivot of History" — with the typical Eurocentric view of his time.[37]

---

35 Jacques Heers, *La Naissance du capitalisme au Moyen Âge. Changeurs, usuriers et grands financiers*, Perrin, 2012, p. 258.

36 François Guizot, *General History of Civilization in Europe*, 1896, on oll.libertyfund.org/title/knight-general-history-of-civilization-in-europe.

37 Halford MacKinder, "The Geographical Pivot of History," *The Geographical Journal*, April 1904.

This is true to some extent, but this common cause should not be confused with political unity or peace among nations. It is undeniable that the Crusades allowed France and England to reduce feudal wars and consolidate themselves as centralized states. But the Crusades did not alleviate the rivalries between European princes. In the colonies they established in Syria, the early crusaders reproduced the only mode of governance they knew: feudalism. Their conquests were divided into four Latin states: the County of Edessa, the Principality of Antioch, the County of Tripoli, and the Kingdom of Jerusalem. Too few in number to truly take possession of the land, they distributed it to vassals who did as they pleased. While theoretically recognizing the suzerainty of the King of Jerusalem (Baldwin of Boulogne), they practically ignored him and quarreled with impunity.

The Third Crusade is an even better example. Before they embarked on the Crusade, the kings of France and England were at war over territorial claims. Although the pope convinced Philip II and Richard I to sign a truce before setting sail for the Holy Land, their relations deteriorated rather than improved during the expedition. Thomas Tout writes: "The Western army had taken with them to Palestine their national jealousies, and the quarrels of the rival claimants for the throne of Jerusalem brought these animosities to a crisis. Philip looked upon Richard with deadly hatred as his most formidable rival."[38] As soon as they were back home (that is, after Richard was ransomed from the jail of Leopold of Austria, who accused him of having arranged the murder of Conrad of Montferrat), they resumed their feud, which would later escalate into the Hundred Years War (1337–1453).

The greatest absurdity of the Crusade is that it aimed to unite Europe around Jerusalem. The popes convinced Europeans that the cradle of their civilization was a city at the eastern end of the Mediterranean, and asked them to fight for it as if the salvation of

38 T. F. Tout, *The Empire and the Papacy (918–1273)*, 4th ed., 1903, p. 302.

Europe depended on it. But there could hardly be a project more contrary to the interests of Europe.

European fascination with Jerusalem did not start with the Crusade, of course, but rather provided one of its incentives. As Jonathan Riley-Smith explains, "the attitude of 11th-century Christians towards Jerusalem and the Holy Land was obsessive. Jerusalem was the centre of the world, the spot on earth on which God himself had focused when he chose to redeem mankind by intervening in history; at the same place, at the end of time, the last events leading to Doomsday would be enacted."[39] However, that obsession had a greater intensity in the West than in the East, probably because the distance added to the myth. As we have already noted, the Carolingian kings developed a strong taste for Old Testament stories. Around 850, the archbishop of Mainz, Rabanus Maurus, attributes to Saint Remigius a prophecy that in the Last Days, a Frankish king, "the last of his race," will make the Roman Empire great again and then "go to Jerusalem, and depose on Mount Olive his scepter and crown. This shall be the end and conclusion of the Roman and Christian Empire." It is hard to measure the influence of this text, but it is certain that the prestige of ancient Israel in the mind of the Frankish kings, and their identification with King David, was a significant factor in the enthusiasm for the Crusade, especially in France.

The pilgrimage tradition also contributed. Since the beginning of the 11th century, many pilgrims left for Jerusalem with the encouragement and practical support of the monasteries. It was Urban II's stroke of genius to package the military expedition as a penitential pilgrimage to Jerusalem. Many of the measures associated with the Crusade, such as the legal protection afforded to the families and property of the crusaders, are consistent with time-tested pilgrimage practices. The cross sewn on the garment also comes from this

39 Riley-Smith, *The First Crusade and the Idea of Crusading*, *op. cit.*, p. 21.

tradition.[40] In this way, Urban II combined into a new synthesis two elements that were traditionally kept separate: Jerusalem as a popular destination for pilgrimage and the warrior ethics of the feudal class.

It must be emphasized that Jerusalem was not the prime concern of the *basileus* Alexios Komnenos when he asked for Western help. The Greeks were not as obsessed with Jerusalem as were the Latins. That may be because they revered Athens as much as Jerusalem (more on this in Chapter III). Moreover, Jerusalem had not been part of the Byzantine Empire since it was conquered by the Arabs in 638, and Syria itself was peripheral to the Empire. Alexios's primary aim was to reconquer Anatolia, starting with Nicaea (today Iznik), which the Turks had conquered in 1081 and made the capital of their *Sultanate of Rum*, a mere hundred kilometers from Constantinople. Alexios also hoped to recover Antioch, a prosperous and strategically important Greek city that had always belonged to the Empire (the crusaders did eventually conquer Antioch, but they kept it for themselves).

Until 1073, Jerusalem had been governed in the name of the Fatimid Caliphs, who respected the authority of the *basileus* and of the patriarch of Jerusalem over Christian shrines, and let Christians worship freely.[41] Orthodox Christians had no complaints, and Syrian Jacobites as well as other non-Orthodox Christians even preferred Muslim rule to Byzantine rule. It was only when the Seljuk Turks took over northern Syria that the situation deteriorated for Jerusalemite Christians and Western pilgrims. But the Fatimids retook Jerusalem from the Seljuks one year before the crusaders came before its walls, and the *basileus* was more than willing to let them rule it again. For Westerners, however, the Crusade was about "liberating" Jerusalem. They rejected the peace offer of the Fatimids, assaulted the Holy City, and massacred its population. Raymond of

40 *Ibid.*, pp. 22, 24.

41 Runciman, *A History of the Crusades*, vol. 1, *op. cit.*, p. 23.

Aguilers, who witnessed the event, wrote: "in the Temple and portico of Solomon crusaders rode in blood up to their knees and the bridles of their horses. Indeed, it was a just and splendid judgment of God, that this place should be filled with the blood of the unbelievers, since it had suffered so long from their blasphemies." This, he claimed, fulfilled Revelation 14:20: "And the winepress was trodden without the city, and blood came out of the winepress, even to the horse bridles."[42] Another chronicler, the anonymous author of the *Gesta Francorum,* wrote: "our men rushed round the whole city, seizing gold and silver, horses and mules, and houses full of all sorts of goods and they all came rejoicing and weeping from excess of gladness to worship at the Sepulchre of our Savior Jesus, and there they fulfilled their vows." This, according to chronicler Robert of Rheims, should be celebrated as "the greatest event since the Resurrection."[43] News of the "liberation" of Jerusalem silenced critics of the project in Europe, and its celebration definitely installed the Crusade as a central paradigm in Western culture. From then on, Westerners saw themselves as the guardians of the center of the world. It became part of their identity. Their obsession only grew with Jerusalem's recapture by Salah al-Din (Saladin) in 1187 (in conditions of discipline and humanity that, by contrast, put Western chivalry to shame), and with every new failed attempt to reverse this fatal development.

One of the greatest ironies of the history of the Crusades is that Jerusalem was temporarily reclaimed in 1229 by Holy Roman Emperor Frederick II, who went there despite the ban and excommunication by Pope Gregory IX and recovered it without a fight. Pierre Boulle writes in *L'Étrange croisade de l'empereur Frédéric II*: "what the imperial galleys carried on June 28, 1228, was not an army of fierce warriors determined to fight to the death; it was a cultural, scientific,

42 Raymond d'Aguilers, *Histoire des Francs qui prirent Jérusalem,* Les Perséides, 2004, p. 165.

43 Tyerman, *God's War, op. cit.,* pp. 158, 168.

artistic, technical mission."[44] Frederick had previously established friendly relations with the emir Fakhr al-Din, ambassador of the Sultan of Egypt, Al-Kamil, and exchanged a profusion of luxurious gifts with the latter. Frederick had been raised in the Kingdom of Sicily in contact with Arab culture. Greatly interested in mathematics, astronomy, medicine, as well as poetry, he wanted to make his "crusade" a sort of international conference for friendship between peoples. "No Western prince has ever evoked so much affection and understanding [among Muslims] as he," wrote Ernst Kantorowicz: "Not only did they admire the encyclopedic learning of the Emperor, who maintained erudite correspondence with the learned men of Egypt and Syria, Iraq, Arabia, Yemen, as well as Morocco and Spain, but they followed all the more important events of his life with unflagging interest."[45] Frederick concluded an agreement with the Sultan in Jaffa on February 18, 1229. The Sultan returned Jerusalem, Bethlehem, Nazareth, as well as other territories in Phoenicia, without any other compensation than retaining possession of the al-Aqsa Mosque. As soon as he was informed, Pope Gregory IX condemned this diplomatic approach, denouncing as a particularly serious sin Frederick's recognition of the rights of Muslims over their mosque. As already said in the first chapter, he launched a crusade against Frederick, granting the possibility for those who had planned to go to the Holy Land to commute their vows in order to fight against Frederick. The relentlessness of the popes' effort to destroy the Hohenstaufen dynasty culminated in the extermination of Frederick's family by Charles of Anjou, brother of King Louis IX and vassal of the pope.

In 1248, after Jerusalem had reverted back to the Muslims, the French King Louis IX led the Seventh Crusade, which ended with

---

44 Pierre Boulle, *L'Étrange croisade de l'empereur Frédéric II*, Flammarion, 1968, p. 137.

45 Ernst Kantorowicz, *Frederick the Second (1194–1250)*, (1931) Frederick Ungar publishing, 1957, p. 196.

his capture by Sultan Turanshah. The very pious Louis IX abandoned his kingdom again for still another crusade in 1270, and died of dysentery in Egypt that same year. It was reported that his last words were for the city he never saw: "Jerusalem! Jerusalem!" All Europe, it seems, has been weeping over Jerusalem ever since. Tyerman writes: "The clerical and lay elites of western Europe found it almost impossible to let go of the Holy Land as a political ambition or vision of perfection. Throughout the fourteenth and fifteenth centuries, governments, moralists, preachers and lobbyists returned again and again to a subject in which practical and moral objectives were fused together."[46]

Jerusalem never left the Western mind. General Bonaparte tried to take it from the Ottomans in 1799, and, although he failed, his heroic attempt boosted his fame. It was not until December 9, 1917 that Jerusalem was finally recaptured by Christian troops. When British General Edmund Allenby entered the city in a solemn procession, he proclaimed "the end of the Crusades," and the London *Punch* published an illustration showing Richard I looking down on Jerusalem and nodding contentedly, "My dream comes true!"[47]

By this time, the Anglican Church and Calvinist Puritans had long rejected papal authority and officially condemned the notion of penitential warfare. But the obsession with Jerusalem remained strong throughout the Victorian era. It combined with a certain Judeophilia which had taken hold of the British elite in the 17th century. Jewish historian Cecil Roth explains: "Puritanism represented above all a return to the Bible, and this automatically fostered a more favourable frame of mind towards the people of the Old Testament."[48] An outgrowth of that interest in ancient Israel was the

---

46 Tyerman, *God's War, op. cit.*, pp. 812, 827.

47 It is reproduced on the cover of Eitan Bar-Yosef's book, *The Holy Land in English Culture 1799–1917*, Clarendon Press, 2005.

48 Cecil Roth, *A History of the Jews in England* (1941), Clarendon Press, 1964, p. 148.

theory known as British Israelism, according to which the English were the direct descendants of the ten lost tribes of Israel. This theory remained influential well into the time of Queen Victoria and her prime minister, Benjamin Disraeli, with, for example, Edward Hine's *The English Nation Identified with the Lost Israel* (1870) fancying that the name "Saxon" derives from "Isaac's sons."

Europe's infatuation with Israel is not unrelated to the British and French support for Zionism at the beginning of the 20th century. This is not to say, of course, that there was no other geopolitical agenda. But the sacralization of biblical Israel in Christian culture obviously constituted a key factor in the support given by Christian nations to the "rebirth" of Israel between 1917 and 1948. Holding it as a revealed truth, or at least as a reasonable idea, that Jews were the chosen people of God in biblical times, European public opinion, both Catholic and Protestant, was rather well disposed toward a project which explicitly aimed at resurrecting this very same Israel.

That being said, it was namely the Crusade and the memory of it embedded in European culture that played the major role in sealing the sacred bond between Western Christendom and Israel, which has largely, even excessively, defined international relations ever since. Crusaders saw themselves as imitating the people of Moses. According to an account by Robert of Reims, Urban II said in his sermon at Clermont: "Take the road to the Holy Sepulchre, rescue that land from a dreadful race and rule over it yourselves, for that land that, as scripture says, flows with milk and honey was given by God as a possession to the children of Israel."[49] In the version of Baldric of Dol, Urban II referred to the Arabs as the Amalekites that Yahweh ordered King Saul to slaughter entirely: "man and woman, babe and suckling, ox and sheep, camel and donkey" (1 Samuel 15:3). "It is our duty to pray, yours to fight against the Amalekites," Urban reportedly said: "With Moses, we shall extend unwearied hands in prayer

49 Tyerman, *God's War, op. cit.*, p. 84.

to Heaven, while you go forth and brandish the sword, like dauntless warriors, against Amalek."[50] Catholics like to blame Protestants for putting too much emphasis on the Old Testament; but it was the Crusade, not the Reformation, that remade Christ in the likeness of Moses and Joshua.

Constantinople Betrayed

The project of Holy War for the Holy Land did not originate with Urban II (1088–99), but rather from his mentor, Gregory VII (1073–85), the most energetic promoter of what became known as the Gregorian Reform. Gregory VII had planned to personally lead an army against the Muslims. Norman Cantor explains his two main objectives: "Such a crusade would be an expression of the supreme pontiff's moral leadership of the western world (which was one of Gregory's cardinal doctrines) and would bring the peoples of the north into closer relations with Rome. Finally, the Latin invasion of the Orient could be expected to take a long step toward the assertion of papal hegemony in Greek Christian lands."[51]

It was left to the charismatic Urban II to bring the project to fruition. In term of the first objective, it was a success. Before he made his famous sermon in November 1095, Urban was in a dire position: he had been expelled from Rome, where Emperor Henry IV had installed his own pope, Clement III. According to Tyerman, "Urban II sought to use the mobilization of the expedition as a cover to reclaim the pope's position in Italy and demonstrate his practical leadership of Christendom, independent of secular monarchs."[52] It was a spectacular show of strength, since in that very same Council

---

50 August Charles Krey, *The First Crusade: The Accounts of Eyewitnesses and Participants*, Princeton UP, 1921, p. 36.

51 Norman Cantor, *The Civilization of the Middle Ages*, HarperPerennial, 1994, pp. 290–291.

52 Tyerman, *God's War*, *op. cit.*, pp. 7–8; also p. 74.

of Clermont, Urban confirmed the excommunication of the king of France, Philip I, for his adulterous marriage with Bertrade of Montfort. Urban thereby demonstrated that he could come into French territory, declare the French king unfit, and mobilize under his own banner the elite of French knighthood. It was a *coup d'état* of sorts—and the real beginning of papal suzerainty over European kings. What is most remarkable, however, as Thomas Tout comments in *The Empire and the Papacy*, is that the pope was able to pull off this move "at a time when all the chief kings of Europe were open enemies of the Papacy. Henry IV was an old foe, Philip of France had been deliberately attacked, and William Rufus of England was indifferent or hostile. But in the eleventh century the power of even the strongest kings counted for very little. What made the success of Urban's venture was the appeal to the swarm of small feudal chieftains, who really governed Europe, and to the fierce and undisciplined enthusiasm of the common people, with whom the ultimate strength of the Church really lay."[53]

In regard to their second great objective, establishing papal supremacy over the Greek Church, the Crusades were a complete failure. They made the schism permanent and irreversible. Tensions built up from the start of the First Crusade, when the *basileus* Alexios Komnenos saw tens of thousands of undisciplined Western warriors gather under his walls. This was not what he had asked for. As Steven Runciman wrote: "No government is unwilling to make allies. But when these allies send large armies, over which it has no control, to invade its territory, expecting to be fed and housed and provided with every amenity, then it questions whether the alliance is worth while. When news of the Crusading movement reached Constantinople it aroused feelings of disquiet and alarm."[54] These feelings proved justified when the Norman Bohemond of Taranto captured Antioch

53 Tout, *The Empire and the Papacy, op. cit.*, p. 138.

54 Runciman, *A History of the Crusades*, vol. 1, *op. cit.*, p. 96.

from the Turks and refused to hand it to the Emperor to whom it rightfully belonged. This was unsurprising; Bohemond was the son of Robert Guiscard who, with the blessing of the pope, had invaded the Balkans and attempted to seize Constantinople in 1081, after having, in 1059, conquered southern Italy and removed it from Byzantine domination.

In addition to his martial prowess, Bohemond was a fine lobbyist and propagandist. In 1105, he went to Rome to convince Pope Paschal II that Emperor Alexios was a usurper who had seized the throne "by treachery and horrible plots," and that he was a greater enemy of the Latins than the Muslims. Then, accompanied by a papal legate, he made a diplomatic tour of France to mobilize a crusade against Constantinople. On this occasion, he distributed copies of the *Gesta Francorum*, an account of the First Crusade written to his glory, which presented "the abominable emperor" as a traitor whose sole motivation for each action was the destruction of the army of the crusaders. This cornerstone of the historiography of the First Crusade contributed more than any other book to the negative image of the Byzantines as effeminate and deceitful. The pope's support for a crusade directed against Constantinople was, according to Runciman, "a turning point in the history of the Crusades. The Norman policy, which aimed to break the power of the eastern Empire, became the official Crusading policy." The Byzantines found their worst suspicions realized: "The Crusade, with the Pope at its head, was not a movement for the succour of Christendom, but a tool of unscrupulous western imperialism."[55] Bohemond marched against Constantinople in 1107, but the confrontation turned to his disadvantage and, by the Treaty of Devol, he was forced to recognize himself a vassal of the Byzantine Emperor for his principality of Antioch, and to commit to re-establishing an Orthodox patriarchate there.

55 Runciman, *A History of the Crusades*, vol. 2, *op. cit.*, p. 48.

However, he died shortly after, and his nephew Tancred, who held Antioch in his absence, refused to implement the treaty.

The Second Crusade, which did not even feign the pretext of helping Constantinople, worsened relations between the Franks and the Greeks. The crusaders accused Emperor Manuel I Komnenos of the worst treachery, but Steven Runciman sets the record straight: "The behaviour of the Crusaders when they were guests in his territory was not such as to increase the Emperor's liking for them. They pillaged; they attacked his police; they ignored his requests about the routes that they should take; and many of their prominent men talked openly of attacking Constantinople. Seen in such a light his treatment of them seems generous and forbearing."[56]

The breaking point was the Fourth Crusade, which ended in the sack of Constantinople. This appalling episode, of incalculable consequences, has been erased from the Western heroic tall tale of the Crusades — it is quite understandable why, but the full story needs to be told here.

The Fourth Crusade

The Fourth Crusade was launched in 1198, a century after the first, at the initiative of Innocent III, a newly elected, dynamic young pope aged 38. Its stated objective was to retake Jerusalem, the heart of the Frankish-Latin Kingdom of Jerusalem founded a century earlier by the First Crusade and recently reconquered by Saladin. As with previous expeditions, the pope guaranteed God's support to the crusaders and complete remission of their sins. Many great lords, mainly French, responded to the call. They elected Marquis Boniface of Montferrat as leader of the expedition. They agreed on a strategy: first to attack Cairo, held since Saladin's death in 1193 by his brother, Al-Adil, and then to march toward Jerusalem by taking the coastal

56 *Ibid.*, p. 275.

towns of southern Syria, because only in this way could the Frankish Kingdom of Jerusalem be permanently secured.

In 1201, the leaders of the Crusade negotiated with the Venetians a contract for the transport and provisioning for one year of 4,500 knights and their horses, 9,000 squires, and 20,000 infantrymen on 50 galleys, all for the price of 85,000 silver marks (25 tons of silver) and half of the conquered territory and spoils of war. The Venetian shipyards set to work, the embarkation toward Cairo scheduled for June 28, 1202. But the crusaders had thought too big: their numbers turned out to be lower than the terms of the contract, and they were unable to raise the 85,000 marks owed. Venice therefore refused to supply the ships. Confined on a small island and harassed by their creditors, the crusaders accepted the following arrangement: the settlement of their debt was to be postponed if they agreed to take the city of Zara (on the eastern shore of the Adriatic, today in Croatia) on behalf of the Venetians. Some knights protested and returned home, because Zara was under the suzerainty of the Catholic king of Hungary. But the commanders of the Crusade accepted the deal: Zara was stormed and pillaged in November 1202.

It was now too late to venture into the Levant, and the crusaders took up their winter quarters in Zara. However, the contract signed with the Venetians only provided for their supplies until the summer of 1203. The crusaders were then forced to comply with a new arrangement: before driving the Muslims from Jerusalem, they had to sail to Constantinople to dethrone Emperor Alexis III, who was hostile to the Venetians, and put on the throne a pro-Western pretender, namely the brother-in-law of Philip of Swabia. To finally convince the crusaders of his noble cause, the suitor in question, Alexis Ange, promised that, once on the throne, he would pay the crusaders 200,000 silver marks, more than double what they owed the Venetians; he would also finance the conquest of Egypt and add a contingent of 10,000 Byzantine soldiers; he would pay for the maintenance of five hundred knights to remain in the Holy Land; and he would ensure the Orthodox Church's submission to Rome. Taken by the throat by the Venetians who demanded repayment, and lured by the prospect of important booty and territories richer than those of Syria and Palestine, Boniface of Montferrat and the majority of the knights sailed toward Constantinople and, by the mere appearance of their formidable army, saw the emperor flee and imposed their puppet, who took the name of Alexios IV.

Naturally, Alexios turned out to be incapable of keeping his promises. His attempt to force the clergy of the city to acknowledge Latin supremacy and the exorbitant tax he demanded from his subjects to raise the promised sum aroused anger, as did the arrogance of the Franks and Venetians who behaved like conquerors in the city. Resentment reached a boiling point in the winter of 1203, and riots broke out. It was then that a son-in-law of the fleeing Emperor Alexios III, Alexios Murzuphle, took the lead of the anti-Latin party, eliminated Alexios IV and his father, and seized the throne under the name of Alexios V, with the city's support. He immediately denounced the agreements with the crusaders.

Confrontation was inevitable. In March 1204, while besieging the city, the crusaders signed a new treaty with the Venetians to share in advance the spoils of the Byzantine Empire. The crusaders would have to concede to Venice three eighths of the Byzantine lands conquered or remaining to be conquered, and three fifths of the city, as well as numerous Syrian ports and new commercial privileges. The crusaders stormed the city in April and carried out what would go down in history as one of the most dastardly pillages of all time. The Byzantine senior official and historian Niketas Choniates, who witnessed the capture and sack of Constantinople before fleeing, left a poignant account. For three days and three nights, the crusaders murdered, raped, pillaged, and destroyed everything they found. However, according to Collin Wells, author of *Sailing from Byzantium*:

> Tragic as the human cost was, this isn't what makes the sack of Constantinople unique. The city had stood inviolate as the capital of Christendom for nearly nine centuries, since its founding as the New Rome in the early fourth century. A peerless collection of fine art, religious relics, and irreplaceable manuscripts filled its churches, monasteries, libraries, and palatial homes. Mosaics, icons, frescoes, ancient bronze and marble statues, precious metalwork, jeweled artifacts, silken wall hangings, painstakingly copied works of ancient and medieval Greek literature — the scale of what the world lost in those three days can only be guessed, never known.[57]

After relishing in the best residences in the city, the conquerors elected Baldwin of Flanders as the new emperor and the Venetian Thomas Morosini as patriarch. The latter imposed the religious authority of Rome and swore "that no one should be received as a canon of Santa Sophia unless he is a Venetian by birth or has served ten years in a Venetian church." Although the pope invalidated that oath, thirty-two of the forty canons whose origins are known were Venetian. Robert Bartlett summates: "This was a colonial church."[58]

How can we explain a military expedition, which had the stated aim of retaking Jerusalem from the Muslims and coming to the aid of Christians, being diverted toward the conquest and looting of the Christian capital of the East? To explain the sack of Constantinople, historians sometimes invoke an unfortunate series of unforeseen events that drew the unwitting crusaders into this criminal enterprise. Applied to contemporary history, this theory would be tantamount to asserting, for example, that the United States destroyed Iraq, Libya, and Syria by mistake or inadvertence.

A more reasonable theory is the "Venetian conspiracy." It was, indeed, the Venetians who, by financing in advance the transport of the Crusade, made the crusaders their mercenaries and could thereby

---

57 Collin Wells, *Sailing from Byzantium: How a Lost Empire Shaped the World*, Bantam, 2008, p. 43.

58 Bartlett, *The Making of Europe, op. cit*, p. 14.

impose their own goal of taking over Constantinople. The Venetians, and the Doge in particular, bore a grudge against the Byzantines. To understand why, we have to go back in time. Venice had developed under the domination and protection of Constantinople until it emancipated itself in the 11th century, becoming the greatest maritime power in the Mediterranean and the main commercial intermediary between East and West. It nevertheless remained the ally of the Byzantine emperor, providing him with his main naval combat force, in exchange for considerable commercial and tax privileges. The economic power of the Venetians ended up exasperating Emperor Manuel Komnenos who, in 1171, withdrew all their privileges, confiscated all their property and expelled them from the empire.

At the turn of the 13th century, when Innocent III launched the Fourth Crusade, Venetian merchants had a dual interest in deflecting the Crusade from Cairo to Constantinople. Not only would they carve out the lion's share of the Byzantine territories and retake their trading posts in northern Syria, but they would also preserve their commercial interests in Muslim Egypt, their most important trading partner since the time of the Fatimids. Four years after the sack of Constantinople, they signed a commercial treaty with the Sultan of Cairo, Saladin's brother. The Fourth Crusade was, in every respect, a great success for the merchant Republic of Venice, which established itself as a true colonial empire.

However, it is too easy to single out the Venetians as the guilty party. After all, it was mainly Franks who destroyed Constantinople. Rome's responsibility is also heavy. It may be true that Pope Innocent III was faced with a *fait accompli*, as Latin chronicles say. When the news of the capture of Zara reached him, he reportedly excommunicated all the crusaders involved. But he quickly pardoned them, maintaining the excommunication only on the Venetians, who were hardly troubled by it. When he learned of the second diversion toward Constantinople, he issued a bull forbidding such an attack on Christians unless they actively opposed the holy war. However, in a letter of 1203 to the leaders of the Crusade, he authorized the pillaging of Greek cities in the event of a lack of supplies provided by the Byzantines. His legates accompanying the crusaders did nothing to discourage the assault on Constantinople, even suggesting that it was morally justifiable since the Byzantine capital was populated by schismatic rebels. As soon as the news of the capture of Constantinople reached him, Pope Innocent III wrote to the new Frankish emperor and the entire crusader army to congratulate them. His letter *Legimus in Daniele* is a hymn of triumph. He rejoiced in the "just judgment of God" against the Byzantines, whose refusal to affirm the *filioque* was comparable to Jews' refusal to recognize the divinity of Christ. God, he said, has restored the daughter to the mother, and the member to the head. The pope even issued a decree releasing all the crusaders from their vow to go to the Holy Land: Latin Constantinople served as the new Jerusalem, and defending it against Byzantine attempts to retake it was worth exactly the same plenary indulgence as the defense of Jerusalem against the Saracens. All of Latin Christendom was invited to rejoice in the victory of Rome: as Jonathan Harris writes, "enthusiasm grew when the precious relics began to arrive for the churches of France and Belgium. Hymns were sung to celebrate the fall of the great ungodly city, *Constantinopolitana Civitas diu profana*, whose treasures were now disgorged."[59]

The new Franko-Latin Empire, established by the crusaders on the ruins in the wake of their rampage, only survived half a century. A Byzantine elite entrenched in Nicaea managed to reconstitute a state and an army, gradually regained control of certain cities, and then, in 1261, under the command of Michael Palaiologos, drove the Franks and Latins out of Constantinople and restored the Byzantine

59 Harris, *Byzantium and the Crusades, op. cit.*, pp. 2, 70, 80; George Demacopoulos, *Colonizing Christianity: Greek and Latin Religious Identity in the Era of the Fourth Crusade*, Fordham UP, 2019, p. 86; Steven Runciman, *A History of the Crusades*, vol. 3: *The Kingdom of Acre and the Later Crusades* (1954), Penguin Classics, 2016, p. 128.

Empire. But the city was only a shadow of its former self: the Greek population had been decimated or exiled, the churches and monasteries had been desecrated, trade was at a standstill, and the city was in ruins, as the Latin emperors did not have the means to restore or maintain it. The city now had only about 35,000 inhabitants, compared to at least 500,000 in 1203 (one million with the suburbs). Moreover, the Empire had been amputated by the loss of its richest provinces to the Franks and the Muslims.

When the Byzantines retook Constantinople in 1261, Pope Urban IV immediately ordered a new crusade to be preached throughout Europe, this time directed explicitly against "the Greeks." His call aroused little enthusiasm except among the Venetians who, once again stripped of their privileges for the benefit of the Genoese, offered free transport for all crusaders. In 1281, Pope Martin IV supported the project of Charles of Anjou (the brother of Saint Louis, who had received from the pope the crown of Sicily) of retaking Constantinople. The popular revolt in Sicily (the Sicilian Vespers) forced Charles to abandon this project.

Consequences

Historians agree that the Fourth Crusade inflicted a mortal wound on the Byzantine Empire, exhausting its capacity to resist Muslim expansion. Before buckling under the onslaught of the Turks, Constantinople called on the West for help one last time. But the West's Middle-Eastern foreign policy was then a department of the Roman Curia, so to speak, and so the popes demanded in exchange Constantinople's religious submission to Rome. With a knife at his throat, Emperor John VIII went in person—accompanied by the patriarch of Moscow—to the Council of Ferrara-Florence in 1439. But the memory of the Fourth Crusade was still so vivid that a large part of the Orthodox clergy, as well as the monks and the population as a whole, fiercely opposed agreements with the Latins. Those who could not flee Constantinople still preferred the Ottoman yoke to Latin humiliation. The conclusion of the great British medievalist Sir Steven Runciman on the consequences of the Fourth Crusade is worth quoting at length:

> There was never a greater crime against humanity than the Fourth Crusade. Not only did it cause the destruction or dispersal of all the treasures of the past that Byzantium had devotedly stored, and the mortal wounding of a civilization that was still active and great ; but it was also an act of gigantic political folly. It brought no help to the Christians in Palestine. Instead it robbed them of potential helpers. And it upset the whole defense of Christendom … In the wide sweep of world history the effects were wholly disastrous. Since the inception of its Empire Byzantium had been the guardian of Europe against the infidel East and the barbarian North. She had opposed them with her armies and tamed them with her civilization. She had passed through many anxious periods when it had seemed that her doom had come, but hitherto she had survived them. At the close of the twelfth century she was facing a long crisis, as the damage to her man-power and her economy caused by the Turkish conquests in Anatolia a century before began to take full effect, enhanced by the energetic rivalry of the Italian merchant cities. But she might well have shown her resilience once again and have reconquered the Balkans and much of Anatolia, and her culture could have continued its uninterrupted influence over the countries around. Even the Seldjuk Turks might well have fallen under its sway and in the end been absorbed to refresh the Empire. The story of the Empire of Nicaea [1205–1261] shows that the Byzantines had not lost their vigour. But, with Constantinople gone, the unity of the Byzantine world was broken and could never be repaired, even after the capital itself was recovered. It was part of the achievement of the Nicaeans to keep the Seldjuks in check. But when a new, more vigorous Turkish tribe appeared, under the leadership of the brilliant house of Osman, the East Christian world was too deeply divided to make an effective stand. Its leadership was passing everywhere, away from the Mediterranean birthplace of European culture to the far north-east, to the vast plains of Russia. The Second Rome was giving place to the Third Rome of Muscovy. Meanwhile hatred had been sown between Eastern and Western Christendom. The bland hopes of Pope Innocent and

> the complacent boasts of the Crusaders that they had ended the schism and united the Church were never fulfilled. Instead, their barbarity left a memory that would never be forgiven them. Later, East Christian potentates might advocate union with Rome in the fond expectation that union would bring a united front against the Turks. But their people would not follow them. They could not forget the Fourth Crusade. … the whole Crusading movement had embittered their relations, and henceforward, whatever a few princes might try to achieve, in the hearts of the East Christians the schism was complete, irremediable and final.[60]

Ultimately, however, rather than a mere aberration, the sack of Constantinople by the crusaders was the predictable outcome of the imperial and hegemonic policies of the popes. For, according to a point of view widely shared today, here expressed by Warwick Ball, "the real issue behind the entire Crusading movement was not so much the fight against Islam, but the supremacy of Rome and the papacy, one of the biggest issues of the European Middle Ages. The fight against Islam was simply a means towards that end: in promoting such a war the popes would be seen as the leaders of Christendom over any other claimants."[61]

As a matter of fact, the unity of the Islamic world did not suffer from the Crusades — quite the opposite. Before the First Crusade, it was fragmented into two rival caliphates (Baghdad and Cairo) alongside a number of independent emirates and city-states. The Frankish aggression stimulated reunification. Archbishop William of Tyre complained about this in the early 1180s: "In former times almost every city had its own ruler … not dependent on one another … who feared their own allies not less than the Christians [and] could not or would not readily unite to repulse the common danger or arm

60 Runciman, *A History of the Crusades*, vol. 3, *op. cit.*, pp. 130–131.

61 Warwick Ball, *Sultans of Rome: The Turkish World Expansion*, Olive Branch Press, 2013, p. 94.

themselves for our destruction. But now ... all the kingdoms adjacent to us have been brought under the power of one man [Nur ed-Din]."[62]

Moreover, before the First Crusade, the Byzantines had been living on good terms with the Fatimid Caliphate, of which Cairo was the capital. "In the middle of the eleventh century the tranquility of the east Mediterranean world seemed assured for many years to come. Its two great powers, Fatimid Egypt and Byzantium, were on good terms with each other."[63] Christians worshiped freely in Jerusalem, and Muslims had their mosque just outside the walls of Constantinople (it was burned by the Franks, and the fire spread to a third of the city). The Seljuk invaders from the East were the common foes of the Fatimids and the Byzantines. But for the unsophisticated crusaders, all Muslims were the same. The Franks' policy of "normative hostility" against Muslims disrupted the policy of the Byzantines, which was "to play off the various Moslem princes against each other and thus to isolate each of them in turn."[64]

The Franks' shortsightedness also hurt their own chances of success. For example, the crusaders' decision to attack Damascus during the Second Crusade was especially ill-advised. "It was a decision of utter folly," Runciman wrote. After all, "Of all the Moslem states the Burid kingdom of Damascus alone was eager to remain in friendship with the Franks; for, like the farther-sighted among the Franks, it recognized its chief foe to be Nur ed-Din. Frankish interests lay in retaining Damascene friendship till Nur ed-Din should be crushed, and to keep open the breach between Damascus and Aleppo. To attack the former was, as the events of the previous year had shown, the surest way to throw its rulers into Nur ed-Din's hands." Moreover, the crusaders made a pitiful retreat from Damascus after only four days

62 Tyerman, *God's War, op. cit.*, p. 343.

63 Runciman, *A History of the Crusades*, vol. 1, *op. cit.*, p. 42.

64 Housley, *Contesting the Crusades, op. cit.*, p. 158; Runciman, *A History of the Crusades*, vol. 2, *op. cit.*, pp. 274–275.

of siege. This was "a terrible humiliation," "a bitter blow to Christian prestige," and a boost to Muslim moral.[65]

As a whole, the Crusades not only dealt a mortal blow to the Eastern Christian empire that they pretended to be rescuing. They also ruined diplomatic relations between Byzantium and the Shiite caliphate of Egypt, indirectly causing the fall of this long-standing ally, which would be absorbed by Saladin under the Sunni banner in 1171. Thus, they strengthened the Sunni power that they were supposed to fight. Ultimately, the Crusades never seriously threatened Muslim rule over the Middle East, but rather catalyzed its unification, and they dug a wide trench of incomprehension and hostility between Christian and Islamic civilizations, thus doubly harming Eastern Christians of all denominations (Orthodox, Copts, Nestorians, Armenians, Jacobites, etc.), who had up until then enjoyed freedom of worship under most Muslim rulers.

Ultimately, the Crusades, with their inherent hypocrisy, harmed the West by corrupting its very soul. At the same time, the Crusades harmed the rest of the world by making the West a dangerous, unrestrained predator. The effect that the ultimate stabbing of Constantinople had on the personality of the West seems hardly a matter of speculation. On this point, Eric Hoffer's thought is insightful: "There is perhaps no surer way of infecting ourselves with virulent hatred toward a person than by doing him a grave injustice. That others have a just grievance against us is a more potent reason for hating them than that we have a just grievance against them."[66] Such hatred will not cease with the destruction of its object. It will have to find new objects, lest it turn into self-loathing. As we shall see in the next chapter, Rome's hatred for Constantinople seems to have survived Constantinople, and redirected itself against Russia.

---

65 Runciman, *History of the Crusades*, vol. 2, *op. cit.*, pp. 281–285.

66 Eric Hoffer, *The True Believer: Thoughts on the Nature of Mass Movements*, 1951, HarperPerennial, 2019, p. 118.

The Crusades in Europe and the Inquisition

The popes used the Crusade for a variety of geostrategic goals, targeting all their enemies for holy war and promising the remission of sins to anyone who agreed to fight them. In this spirit, crusades were even launched against the pope's enemies within Western Christendom. Such actually began before the First Crusade, if we count as a crusade the conquest of Sicily in 1060 by the Norman Roger I, which was carried out with the blessing of Pope Nicholas II, who gave Roger the "banner of Saint Peter" (*vexillum Sancti Petri*) for the occasion. The conquest of England by another Norman warlord was, in every respect, a crusade against the Anglo-Saxons, who were Christians but beyond the control of the pope. Interestingly, the last Saxon King of England, Harold Godwinson, who was killed at the Battle of Hastings (1066), is honored by the Russian Orthodox Church as a martyr. That is because his daughter, Gytha of Wessex, had married Vladimir II Monomakh, Grand Prince of Rus' of the Rurikid dynasty in Kiev. She bore him five sons, who went on to participate in the expansion of the Kievan kingdom and founded the city of Moscow. The Rurikids were then in communion with Byzantium (Vladimir II married a Byzantine princess). Saxon England had every reason to remain within the Russian-Byzantine orbit. This displeased the pope and motivated his support for the conquest of England by William of Normandy. Harold was excommunicated with his supporters, and William was given a banner of the Roman Church and a priceless ring containing a hair of Saint Peter set under a diamond. Religious conquest immediately followed military conquest, as Bernard Cottret describes: "The native Church, its saints, its martyrs, and their pious relics appeared suspect. Clergymen from across the sea agreed to replace Saxon priests in positions of responsibility, particularly among the senior clergy."[67] Liturgical reform was adopted along with submission to

67 Bernard Cottret, *Histoire de l'Angleterre, de Guillaume le Conquérant à nos jours*, Texto/Tallandier, 2019, pp. 19, 26.

the pope. A number of Saxon nobles fleeing William's ethnic cleansing found refuge in Byzantine lands. In 1075, they were rewarded by the emperor for helping repel the Seljuk Turks from Constantinople. They joined the Varangian Guard, an elite corps dedicated to the protection of the emperor. Other Saxons found refuge in Ireland.

Ireland, by the way, had a very ancient monastic tradition, rich in Christian erudition, but remained out of papal control. The independence of the Irish Church ended with the conquest of Ireland by Henry II Plantagenet, grandson of William the Conqueror, again behind the papal banner. Bernard Cottret explains: "[Henry] landed in Waterford in October 1171. By his bull *Laudabiliter*, Pope Adrian IV had conceded, around twenty years earlier, the lordship of the country to the king of England, charging him with defending the truths of the Christian religion in the midst of a frustrated, vicious, ignorant, and quarrelsome people. Alexander III reiterated these grievances: if Ireland, in theory, had already been Christianized, it had, he insisted, long resisted the civilizing influence of Rome." The Irish were accused of not paying tithes, of eating meat during Lent or, more damning, of "being incestuous, and living in cohabitation with several sisters, or with their sisters-in-law"[68]—in other words, they were clannish, and the clan is the enemy of the Church, as we shall see in the last chapter.

The most infamous crusade launched by a pope against Christians was the Albigensian Crusade (1209–29) in the southern part of what was still understood as "Gaul." It was proclaimed by Innocent III as soon as the Franks and Venetians had conquered Constantinople. The coveted lands were those of the immense county of Toulouse, whose sovereign was a vassal of the king of France only by a thin legal fiction, and for only part of his domains. The Occitan language spoken there was almost incomprehensible to the northern Franks. Culturally, Occitania was more Hispanic than French, and Count Raymond VI had strengthened the Barcelona-Toulouse axis by

68 *Ibid.*, p. 47.

marrying a sister of Peter II of Aragon, while his son Raymond VII married another (becoming the brother-in-law of his own father).

Before the Crusade, the whole south of France enjoyed a certain Byzantine atmosphere, manifestations of which can still be seen in the dome basilicas of the Southwest (Périgueux, Angoulème, Cahors, Souillac, Solignac, Cognac, Saintes), which were built on Byzantine models, probably by Byzantine architects. In the mid-19th century, the French archaeologist Félix de Verneilh expressed surprise when examining the 12th-century cathedral in Périgueux: "a Byzantine building is transplanted, all in one piece, deep in our provinces, in one of our small towns. … How, by what combination of extraordinary circumstances could this have happened?"[69] There was also, in the county of Toulouse, a rare religious tolerance allowing for heterodox anti-papist communities to live in peace. Those most directly targeted by Rome were known as the Cathars — from the Greek *catharos*, "pure." What most preoccupied the papacy was that they recruited from the urban elite and the lower nobility.[70] Although their adversaries did everything to erase or sully their memory, we know that the Cathars considered themselves simply "good Christians." They were certainly dissidents with regard to the dogma and the liturgy defined by the Great Church, but, as Michel Roquebert explains, they were "Christians all the same, to the exact extent that for them there was only one revelation, of which Christ was the bearer, and that their only reference was the New Testament, completed by what served their demonstrations in the Old Testament."[71] It is generally assumed that the Cathars were the spiritual heirs of the Bogomils who appeared in Bulgaria around 950 and were still enjoying the relative tolerance of the Orthodox Byzantines in the 11th century. They

69 Félix de Verneilh, *L'Architecture byzantine en France. Saint-Front de Périgueux et les églises à coupoles de l'Aquitaine,* 1851, p. 124.

70 Jacques Berlioz, ed., *Le Pays cathare. Les religions médiévales et leurs expressions méridionales,* Seuil, 2000, pp. 17–79.

71 Michel Roquebert, *Histoire des cathares,* Perrin/Tempus, 1999, p. 24.

were still numerous in Bosnia when the Turks arrived in the second half of the 15th century, following which the majority converted to Islam. When, in May 1167, the Cathars of Toulouse organized a council, their "pope" Nicetas made a special visit from Constantinople (although the truth about this account is disputed[72]). What made the Cathars especially hated by Rome was their Gnostic dualism, which caused them to be denounced as "Manicheans," although no Persian influence can be detected in their doctrine. Not all Cathars professed absolute dualism, but they regarded the Roman Catholic hierarchy as an agent of the devil, the prince of this world; they would soon find confirmation of this in the Crusade against them and in the Inquisition.

The Cathars were not the only dissidents who obstructed papal supremacy. The Toulouse cleric Guillaume of Puylaurens, a witness and chronicler of the Albigensian Crusade, wrote: "There were Arians, Manichaeans, and also Waldensians. ... Although they were divided among themselves, they all conspired to destroy souls against the Catholic faith."[73] What all these "heresies" protested against was the defilement of the Church in secular affairs, luxury and corruption. "The Waldensians (followers of Peter Waldo of Lyons) believed that the authority of the Roman Church was annulled when Pope Sylvester had accepted temporal possessions from the Emperor Constantine"[74]—they could not have known that the Donation of Constantine was a forgery. Many "heretics" also contested the legitimacy of the regular priesthood, the validity of the sacraments, and especially the quasi-magical theory of "transubstantiation" (the physical, and not just symbolic, transformation of the Sacred host during mass). The Cathars also rejected the doctrine of eternal Hell

---

72 Janet and Bernard Hamilton (ed.), *Christian Dualist Heresies in the Byzantine World c.650–c.1405*, Mancheseter UP, 1998, pp. 42–64.

73 Roquebert, *Histoire des cathares, op. cit.*, p. 51.

74 Sayers, *Innocent III, op. cit.*, p. 154.

as contrary to God's love, as well as the recently established Purgatory (also rejected by the Greek Orthodox).

Innocent III urged Philip II of France to seize the lands of these rebellious peoples: "Confiscate the property of counts, barons and citizens who do not want to eliminate heresy from their lands or who dare to maintain it. Do not delay in attaching their entire country to the royal domain." He insisted in a second letter: "In the name of Moses and Peter, seal this alliance of royalty and priesthood." The king did not respond. In March 10, 1208, the pope proclaimed the forfeiture of the Count of Toulouse, Raymond VI, this "minister of the devil," and the exposure of his domains to prey: "Let all those who are linked to the said count by an oath of loyalty, association or alliance be declared by our apostolic authority relieved of this oath. May it be permitted to every Catholic ... not only to fight the count in person, but also to occupy and keep his property, so that the wisdom of a new possessor purges this land of the heresy by which it has been shamefully soiled until now, by the count's fault."[75]

Understanding that such a precedent would undermine the stability of the entire feudal pyramid, Philip II protested: "You have no right to act like this," he wrote to the pope. But the pope could count on the efficiency of his war propaganda among knights and adventurers of all kinds, although these people also had their own motivations which the Church could not always manage to channel. Simon de Montfort, a small lord of Île-de-France who had responded to the pope's calling, seized the vast viscounty of Carcassonne and other vassal principalities of the count of Toulouse, subjecting them to his "Statutes of the Conquered Land" (Statutes of Pamiers, 1212), which included the obligation for all to attend Latin mass on Sunday "and to hear the entire mass and sermon there." But Simon overstepped his mandate and carved out a fiefdom larger than his king's domain and then resisted the pope's injunctions to give back part of it. Nicknamed

75 Roquebert, *Histoire des Cathares, op. cit.*, pp. 113–139.

"the executioner of Languedoc" for his thousands of executions by rope, iron, and fire, and his destruction of hundreds of villages, castles, vineyards, and orchards, Simon de Montfort is the archetypal figure of the crusader who found in the Crusade a divine justification for his satanic greed. However, it was not Simon but Arnaud Amaury, the abbot of Cîteaux whom Innocent III appointed leader of the Crusade, who uttered in Béziers the famous sentence (often distorted): "Massacre them all, for the Lord knows his own!" He wrote in his report to the pope: "Our troops, sparing neither rank, nor sex, nor age, put to death by the sword approximately twenty thousand people; after a huge massacre of the enemies, the entire city was pillaged and burned. Divine vengeance struck it wonderfully."[76] Here comes Yahweh again.

Urged to intervene, King Philip sent his son, the future Louis VIII, on an observation mission. Shortly after the death of his father in 1223, Louis VIII took the cross against the count of Toulouse, but died before the end of his expedition. It is rumored that his allegiance to the pope was due to the influence of his wife, the pious Blanche of Castile. After her royal husband's death, she held the regency for her son Louis IX, brought to the throne at nine years old. It was this future Saint Louis who reaped the fruit of the alliance between Rome and Paris, with the Treaty of Paris (1229) by which Raymond VII of Toulouse surrendered half of his states to the Capetian crown and, by the marriage of his daughter to a brother of the king under precise inheritance clauses, guaranteed the annexation of the other half in the short term. Occitania became fully French in 1271.

The Crusade did not overcome heresy. For this, the Inquisition was founded in 1231 by Pope Gregory IX and entrusted to Dominique of Guzman, founder of the Dominican Order. In 1252, by the bull *Ad extirpanda*, Pope Innocent IV authorized the use of torture to obtain confessions from heretics—these "murderers of souls as well

76 *Ibid.*, pp. 136, 120.

as robbers of God's sacraments and of the Christian faith"—on the reasoning that, since they are destined for eternal torture in hell, it is an act of kindness to subject them to some temporary torture in this world in an attempt to reconcile them with the Church. Michel Roquebert makes the point that the Inquisition was "the first historical emergence of a system of exhaustive ideological control of an entire population by means of investigations, institutionalized denunciation, interrogations and the creation of intelligence files."[77]

Our survey of the crusades would not be complete without mention of the crusade in Bohemia against the Hussites in the early 15th century. Bohemia was a mighty kingdom under the Luxembourg dynasty, one of whose members became Holy Roman Emperor Charles IV (1347–78). The Bohemian Church, under Rome's jurisdiction, was particularly rich, corrupt, and debauched at the end of the 14th century. Jan Hus, supported by a segment of the nobility and of the lower clergy, inaugurated a protest movement demanding the freedom to preach, the Church's renunciation of earthly possessions, the punishment of sinners, and communion with the two kinds of bread and wine for laymen as well as priests. This Bohemian reform movement was influenced by the Englishman John Wycliff (1330–84), who had defied the Church's ban by translating the Bible into English (from Latin). Wycliff and Hus did not openly reject the authority of the pope, but they urged the Church to renounce political power and worldly possessions. Although he went under safe conduct to the Council of Constance to answer his accusers, Jan Hus was arrested, tortured, and burned alive in 1415, followed a year later by his disciple Jerome of Prague. Far from dying out, the Hussite movement developed into a dissident church which the papacy addressed by launching a crusade that devastated the country for twelve years (1420–1431). The heretics were subdued physically, but not spiritually. Some of them established contacts with the Byzantine Church. In

77 *Ibid.*, pp. 18–19.

1451, according to Steven Runciman, "a Bohemian whom the Greeks called Constantine Platris and surnamed the Englishman—he was probably the son of a Lollard refugee settled in Bohemia—came to Constantinople with letters to the Orthodox authorities. ... Friendly messages, full of denunciations of Roman pretensions, were exchanged. But the fall of the city little more than a year later prevented further negotiations."[78] A century later, a large part of Bohemia responded to Martin Luther's call for religious emancipation from Rome. Jan Hus and Jerome of Prague are national heroes in the Czech Republic and saints for the Orthodox tradition.

The Beginning of Colonization

In *The Latin Kingdom of Jerusalem: European Colonialism in the Middle Ages,* Joshua Prawer presents medieval crusading as a foreshadowing of later European colonialism. He contends that the institutions and economy of the Latin states are best understood in the light of their colonial status: "Though colonization is not a new phenomenon in European history, only since the Crusades is there continuity and filiation between colonial movements. Ever since, colonialism has remained a major factor in European and non-European history. In this sense it is justified to regard the Crusader kingdom as the first European colonial society."[79] The Northern Crusades in the Baltic regions, launched in the early 13th century with the full benefit of papal indulgences and privileges, fit modern definitions of colonization very well. The appeal of Archbishop Adalgot of Magdeburg in 1108 makes it clear:

---

78 Steven Runciman, *The Great Church in Captivity,* Cambridge UP, 1968, p. 238.

79 Joshua Prawer, *The Latin Kingdom of Jerusalem: European Colonialism in the Middle Ages*, Weidenfeld & Nicolson, 1972, p. ix. See also George Demacopoulos, *Colonizing Christianity: Greek and Latin Religious Identity in the Era of the Fourth Crusade,* Fordham UP, 2019.

> These gentiles are most wicked, but their land is the best, rich in meat, honey, corn and birds, and if it were well cultivated none could be compared to it for wealth of its produce ... And so, most renowned Saxons, French, Lorrainers and Flemings and conquerors of the world, this is an occasion for you to save your souls and, if you wish it, acquire the best land in which to live. May He who with the strength of his arm led the men of Gaul on their march from the far West in triumph against his enemies in the farthest East give you the will and power to conquer those most inhuman gentiles who are nearby and to prosper well in all things.[80]

The filiation between the Crusades and colonization is transparently clear in the Americas. In *Columbus and the Quest for Jerusalem,* Carol Delaney reveals a little known fact: "The quest for Jerusalem was Columbus's grand passion; it was the vision that sustained him through all the trials and tribulations he felt, like Job, that he endured ... He had dedicated his life to the liberation of Jerusalem; on his deathbed, realizing he would never see his project fulfilled, he ratified his will that left money to support the crusade he hoped would be taken up by his successors."[81] Columbus was also obsessed with gold. He was hoping to reach the Cipango (Japan) of Marco Polo, so rich in gold that roofs and furniture were made of it. But the gold, in Columbus's mind, was for Jerusalem. He wrote in his diary on December 26, 1492 that he wanted to find gold "in such quantity that the sovereigns ... will undertake and prepare to go conquer the Holy Sepulchre."[82] On returning from his first voyage, he wrote to King Ferdinand and Queen Isabella "that in seven years from today I will be able to pay Your Highnesses for five thousand cavalry and fifty thousand foot soldiers for the war and conquest of Jerusalem, for which purpose this enterprise was undertaken." Ten years later, he was still dwelling on the same theme. In a letter written in Jamaica during his fourth expedition, he stated: "Gold is a metal most

80 Tyerman, *God's War, op. cit.*, p. 676.

81 Carol Delaney, *Columbus and the Quest for Jerusalem,* Free Press, 2012, p. 27.

82 *Ibid.*, p. 10.

excellent above all others; of gold treasures are formed, and he who has it makes and accomplishes whatever he wishes in the world, and finally uses it to send souls into Paradise."[83] As we have seen, the idea that souls could be saved by gold was born from the Crusades.

The Spanish and Portuguese conquistadors had been immersed all their lives in the ideology of the *Reconquista,* a series of crusades against the Muslims of Iberia. As Norman Cantor explains: "The *Reconquista* was the dominant, almost the exclusive, theme of medieval Christian Spanish history, and some historians have seen it as the determining factor in the molding of the peculiar Spanish character. All Iberian society originated in a grim war of five centuries against Islam, and the Spanish institutional structure was organized around the warlord and the necessities of aggressive warfare."[84] No wonder, then, that the conquistadors saw themselves as crusaders. And there is no way around the fact that the papacy legitimated the conquest and colonization of the New World. By the 1494 Treaty of Tordesillas, Pope Alexander VI declared that the line of longitude 46° 37' west of Greenwich (as translated into modern terms) defined the hemispheres of Spanish and Portuguese settlement and conquest overseas.[85] Latin American countries have never escaped their colonial status, and have simply transitioned from European colonization to the ongoing endeavors of American colonization.[86] This is why they did not inherit the spirit of the Crusades—and, as a result, are not considered part of the "collective West."

Among the factors that shaped European colonialism, let us not forget the competition between colonizing states examined in the

83 Carol Delaney, "Columbus's Ultimate Goal: Jerusalem," on www.amherst.edu/system/files/columbus.pdf.

84 Cantor, *The Civilization of the Middle Ages, op. cit.*, p. 290.

85 John Hale, *The Civilization of Europe in the Renaissance*, Fontana Press, 1994, p. 131.

86 As famously argued by Eduardo Galeano in *The Open Veins of Latin America,* first published in Spanish 1971.

previous chapter. It is in the nature of an empire to seek to expand its cultural, economic and political influence. But in the case of Europe, it was not one empire expanding, but a pack of rival states pouncing on their prey with the primary motivation of plundering more resources than their rivals. In this sense, colonialism, in its most brutal and destructive character is yet another consequence of Europe's inability to unify politically into an empire. As noted in the first chapter, colonial empires were European nations' attempts to fulfill Europe's imperial destiny that they could not fulfill in Europe itself, and it is significant that among Europe's great nations, the one that least indulged in colonialism was Germany.

Ultimately, the Crusade would be the fairy godmother that bent over the cradle of the United States. In the 19th century, after having accomplished its "Manifest Destiny" and pushed its Frontier to the Pacific Ocean at the expense of the Mexican Empire, the U.S. remained overflowing with crusading spirit. Those who made their fortune in China through the opium trade, as did Franklin Roosevelt's maternal grandfather, Warren Delano, did so in the company of missionaries and with the good conscience of contributing to the salvation of Chinese souls.[87] In the postcolonial age, American neocolonialism resorted again to the rhetoric of the crusades, this time for the new religion of liberal democracy. President Woodrow Wilson declared in 1912: "We are chosen, and prominently chosen, to show the way to the nations of the world how they shall walk in the path of liberty."[88] In 1951, six years after nuking Hiroshima and Nagasaki and firebombing to ashes 67 other Japanese cities, Truman declared: "Divine Providence has played a great part in our history. I have the feeling that God has created us and brought us to our present position of power and strength for some great purpose. … It is given to us to defend the spiritual values — the moral code — against the vast

87 James Bradley, *The China Mirage: The Hidden History of American Disaster in Asia*, Black Bay Books, 2015.

88 Wilson Center [www.wilsoncenter.org/about-woodrow-wilson].

forces of evil that seek to destroy them."[89] Dwight Eisenhower entitled his WWII memoirs *Crusade in Europe*, which is especially ironic: Europe, which had launched so many crusades to the East, now became the target of a crusade from the new West, to be "liberated" from Germany and thereby turned into an American colony.

NATO's destruction of Yugoslavia in 1999 also fits the crusading pattern, as Diana Johnstone remarks in her book *Fools' Crusade*: "When the Soviet Bloc collapsed, non-aligned Yugoslavia lost its value to the West as a strategic asset. As a nominally socialist country with considerable Third World relationships thanks to its leading role in the Non-Aligned Movement, Yugoslavia could be seen as a potential alternative model. If the country held together, it might stand in the way of Western plans for the region. Perhaps the potential Yugoslav 'threat' was an illusion. But its disintegration settled the matter, and destroying the country provided a useful exercise for future operations."[90]

What happened to Yugoslavia was uniquely devastating, but many other countries are targeted with similar base motives and false pretexts (at the present time of writing: Venezuela). Most American military adventures fit Christopher Tyerman's definition of the medieval Crusades as "wars justified by faith conducted against real or imagined enemies defined by religious and political elites as perceived threats to the Christian faithful."[91] That today's crusades are launched in the name of Democracy rather than Christianity is the only difference. John Mearsheimer, who defines the culture of U.S. policymakers as "progressive liberalism," notes that liberal states "have a crusader mentality hard-wired into them that is hard to restrain."[92]

---

89 Truman Library [www.trumanlibrary.org/publicpapers/index.php?pid=280].

90 Diana Johnstone, *Fools' Crusade: Yugoslavia, NATO and Western Delusions*, Pluto Press, 2002, p. 11.

91 Tyerman, *God's War, op. cit.*, p. xiii.

92 John P. Mearsheimer, *The Great Delusion: Liberal Dreams and International Realities*, Yale UP, 2018, p. 2.

III

New Romes: The Ghosts of Byzantium

Until very recently, most Western medievalists wrote as if Constantinople was of little or no concern to them. When they did mention it, it was often in derogatory terms taken directly from the Latin chronicles of the Crusades. British historian Steven Runciman, the exception to this trend, wrote: "Ever since our rough crusading forefathers first saw Constantinople and met, to their contemptuous disgust, a society where everyone read and wrote, ate food with forks and preferred diplomacy to war, it has been fashionable to pass the Byzantines by with scorn and to use their name as synonymous with decadence."[1]

Fortunately, Anglo-American academia has now overcome this prejudice. Runciman did much to promote knowledge of Byzantine history and of the Byzantine experience of the Crusades. His *History of the Crusades* in three volumes is still essential reading. The American Paul Stephenson, who in 1972 denounced "the excision of Byzantine history from European medieval studies" as "an unforgivable offense against the very spirit of history," has also made important contributions. More recently, Anthony Kaldellis, an American of Greek heritage, has provided insightful and innovative analyses

1 Steven Runciman, *The Emperor Romanus Lecapenus and His Reign: A Study of Tenth-Century Byzantium*, Cambridge UP, 1988, p. 9.

which have earned him the epithet "Byzantine revisionist." This chapter will draw heavily on his work.

Byzantium is a lost civilization. And yet it is a fascinating historical subject because, in so many ways, the long struggle between Rome and Constantinople that culminated with the sack of 1204 still resonates in contemporary geopolitics. When Byzantium died, its immortal spirit was recollected by Russia. Russian civilization was born as a daughter of Byzantine civilization, and learned almost everything from it. It never forsook its filial loyalty and, after Constantinople fell to the Ottomans, the Russian tsars picked up the Byzantine banner with the double-headed eagle. Moscow called itself the Third Rome, and it never gave up the hope of rescuing the Second Rome from Muslim domination. Moreover, although Westerners are unaware of it, Russians today have an acute sense of the West's hostility towards them as being the continuation of Rome's treacherous war against Constantinople. How the actual showdown will end in the near future will tell us if there are karmic forces working in history.

Byzantine Revisionism

If «Byzantine revisionism» means anything, it means listening to the Byzantine version of its long struggle with the West and recognizing that the victor's narrative is misleading, as it always is. We were told, for example, that the Crusades were the West's generous response to the Byzantines' appeal for help. And if an indiscreet Western historian tells you about the sack of Constantinople by the crusaders in 1204, he will often present it as a regrettable blunder, the fault of the Venetians, and will gloss over it. Byzantine revisionism underscores the cataclysmic effect of this event in East-West relations. The above-quoted Steven Runciman insisted in *Byzantine Civilisation*: "It is hard to exaggerate the harm done to European civilisation by the sack of Constantinople. The treasures of the City, the books and works of art preserved from distant centuries, were all dispersed and most destroyed. The Empire, the great Eastern bulwark of Christendom, was broken as a power. Its highly centralised organisation was ruined. Provinces, to save themselves, were forced into devolution. The conquests of the Ottoman were made possible by the Crusaders' crime."[2]

Byzantine revisionism must begin by reinstating Constantinople geographically at the heart of the great Eurasian immensity, and historically as a dominant power during the medieval millennium. First, we need to put Constantinople in the center of our map. It was by far the largest city in the Christian world throughout the Middle Ages. Around the year 1000, its walls could have contained the ten largest cities in Western Europe, including Rome. Its population approached a million, counting the suburbs. Here is how Anthony Kaldellis describes Constantinople at the very beginning of the central Middle Ages:

> At the turn of the first millennium the empire of New Rome was the oldest and most dynamic state in the world and comprised the most civilized portions of the Christian world. Its borders, long defended by native frontier troops, were being expanded by the most disciplined and technologically advanced army of its time. The unity of Byzantine society was grounded in the equality of Roman law and a deep sense of a common and ancient Roman identity; cemented by the efficiency of a complex bureaucracy; nourished and strengthened by the institutions and principles of the Christian Church; sublimated by Greek rhetoric; and confirmed by the passage of ten centuries. At the end of the reign of Basileios II (976–1025), the longest in Roman history, its territory included Asia Minor and Armenia, the Balkan peninsula south of the Danube, and the southern regions of both Italy and the Crimea. Serbia, Croatia, Georgia, and some Arab emirates in Syria and Mesopotamia had accepted a dependent status.[3]

---

2 Steven Runciman, *Byzantine Civilisation*, Arnold & Co., 1933, pp. 54–55.

3 Anthony Kaldellis, *Hellenism in Byzantium: the Transformation of Greek Identity and the Reception of the Classical Tradition*, Cambridge UP, 2007, p. 189.

In 1018, the same Basileios (or Basil) II was "the most powerful and victorious ruler in the Christian world."[4] That is the reason why Vladimir the Great married his sister and adopted his faith. The young German Emperor Otto III, already half-Byzantine through his mother Theophano, was about to marry Basil's niece when he died at the age of 21. Everything at the Ottonian court was modeled on Byzantine protocol—even the title of *kaiser*, borrowed not from the Latin *caesar*, but from the Greek *kaisar*. From Charlemagne to the Hohenstaufen, Western imperial ceremonial was of Byzantine inspiration, and the whole of Europe was drawn into the civilizational field of Constantinople. The size, wealth, and splendor of this city so impressed Western visitors that, in one of the earliest French "romances," *Partonopeu de Blois* (late 12th century), Constantinople is the name of paradise—a fairy paradise not devoid of eroticism. Robert of Clari, who was among the crusaders who sacked it in 1204, marveled: "Since the creation of this world, such great wealth has never been seen or conquered. … there has never been, in the forty richest cities in the world, as many goods as those found inside Constantinople."[5] Until this catastrophe, Constantinople was probably the largest commercial hub in the world, connecting China, India, Arabia, Africa, Europe, Russia, and the Baltic states. Many of the luxury goods that reached Europe (silk or cotton fabrics, porcelain, ivory, gems, tea, spices, perfumes and ointments, dyes, not to mention ideas) transited through Constantinople.

The importance of the Eastern Roman capital must be measured not only synchronically around the year 1000, but also diachronically for over 1000 years. Byzantine revisionism means restoring Constantinople to its rightful place on the long timeline. Kaldellis writes:

---

4 Anthony Kaldellis, *Streams of Gold, Rivers of Blood: The Rise and Fall of Byzantium, 955 A.D. to the First Crusade*, Oxford UP, 2019, p. 81.

5 Robert de Clari, *La Conquête de Constantinople*, Champion, 2004, p. 171.

> Byzantine civilization began when there were still some people who could read and write in Egyptian hieroglyphics; the oracle of Delphi and the Olympic games were still in existence; and the main god of worship in the east was Zeus. When Byzantium ended, the world had cannons and printing presses, and some people who witnessed the fall of Constantinople in 1453 lived to hear about Columbus's journey to the New World. Chronologically, Byzantium spans the entire arc from antiquity to the early modern period, and its story is intertwined with that of all the major players in world history on this side of the Indus river.[6]

From this point of view, the expression "the Middle Ages," coined during the Renaissance, seems quite inappropriate. These thousand years should be renamed "the Byzantine era." Unlike the Middle Ages, whose contours are vague and the subject of endless debate, the Byzantine era is extremely easy to identify. "There is no ambiguity or chronological fuzziness here." If the term "Middle Ages" is "inherently problematic," says Kaldellis, then the more recent invention of "Late Antiquity" has only added to the confusion: "late antiquity drove a wedge between Byzantium and its ancient roots." It also "appropriated for itself major areas of Byzantine innovation that had world impact."

If Byzantium fits poorly within the framework of Late Antiquity and the Middle Ages, it is because these Eurocentric categories were created to obscure or marginalize Byzantium. We were taught that Byzantium was a pale copy of the late Roman Empire, slowly declining into insignificance. But what can a thousand-year long decline possibly mean? The reality is that Byzantium was the Roman Empire until the West erased it from its history books. "Byzantium in the tenth century resembled the Roman empire of the fourth century more than it resembled any contemporary western medieval state," Kaldellis writes.[7] And what we call "the fall of the Roman Empire" never happened in the East until 1453 (the capture of Constantinople

6 Anthony Kaldellis, *Byzantium Unbound,* ARC Humanities Press, 2019, p. 34.

7 *Ibid.*, pp. 62, 43.

by the Ottoman Turks). From 330 until then, there had been no discontinuity in Roman civilization in the East.

The Byzantines always referred to themselves as Romans (*Rhomaioi*). The Persians, Arabs, and Turks called them *Rumi*. The term "Byzantine" was introduced in 1555 and became commonly used in the 19th century. It was a way of depriving the Eastern Romans of their Romanness, and it was the continuation of propaganda that had started in the 8th century, when the popes turned away from Constantinople and sought the patronage of the Franks. From that time, Kaldellis writes, "the term *Graeci* began to displace *Romani* in western references to the eastern empire. This intensified when some Frankish kings began, if at first only sporadically and uncertainly, to claim for themselves the title of emperor of the Romans. By the ninth century, both popes and western emperors were, in their official correspondence, actively questioning the right of the eastern emperor to call himself emperor of the Romans." Thus, Kaldellis continues, "the easterners were increasingly reclassified as *Graeci*, a term that in ancient Latin literature conveyed negative connotations that were now reactivated, connotations of treachery, effeminacy, excessive sophistication, love of luxury, verbal trickery, and cowardice."[8] The soft-power war behind this naming is illustrated by a letter from Louis II, great-grandson of Charlemagne, to Basil I, the founder of the Macedonian dynasty: "The Greeks have ceased to be emperors of the Romans on account of their bad opinions when it comes to religious faith. Also, not only have they abandoned the city and the seat of empire, they have also abandoned the Roman people and the language itself, having migrated in all ways to a different city, seat, people, and language." Louis adds that he has a better claim to the title of Roman Emperor because it was bestowed on him by the pope, whereas the Greek *basileus* is sometimes acclaimed by the senate, the people, or the armies. In making this argument, as Kaldellis remarks, "Louis

8 Anthony Kaldellis, *Romanland: Ethnicity and Empire in Byzantium*, Belknap Press, 2019, pp. 13–14.

displayed how out of touch he was with ancient Roman tradition. In this particular aspect, eastern practice adhered to authentic Roman notions of acclamation, whereas western practice did not."[9]

The Byzantine Republican Monarchy

The Easterners, for their part, thought that their political tradition was more Roman than the Franks'. And they were right, as Kaldellis argues in *The Byzantine Republic.* Here again, he puts an end to centuries of prejudice: "An imaginary modern construct labeled 'Byzantium,' identified with theocracy and absolutism, has come to stand between us and the vibrant political culture of the east Romans." Byzantium was a *basileia* (kingdom) in the service of a *politeia* (the Greek equivalent of *res publica*): a republican monarchy in which popular acclamation made the emperors and popular disapproval unmade them. This was not always the case in practice, but it was at least "a deeply embedded ideology; that is, this was the only acceptable framework for the legitimation of imperial power in Byzantium." Certainly, there were dynasties, but "dynastic claims were not a right but only one among many rhetorical arguments that an emperor (or potential emperor) could make." "Just as the people could turn out in numbers to end a dynasty (in 695, 1042, and 1185), so too could they rally to defend it when it was popular and they perceived it as being under threat."[10]

According to Kaldellis, "the explicit or underlying assumption of all narratives, speeches, pronouncements, and documents relating to the *basileia*" is that "the emperor was supposed to work hard for the benefit of his subjects." And so in 491, when Anastasios I was elected emperor by popular acclaim in the hippodrome, he declared: "I am not unaware how great a burden of responsibility has been

9 *Ibid.*, p. 20.

10 Anthony Kaldellis, *The Byzantine Republic: People and Power in New Rome*, Harvard UP, 2015, pp. 199, 109, 139, 215, 130.

placed upon me for the common safety of all. … I entreat God the Almighty that you will find me working as hard at public affairs as you had hoped when you universally elected me now." In 511, when a controversy pitted him against Patriarch Makedonios, and civil war was a looming possibility, "Anastasios appeared in the hippodrome without his crown and offered to abdicate, which calmed the crowd. When the people told him to put his crown back on, they were symbolically reinvesting him with imperial authority." The elective character of royalty should of course not be confused with the use of the secret ballot. "Election" meant popular acclamation, and that made the hippodrome, adjacent to the imperial palace, the political heart of the Byzantine Republic. In fact, Kaldellis argues, "Byzantium was probably more republican than its predecessors, the Principate [27 BC–284 AD] and the Dominate [after 284 AD]."[11]

As for the Byzantine plebeians, they were not passive subjects: "They were on the alert for opportunities to intervene in the politics of the City and could mobilize within hours." Kaldellis mentions episodes in which "the people of Constantinople took the initiative to defend and enforce their views when it came to religious, political, fiscal, and dynastic matters, or when they disliked an emperor and wanted to get rid of him. … While there were no regular legal mechanisms by which the people could exercise power, there were also no formal agreements that could shield an emperor from the anger of the people or other elements of the republic when they had recourse to extralegal measures." This could lead to civil wars, which are considered in Byzantine chronicles as unfortunate but legitimate manifestations of the republican spirit. This explains that "no state in history ever had more civil wars that changed nothing about the structure or the ideology of the polity. Byzantine civil wars were usually only about personnel."[12]

11 *Ibid.*, pp. 55–56, 120, 146.

12 *Ibid.*, pp. 137, 124, 181, 138.

The political hierarchy of Byzantium, Kaldellis writes, was "an aristocracy of service, not blood, despite the occasional rhetoric." There never existed a hereditary nobility in Constantinople. Meritocracy was cultivated instead. The elite "was marked by high turnover and had no hereditary right to office or titles, and no legal authority over persons and territories except that which came from office." Although the senatorial class of the old Western Empire was jealous of its blood, Constantine had recruited locally for the new Rome a class of administrators whose value system became more based on public service. Certainly, there were rich and powerful families, but they became so by their political involvement, and only remained so as long as they retained the emperor's favor. Thus, Constantinople was "a place of opportunity." For example, Basil I, the founder of the Macedonian dynasty, "was a peasant who went to the City to escape poverty, and maneuvered his way to the throne."[13]

In conclusion, there are important lessons of political philosophy to be learned from Byzantium. Runciman writes in *Byzantine Civilisation*: "That the Byzantine Empire should have endured for eleven hundred years was almost entirely due to the virtues of its constitution and administration. Few states have been organised in a manner so well suited to the times and so carefully directed to prevent power remaining in the hands of the incompetent."[14]

Byzantine Romanness and Hellenistic Civilization

The Byzantines called their own language Romaic (*romaika*), whereas we now call it Greek. Strangely enough, they considered themselves Roman even from an ethnic point of view, but not because they thought of themselves as having Italic ancestors. Among eight "snapshots" that Kaldellis provides to "highlight the ethnic aspects of Romanness in Byzantium," none of them indicate that the Byzantines

13 Kaldellis, *Streams of Blood, op. cit.*, p. 5.

14 Runciman, *Byzantine Civilisation, op. cit.*, p. 61.

thought their ancestors came from Rome in Italy. Three of them indicate rather that they considered their own eastern *Romania* (from the Balkans to Anatolia) as the cradle of Romanness. For example, in 1246, the population of Melnik asked to be ruled by the Roman *basileus* rather than the Bulgarian tsar because, they said, "we all originate in Philippopolis and we are pure Romans when it comes to our *genos*."[15] Philippopolis is a Greek city founded by Philip II of Macedon (the father of Alexander the Great), about 200 miles west of Constantinople, in present-day Bulgaria. We must understand, therefore, that Romanness was for the Byzantines synonymous with what we call Hellenistic civilization, which radiated from the Balkans. For them, Alexander the Great was a Roman. Why wouldn't he be? The Roman Emperor Constantine the Great was himself born in the Balkans, as were all the Eastern emperors after 450, with the exception of Zeno.

We must assume that the Byzantines were aware that the "Roman Empire" had been founded in Rome, Italy. But they also knew that Rome, like many other Western cities, had been founded in the first place by settlers from the Balkans and the west coast of Anatolia, so that when Constantine founded the New Rome, it was somehow a return to the source of Romanness. Italic Romans themselves were aware of the Eastern origin of their city. According to Virgil's *Aeneid*, the founder of Rome came from Troy on the Anatolian coast, in the immediate vicinity of the Bosphorus. According to another legend that the Italian Romans entertained, Rome was founded by Romos, the son of Odysseus and Circe.[16] *Romos* is a Greek word meaning "strong." Strabo reports in his *Geographia* (V,3) that "another, more ancient tradition makes Rome an Arcadian colony," and insists that "Rome itself was of Hellenic origin." Dionysius of Halicarnassus in his *Roman Antiquities* (I,89,2) declares: "Rome is a Greek city." His

15 Kaldellis, *Romanland, op. cit.*, pp. 8, 11, 35.

16 Sander Goldberg, *Epic in Republican Rome*, Oxford UP, 1995, pp. 50–51.

thesis is summed up by the syllogism: "The Romans descend from the Trojans. The Trojans are of Greek origin. Therefore the Romans are of Greek origin." The same Dionysius claimed that "the language spoken by the Romans" derives from Aeolic Greek, a theory called "Aeolism" and later defended by Renaissance scholar Janus Lascaris.[17] In his *History of the Empire* (I,11), the Greek-speaking Roman historian Herodian tells the story of Italian Romans going to Pessinus in Phrygia (Anatolia) to bring back a statue of the goddess Cybele. They succeeded "by reminding the Phrygians of their kinship and by recalling to them that Aeneas the Phrygian was the ancestor of the Romans."

Rome's initial situation in relation to the Greek or proto-Byzantine world was that of a colony, much like Carthage in relation to Phoenicia. Just as Carthage became the capital of the Phoenician world after the destruction of Tyre by Alexander the Great in 333, Rome became the capital of the Hellenistic world after the collapse of the Ptolemaic and Seleucid empires. Rome became hegemonic during a brief period marked by a power vacuum in the eastern part of the Mediterranean region in the 1st century BC, and already lost its dominant position by the beginning of the 4rd century AD, when the center of the Roman *oikumene* started shifting back east. "For the entire period between A.D. 535 and 800, Rome was a frontier city. It lay on the western periphery of a great, eastern empire."[18] Geographically, the Italian peninsula is not in the western part of the Mediterranean, but rather in the middle: the city of Rome belongs to the West, but the eastern Adriatic coast of Italy, with Ravenna and Venice belongs

17 Han Lamers, "Janus Lascaris' Florentine Oration and the 'Reception' of Ancient Aeolism," in Giancarlo Abbamonte and Stephen Harrison (eds.), *Making and Rethinking the Renaissance: Between Greek and Latin in 15th–16th Century Europe*, De Gruyter, 2019.

18 Peter Brown, *The Rise of Western Christendom: Triumph and Diversity, A.D. 200–1000*, Preface to the Tenth Anniversary Revised Edition, Wiley-Blackwell, 2013.

to the East. And the southern half of the peninsula, with Sicily included, was part of the Byzantine Empire until the Norman conquest in the 11th century.

In short, the Western Roman world was essentially the western extension of Hellenistic civilization which, always centered around the Balkans and Anatolia, predated and outlived it. Even though its main language was Latin, Greek was considered the language of higher culture in Rome well into the second century under the Nerva-Antonine dynasty. Marcus Aurelius, of course, wrote his *Meditations* in Greek. Before him, "Hadrian," wrote Christopher Kelly, "had long paraded his love of Greek culture," taking "a sustained and active intellectual interest in the ancient history and monuments of the eastern Mediterranean world." In Athens he built a new library that "dwarfed the buildings of the ancient Agora," and he completed the construction of "the largest temple ever constructed in the Roman empire" (the Olympieion). He also inaugurated a new organization of Greek cities, the Panhellenion (literally " All-Greek"), which covered five Roman provinces, with Athens as its headquarters. "Hadrian's benefactions ensured that Athens was now the unchallenged capital of a brave new Panhellenic world which stretched from Asia Minor to North Africa."[19] During this period, which marks the culmination of Roman prestige, the Roman Empire took on a decidedly Hellenic identity.

This helps us to understand why the Eastern Romans never considered themselves the heirs of Western Rome. Their civilization was the continuation of the Hellenistic civilization whose roots were in Athens, and whose expansion was due to the conquests of Alexander the Great. The common representation of the Byzantine Empire as the final phase of the Roman Empire, whose capital was transferred from Latium to the Bosphorus, is a biased Western perspective. Politically, culturally, linguistically, and religiously, Byzantium owed

19 Christopher Kelly, *The Roman Empire: A Very Short Introduction*, Oxford UP, 2006, pp. 61–69.

almost nothing to the Italian Rome. "Believing that their own culture was vastly superior to Rome's, the Greeks were hardly receptive to the influence of Roman civilization," notes a recent *Atlas of the Roman Empire*, mentioning only gladiator combats as a possible, yet marginal, Byzantine debt to the Romans (though the Byzantines preferred horse races).[20] What is beyond dispute is that the Byzantines did not consider Italy to be the origin of their Roman civilization.

Why the Byzantines appropriated the name of Romans while denying it to the Italians remains somewhat a mystery, even to Anthony Kaldellis.[21] There might have been an element of mimetic rivalry: the Byzantines insisted on being Romans when the Western Romans started to dispute their right to do so and called them Greek. Another factor, I would suggest, is that the word "Roman" replaced the word "Hellene" when the latter was appropriated by the anti-Christian resistance. On this point, Michael Tierney made this interesting remark:

> The profound difference in civilization and character between the Eastern and Western halves of the Roman Empire is nowhere more clearly shown than in the words by which each of them designated the old-world religions displaced by Christianity. Whereas in the west the ancient cults were indifferently lumped together as the practices of *pagani*, country villagers, to be distinguished from the civilized and educated worship of the towns, in the east the exact opposite happened. The names *Hellen* and *Hellenism*, which since the time of Isocrates and the conquests of Alexander the Great had come to be applied to Greek culture rather than to the Greek race, were there retained for the adherents of the old religion and its practice.[22]

Europe's amnesia of Byzantine civilization is no accident. The West repressed the memory and the guilty conscience of having

---

20 Claire Levasseur and Christophe Badel, *Atlas de l'Empire romain*, Éd. Autrement, 2020, p. 76.

21 Kaldellis, *Romanland, op. cit.*, p. 59.

22 Michael Tierney, "Julian the Apostate and the Religion of Hellenism," *Studies: An Irish Quarterly Review* 20, no. 80 (1931), pp. 583–597.

assassinated the East. We, Westerners, believe (and have led the rest of the world to believe) that the Roman Empire—the real one, the Western one—gave everything to the Eastern Roman Empire, and took nothing from it. For example, we consider Roman law the foundation of our legal system. But we are bound to be seized by severe cognitive dissonance when we learn that Roman law was only (re) discovered in the West when a Byzantine copy of Justinian's *Digesta* came into the hands of Bolognese scholars around 1080. Specialists like Harold Berman or Aldo Schiavone are positive that there had been no knowledge of Roman laws for the preceding 700 years in Western Europe.[23]

We, Westerners, admire our splendid "Roman basilicas" (from the Greek *basilikos*, "royal"), with no awareness that they were originally built by Byzantine architects. We also cherish our medieval fortified castles, but have no idea that our ancestors learned how to build them from the Byzantines during the Crusades, as Frances and Joseph Gies explain in *Life in a Medieval Castle*: "The Crusaders made use of the building skills of their sometimes Greek allies and their Turkish enemies, improved by their own experience. The results were an astonishing leap forward to massive, intricately designed fortresses of solid masonry. The new model of castle spread at once to western Europe, including England."[24]

Daughter of Athens

In addition to being located at the heart of the Hellenistic civilization, Constantinople is also close to the cradle of Christianity, which spread from Anatolia and the Balkans with Paul. In fact, Christianity

---

23 Harold J. Berman, *Law and Revolution: The Formation of the Western Legal Tradition*, Harvard UP, 1983; Aldo Schiavone, *The Invention of Law in the West*, Harvard UP, 2012.

24 Frances and Joseph Gies, *Life in a Medieval Castle*, Harper Perennial, 2015, pp. 12–17.

was already an Eastern religion for the Byzantines, with Edessa (modern Urfa) being one of its first strongholds. Constantinople was born Christian, while Rome was reluctantly converted late in its history. It was in and around Constantinople that the unity of the Church was achieved by the "ecumenical councils" between the 4th and 6th centuries, convened and presided over by the Byzantine Emperors and attended almost exclusively by Easterners. As Kaldellis points out, "the majority of Christians during the medieval period lived in the east, in the Slavic, Byzantine, and Muslim-ruled lands, and farther east than that too."[25] It was Constantinople that gave Christianity to Rome, not the other way around. The Catholic medievalist Christopher Dawson emphasized this point in *Religion and the Rise of Western Culture*: "we must remember that at the time of the fall of the Roman Empire in the West the main centres of Christian culture and the majority of the Christian population were still non-European. The mother tongue of the Church was Greek and its theological development was mainly due to Asiatic Greek councils and Asiatic Greek theologians, at a time when in the Latin West paganism was still strong, and the ruling classes, and, far more, the rural population, were still largely non-Christian in culture and tradition."[26] After the great ecumenical councils, Rome entered the period of the "Byzantine papacy" (537–752). Each pope was appointed by the Byzantine Emperor, generally from among the "apocrisiaries" (ambassadors to Constantinople) of the previous pope. Only after the Byzantine imperial administration lost control of Italy in the 8th century did the Church of Rome start asserting its independence, and the antagonism came to a head in the 11th century with the Gregorian Reform.

Let us turn again to Byzantium's Hellenistic heritage, which remains less known than its Christian heritage. Anthony Kaldellis

25 Kaldellis, *Byzantium Unbound, op. cit.*, p. 61.

26 Christopher Dawson, *Religion and the Rise of Western Culture*, Doubleday, 1950, pp. 29–30.

argues that Christianity, while essential to Byzantine identity, was not as central to it as our ecclesiastical sources led us to believe. Even in the 6th century, known as an era of intolerant orthodoxy, many high officials and intellectuals did not feel obliged to profess the Christian faith: Zosimas of Palestine, the author of the *New History* in six volumes, was a self-proclaimed "Hellene." The great historian Procopius mentions "Christians" only to exclude himself from this group, and states contemptuously that he finds it "incredibly stupid and presumptuous to investigate the nature of God" (*Justinian's Wars* V,3).

Byzantine civilization stood on two pillars: Jerusalem and Athens. The importance of the second pillar could not be better symbolized than by the large statue of the goddess Athena which stood in the very center of the capital city, in the Forum of Constantine. It had been moved to there from the Acropolis around 465, and would be destroyed only by the crusaders eight centuries later.[27] Although favoring Christianity over pagan cults, Constantine and his sons made their city the conservatory of the ancient Greek heritage. Constantius built the first Imperial Library, containing an estimated 100,000 volumes, which preserved the knowledge and poetry of the ancient Greeks and Romans for almost 1,000 years, until it was looted and destroyed by the raids of the Fourth Crusade. In a short book on the Byzantines' love for Athens and her Parthenon, Anthony Kaldellis states: "after antiquity Athens and the classical legacy that it still represented in the minds of many Byzantines did not vanish from the stage of history as has been asserted. The Parthenon, converted into a church, became an important site of pilgrimage whose fame spread throughout the Christian world. … what attracted pilgrims and adoration were not any sacred relics or icons that were kept thereby rather the Parthenon itself, the building, whose classical past was known and, indeed, quite visible."[28]

---

27 Runciman, *Histoire des Croisades*, vol. 2, *op. cit.*, p. 109.

28 Anthony Kaldellis, *The Christian Parthenon: Classicism and Pilgrimage in Byzantine Athens*, Cambridge UP, 2009, p. xii.

Tertullian and Augustine abhorred Hellenistic culture, but the Greek Fathers didn't. In the 4th century, Gregorios of Nazianzos argued that classical texts were not intrinsically religious and could therefore be profitably studied by Christians. His friend Basil of Caesarea wrote a treatise on the same topic, *To Young Men on How They Might Benefit from Greek Literature.* He argued that the ancient poets, historians, and philosophers deserved a place in the education of Christians because they praised virtue. This little book, writes Collin Wells, "would do much to keep the peace between Athens and Jerusalem in the coming millennium. … Over time, Basil's approach was adopted as the mainstream attitude in the Byzantine East. As such, it remained in force for more than a millennium." Homer always remained "the poet" for the Byzantines: "his works, the beginnings of Western literature, survive today because they remained on the Byzantine educational curriculum. The same holds true for other ancient Greek authors."[29]

Photios, Patriarch of Constantinople from 858 to 867 and 877 to 886, is honored in the Orthodox Church as Saint Photios the Great, although he is best known for promoting the study of pre-Christian Greek literature. Even the works of the anti-Christian emperor Julian (361–63), known as "Julian the Apostate" in the West, but as "Julian the Philosopher" or "the Hellene" in the East, were copied and preserved. Anthony Kaldellis informs us in *Hellenism in Byzantium* (2007): "His legacy was a constant reminder that Hellenism was not, as many wanted to believe, merely a docile handmaiden of the faith but rather could be activated as a powerful alternative. Julian's writings, preserved as a model of style by Christians drawn to his engaging personality, remained available to the curious."[30]

Greek culture radiated from Constantinople to the four corners of the known world, from Persia to Egypt and from Ireland to

29 Collin Wells, *Sailing from Byzantium: How a Lost Empire Shaped the World, op. cit.*, pp. 48–51.

30 Kaldellis, *Hellenism in Byzantium, op. cit.*, p. 144.

Spain. In a book on the Greek roots of Christian Europe, Sylvain Gouguenheim has argued against the common assumption that the diffusion of Greek philosophy and science to the West in the 11th and 12th centuries must be credited to the Muslims. Much of this heritage was transmitted to Italian cities directly from Constantinople, and if the Arabs contributed to its preservation and circulation, it is because they had found it in the libraries of Eastern Christendom.[31] In *Greek Thought, Arabic Culture* (1998), Dimitri Gutas has also demonstrated a direct correlation between early manuscripts copied during the 10th-century Macedonian Renaissance in Constantinople and the texts studied and disseminated by the Arabs. This is not to denigrate the scientific contribution of the Arabs: it is a fact that, in the Middle Ages, Islam was more friendly to science than Christianity (the deeper reason, I presume, being that the study of natural laws challenges the founding miracles of the Christian faith, but does not threaten the foundations of Islam). The contribution of the Arabs in mathematics, as well as in astronomy and physics, is indisputable, as is illustrated by the Arabic origin of words like "algebra" and "algorithm."[32] But the Arab contribution is inconceivable without the Greek heritage preserved by Byzantine librarians and scholars.

Furthermore, although the Fourth Crusade caused the destruction of priceless treasures (two-thirds of the non-Christian books mentioned by Photios in his reading notes, or *Bibliotheca*, were lost forever), it was the starting point of a cultural transfer which culminated at the council of Florence in 1438: the Byzantine emperor and patriarch came accompanied by a retinue of 700 Greek scholars bringing with them an extraordinary collection of classical books still unknown in the West, including manuscripts of Plato, Aristotle, Plutarch, Euclid and Ptolemy. It is hardly an exaggeration that the

31 Sylvain Gouguenheim, *Aristote au Mont Saint-Michel. Les racines grecques de l'Europe chrétienne*, Seuil, 2008.

32 Valerie Hansen, *The Year 1000: When Explorers Connected the World—and Globalization Began*, Penguin, 2020, p. 12.

Byzantine visitors to Florence sparked the Italian Renaissance. Jerry Brotton writes in *The Renaissance Bazaar*: "Culturally, the transmission of classical texts, ideas, and art objects from east to west that took place at the Council was to have a decisive effect on the art and scholarship of late 15th-century Italy."[33] And when, after 1453, the last custodians of high Byzantine culture fled Ottoman domination, many came to contribute to the Italian Renaissance.[34] "Virtually all Greek texts," Kaldellis summarizes, "had to pass through Byzantium in order to reach us."[35]

Among the Byzantine emigrants who made ancient Greek literature known to the West, we must cite Georgios Gemistos, known as Plethon, who died in 1452. He was the true initiator of Platonic studies in the West. His speeches on Plato so fascinated the Florentine court of Cosimo de' Medici that the latter decided to found the Platonic Academy in Florence under the direction of Marsilio Ficino. Around the same time, the Byzantine scholar Bessarion helped Pope Nicholas V establish the Vatican Library, then, in 1468 donated to Venice his invaluable collection of six hundred Greek manuscripts, which constituted the initial core of the Biblioteca Marciana. "Books," he told the Doge and Senate, "are full of the voices of the wise, full of lessons from antiquity ... so great is the power of books ... that without them we would all be rude and ignorant. Without books, we should have almost no memory of the paste, no examples to follows."[36] His goal was to save ancient Greek literature by transplanting it to the West. It is no exaggeration to say that Byzantine

---

33 Jerry Brotton, *The Renaissance Bazaar: From the Silk Road to Michelangelo*, Oxford UP, 2010, p. 103.

34 Jonathan Harris, *Greek Émigrés in the West, 1400–1520*, Porphyrogenitus, 1995; Nigel G. Wilson, *From Byzantium to Italy: Greek Studies in the Italian Renaissance*, 1992, 2nd ed., Bloomsbury, 2017.

35 Kaldellis, *Byzantium Unbound*, *op. cit.*, p. 46.

36 John Hale, *The Civilization of Europe in the Renaissance*, Fontana Press, 1993, p. 395.

scholarship made the West the "civilization of books" that it was to become. "The Byzantine contribution of the Greek classics allowed the promise of Renaissance humanism to be fulfilled, by letting the West reclaim the body of literature that makes up the foundation of Western civilization," Collin Wells writes.[37]

Westerners, however, decided to ignore this debt, pretending instead to have received the Greek classics directly or via the Arabs. Steven Runciman wrote in *The Fall of Constantinople*: "Western Europe, with ancestral memories of jealousy of Byzantine civilization, with its spiritual advisers denouncing the Orthodox as sinful schismatics, and with a haunting sense of guilt that it had failed the city at the end, chose to forget about Byzantium. It could not forget the debt that it owed to the Greeks; but it saw the debt as being owed only to the Classical age."[38] In Anthony Kaldellis's words: "For the past 500 years the West has imagined its relation to ancient Greece as a dynamic and vitally intellectual one, but even recent works continue to cast Byzantium not as a genuine participant but only as the caretaker of the classical tradition for the ultimate benefit of the West, its 'true heir.' So the history of manuscripts passes through Byzantium and the Arabs, but its history of ideas and literature routinely jumps from St. Augustine to the Renaissance." In reality, "the classical tradition was never lost in Byzantium, which is why it could not be rediscovered." If Western civilization defines itself as the heir to ancient Greek civilization, then "Byzantium emerges as the quintessentially western civilization."[39]

Although there had always been tensions between the Christian and Hellenistic cultures in the East, their equilibrium kept Orthodox Christianity from sinking into the persecuting totalitarianism that

---

37 Wells, *Sailing from Byzantium, op. cit.*, pp. 12–19.

38 Steven Runciman, *The Fall of Constantinople 1453*, Cambridge UP, 1965, p. 190.

39 Kaldellis, *Hellenism in Byzantium, op. cit.*, pp. 4, 2.

characterized Roman Catholicism.[40] The average level of classical education in the Byzantine Empire was much higher than in the medieval Europe of the same period. Byzantine imperial power could always count on an abundant pool of lay officials trained in classical erudition. One major consequence of this was that the political philosophy that guided the ruling elite was classical, whereas in the West, political theology since Charlemagne had been strongly biblical, with kings and emperors often posturing as a new Moses, Joshua, or David (never as a new Jesus).

In conclusion, the notion of Constantinople being a pale copy of Rome lacks historical perspective. Constantinople was the daughter of Athens more than of Rome. It was Constantinople that transmitted the literary, philosophical, and scientific heritage of Greece to Rome, not the other way around. Without the conservation of the Imperial Library of Constantinople, we would hardly know Plato, Aristotle, Thucydides, Herodotus, Aeschylus, Sophocles, Euripides, Euclid and many others. In Constantinople, the light of classical Greece never suffered an eclipse. The name of the cathedral Hagia Sophia, a jewel of Constantinople which still amazed the Franks in the 12th century, clearly indicates the importance of this heritage: Sophia simultaneously designated the goddess of Wisdom, Athena, and the quest of *philosophia* (the Saint Sophia martyred in Rome in 137 along with her three daughters Faith, Hope, and Charity, is obviously a later historicization of the cult of the Divine Wisdom.) Constantinople knew the struggle between Christianity and humanism, but the dual culture encompassing and shaped by such was never called into question.[41]

---

40 Robert I. Moore, *The Formation of a Persecuting Society: Authority and Deviance in Western Europe 950–1250*, Wiley-Blackwell, 2006.

41 Harris, *Byzantium and the Crusades*, *op. cit.*, p. 9.

From Constantinople to Istanbul?

Insofar as the Italian Renaissance was sparked by the rediscovery of Hellenism, it was a legacy of the Byzantine Empire. And if we are prepared to admit that the Renaissance was the true birth of this European civilization that enlightened the world with its science, arts, and technology, then the West emerges as both the murderer and the heir of Byzantium. But two other civilizations can claim the heritage of Byzantium: Istanbul and Moscow. We must understand these two legacies in order to have a comprehensive perspective, both in time and space, of the transformations of the world over the last millennium.

To grasp the extent of Istanbul's Byzantine heritage, we must first form a general understanding of the relationship between the Byzantine world and the Islamic world. The early Muslim expansion undoubtedly dealt a severe blow to the Eastern Roman Empire, depriving it of its richest provinces and, consequently, of a large part of its tax revenue on which its military capacity depended. But there were periods of peaceful exchange. For example, at the end of the 7th century, Emperor Justinian II and Caliph Abd al-Malik signed an agreement on the island of Cyprus: for the next 300 years, Cyprus was jointly governed by the Arabs (politically, fiscally, and militarily) and the Byzantines (religiously and administratively).

In the 10th century, the Fatimids took Sicily, southern Syria, and Palestine from the Byzantines and expanded across much of North Africa, even reaching up the Nile Valley to Sudan. In 1001, Emperor Basil II signed a ten-year truce with the Fatimid Caliph, which was renewed into a peace that lasted more than half a century without serious clashes. The Fatimids pursued a policy of religious tolerance. Christians of all denominations were free to worship within their territory, and in 1027, the Caliph authorized the *basileus* to restore the Church of the Holy Sepulcher in Jerusalem. In return, Constantinople was home to a large mosque under the authority of the caliph (it was burned down by the Crusaders in 1203). Steven Runciman writes: "In the middle of the eleventh century the lot of the Christians in Palestine had seldom been so pleasant. The Moslem authorities were lenient; the emperor was watchful of their interests. Trade was prospering and increasing with the Christian countries overseas. And never before had Jerusalem enjoyed so plentifully the sympathy and the wealth that were brought to it by pilgrims from the West."[42]

In 1071, the Oghuz Turks, nomads from the steppes who, after serving the Caliph of Baghdad as mercenaries, broke away under the command of the Seljuk clan and took control of the Caliphate, defeated the Byzantine army at the Battle of Manzikert and established the Sultanate of Rum (i.e., Rome) in Anatolia. They then took Jerusalem and part of Syria from the Fatimids. The Byzantines and Fatimids allied against them, and when the latter recaptured Jerusalem in August 1098, a year before the Crusaders reached its walls, it was a return to an acceptable situation for the *basileus* Alexius Comnenus. But the Franks, making no distinction between Arabs and Turks, besieged the Fatimids, took the city, and massacred its population. This caused irreparable damage to relations between Islam and the Latin West, as Steven Runciman points out: "Many even of the Christians were horrified by what had been done; and amongst the Moslems, who had been ready hitherto to accept the Franks as another factor in the tangled politics of the time, there was henceforward a clear determination that the Franks must be driven out. It was this bloodthirsty proof of Christian fanaticism that recreated the fanaticism of Islam. When, later, wiser Latins in the East sought to find some basis on which Christian and Moslem could work together, the memory of the massacre stood always in their way."[43]

---

42 Steven Runciman, *A History of the Crusades*, vol. 1, Cambridge UP, 1994, p. 31.

43 *Ibid.*, pp. 237–238.

In the 13th century, as the Sultanate of Rum was agonizing under the yoke of the Mongols, a new warlike Turkish tribe, the Ottomans, emerged and formed a small emirate in northern Anatolia, from where they spread throughout Asia Minor and then to the Balkans. Ottoman Sultan Murad I moved his capital to Adrianople (renamed Edirne) in 1362, after which the Ottoman ruling class gradually became Hellenized. The Ottomans did not hate Constantinople, but admired it and wanted to rule it. Before the capture of Constantinople in 1453, there had been so many mixed marriages between the Byzantine and Ottoman royal houses that Mehmet II believed he had a legitimate claim to the Byzantine throne. Upon entering the city, he proclaimed himself *Kayser-i Rum,* meaning "Caesar of the Romans." It is important to note, as Warwick Ball reminds us in *Sultans of Rome*, that "Constantinople was conquered by the Turks from the west, not from the east": "the Ottomans became a European power before they became a Middle Eastern one and remained a primarily European power throughout, ruling up to twenty percent of mainland Europe from a European power-base." Ball also highlights the religious tolerance of the Ottomans: "Ottoman regard for and protection of Orthodox Christianity was contrasted with the Latin narrow-mindedness, brutality and open persecution." In 1360, Rome launched a crusade against the Bulgars, who were faithful to Byzantine orthodoxy but now had Latin Catholicism forced upon them. "Faced with this, the Bulgarians could hardly fail to welcome the Ottomans, who allowed freedom of worship and extended their protection to the Bulgarian church." The same happened later to the Greeks of Constantinople. "Better the Sultan's turban than the Pope's mitre," Patriarch Gennadius stated sadly but objectively. The Ottomans also incorporated many Byzantines into their administration. One nephew of the last Roman Emperor, Constantine XI, became admiral of the Ottoman Fleet, then the Sultan's grand vizier (i.e., prime minister), while another one was made the governor-general of the Balkans. "Of the grand viziers in the sixty years after the conquest, most were former Christians draw from the Byzantine, Serbian, Bosnian and Albanian aristocracy."[44]

Although the Byzantine Empire was officially pronounced dead with the Ottoman conquest of Constantinople in 1453, it might also be regarded as having simply converted to Islam. In his book *Byzantium after Byzantium* (1934), the Romanian historian Nicolae Iorga even spoke of a "Byzantine renaissance" under the Ottomans, arguing that, unlike the Latins, the Ottomans were lovers of Hellenic culture and admirers of Constantinople. Not only was the city not sacked following the Ottoman victory in 1453—the starkest contrast to what Westerners did to it in 1204—but it was actually "enlarged, repopulated, and deeply loved and respected, with care for all its needs and passions, by the emperors of Ottoman origin," Iorga writes. Furthermore:

> Byzantium, with all it represented—not as the authority of a dynasty, or as the domination of a ruling class, things that could disappear in a catastrophe, but as a complex of institutions, a political system, a religious formation, a type of civilization, comprising the Hellenic intellectual legacy, Roman law, the Orthodox religion, and everything it created and preserved in terms of art—did not disappear, and could not disappear with the fall, in succession, in the fifteenth century of its three capitals: Constantinople, Mistra, and Trebizond. The Ottoman Turks did not bring with them new ways of life. … It was the Byzantine Empire that, with everything it preserved in terms of memories, means, and indestructible ideals, transformed, day by day, those who had come from Bursa and Adrianople to establish themselves in the great city of Constantinople, capable of using and exhorting all nations.[45]

The Ottoman state imitated Byzantine meritocracy. The Habsburg ambassador in Istanbul, Ogier de Busbecq, wrote of the government of Suleiman the Magnificent (1520–66): "In all that great assembly

44 Warwick Ball, *Sultans of Rome: The Turkish World Expansion,* Olive Branch Press, 2013, pp. 90, 95–97, 102.

45 Nicolae Iorga, *Byzantium After Byzantium,* Histria Books, 2022, p. 25.

no single man owed his dignity to anything but his personal merits and bravery; no one is distinguished from the rest by his birth, and honour is paid to each man according to the nature of the duty and offices which he discharges. … Those who hold the highest posts under the Sultan are very often he sons of shepherds and herdsmen, and, so far from being ashamed of their birth, they make it a subject of boasting."[46]

Before concluding this excursion into the Ottoman Empire, let us note that the Ottoman contribution to European culture was ultimately, virtually nil mainly for the reason that, in 1483, the Sultan banned printing on pain of death—and Arabic characters, which were held as sacred, posed insurmountable difficulties for typographers. This allowed the art of manuscript writing to flourish in the Ottoman Empire until the early 20th century, but it downgraded the Ottoman world intellectually. When printing was authorized in 1727, the Muslim world had already fallen irretrievably behind the production and distribution of scholarship in Europe.

Because of the totalitarian nature of Islamic law and religious culture, not much in Ottoman civilization remained recognizably Byzantine after the 16th century, with the exception of architecture. If the Renaissance was Byzantium's gift to the West, then the Ottoman Empire and its radical shift away from modernity emerges as fundamentally anti-Byzantine. In *The Inheritance of Rome,* Chris Wickham has made the interesting remark that one of the reason why the Byzantine Empire has been largely ignored by 19th-century historians is that it is not considered the ancestor of any modern nation-state.[47] Indeed, modern Turks do not regard themselves as the heirs of Byzantium. Consequently, the Ottoman Empire contributed to erasing the memory of Byzantium rather than preserving it.

---

46 *Ibid.*, pp. 110–111.

47 Chris Wickham, *The Inheritance of Rome: A History of Europe from 400 to 1000*, Penguin Books, 2010, p. 23.

Russian Byzantinism

Russians, by contrast, do consider their nation (or rather "people," *narod*, as the Western category and experience of "nation" has remained foreign and constantly disputed in Russian civilization) to be the true spiritual heir of the Byzantine Empire. Understanding why they think so is important for deciphering the relationship between Russia and the West up to this day, as well as for developing a vision of a possible future for this relationship.

Let us review the background. According to the oldest Russian chronicle, known as the *Primary Chronicle*, Vladimir I, Grand Prince of Kievan Rus', received baptism in 988 after considering, and ultimately passing over, the options of Islam and Judaism. He rejected the religion of the Jews because their loss of Jerusalem was, he thought, proof that God had abandoned them. What turned him away from Islam, says the chronicle, was the ban on alcohol: "In Rus'," he said, "we have the joy of drinking, without it we could not exist." He therefore opted for Christianity, but still hesitated between the Roman and the Byzantine rites. He was convinced in favor of the latter by the report of his emissaries who found the German churches gloomy but were dazzled by the beauty of the Byzantine churches and liturgy: "we knew not whether we were in heaven or earth, for on earth there is no such splendor or such beauty."[48] Whatever the truth of that story, it reflects the Russian fascination with Constantinople and its cathedral Hagia Sophia on the eve of the second millennium AD.

Vladimir received baptism, married a sister of the prestigious Emperor Basil II, and began the construction of a Hagia Sophia cathedral in Kiev. It was completed by his son Yaroslav the Wise (1016–54). From then on, John Meyendorff explains in *Byzantine and the Rise of Russia*, "Byzantine influence on Russia became the

48 Scott Kenworthy and Alexander Agadjanian, *Understanding World Christianity: Russia*, Fortress Press, 2021, p. 64.

determining factor in Russian civilization.»[49] Yaroslav enjoyed great prestige in the West and married three of his sisters to Western sovereigns: Anne of Kiev was married to King Henry I of France, while Elizabeth became Queen of Norway, and Anastasia Queen of Hungary.

The Patriarchate of Constantinople granted the clergy of Moscow the right to adapt the liturgy into Slavonic. It bears highlighting this difference between Orthodoxy and Catholicism: until recently, the Roman Church imposed Latin throughout the world, although Latin has no scriptural credential, unlike Greek. When the duke of Bohemia asked the right for his people to worship in Slavonic, as the Russians did, Pope Gregory VII replied that it was out of question: "It is evident to those who consider the matter carefully that it has pleased God to make Holy Scripture obscure in certain places lest, if it were perfectly clear to all, it might be vulgarized and subject to disrespect or be misunderstood by people of limited intelligence as to lead them into error."[50]

Thanks to both linguistic and geographical distance, the Russian national Church was able to develop relative independence from Constantinople while remaining in filial piety to the Mother Church. The architecture of Russian churches perfectly symbolizes this relationship: the colorful onion domes derive from Byzantine domed basilicas, yet they remain instantly recognizable as Russian. Being established long after the Christological controversies, the Russian Church was never disturbed by them. The Serbian Church, also born in the shadow of Byzantium, followed a similar trajectory. After the schism of the 11th century, and through all the vicissitudes of Constantinople, Russia resisted Rome's diplomatic pressure and remained faithful to the Byzantine rite. Even after Constantinople had been mortally wounded by the papal hordes, Eastern Orthodoxy retained its prestige and influence in the Grand Principality of Moscow.

49 John Meyendorff, *Byzantium and the Rise of Russia*, Cambridge UP, 1981, p. 10.

50 Malcolm Barber, *The Two Cities: Medieval Europe 1050–1320*, Routledge, 1992, p. 27.

On the model of Byzantium, Russian high culture enjoyed a relatively peaceful coexistence between theology and philosophy, even to the point that, all the way to the end of the 19th century, it would be hard to find a Russian philosopher who was not also a theologian, albeit one deemed heretical by the guardians of orthodoxy. My favorite example is Vladimir Soloviev (alternatively rendered Solovyov, 1853–1900), a poet, mystic, philosopher, and theologian who is especially known for his "Sophiology," a theological theory of Wisdom as the Feminine World Principle. In general, the struggle between Orthodoxy and heresy was less violent than in the West—the two notable exceptions of bloody repressions being that of the Judaizers in the 15th century, and that of the Old Believers in the 17th century, both of which cases entailed significant political stakes.

Following the fall of Constantinople in 1453, Moscow assumed the role of Third Rome. Ivan the Great (1462–1505) married the niece of the last *basileus* and placed the Byzantine double-headed eagle on his coat of arms. His grandson, Ivan the Terrible (1533–84), took the title of *Czar* or *Tsar*, the Russian equivalent of the Greek *kaisar* (Latin *caesar*). At once exalted and cruel, he embodied the principle of autocracy which would subsequently characterize the Russian political tradition: almost unlimited power, barely balanced by an aristocracy and even less by a parliament, but sacralized by the Church and representing, for Russian peasants, an all-powerful paternal figure.

Russia has never forgotten her political and religious ties to Constantinople. Catherine the Great, Empress of Russia from 1762 to her death in 1796, projected to rebuild the Byzantine Empire by including Greece, Thrace, and Bulgaria, and to pass it on to her grandson, appropriately named Constantine. If the Ottoman Empire survived this Russian ambition, it was mainly thanks to the British. In the Crimean War (1853–56), the Sultan received assistance from the United Kingdom and France, who imposed the Treaty of Paris on Russia. Twenty years later, Tsar Alexander II once again entered into war against the Ottomans, who had just drowned uprisings of the Serbs and Bulgarians in blood. The Ottomans capitulated with the Russians at the gates of Istanbul. Dostoevsky wrote that since Russia "unhesitatingly accepted the banner of the East, having placed the Byzantine double eagle over and above its ancient coat-of-arms, ... Constantinople must be ours, conquered by us, Russians, from the Turks, and remain ours forever."[51] But the British Empire, this time with Austria-Hungary, came to the Ottomans' rescue and, at the Congress of Berlin, returned to them the Christian nations that the Tsar had just emancipated — including Armenia, to her great misfortune.

From Samuel Huntington, *The Clash of Civilizations* (1996).

51 Fyodor Dostoievsky, *The Diary of a Writer, op. cit.*, pp. 629, 904.

It is striking that, ever since the fall of Constantinople, the West has behaved toward Russia in the same way as it previously behaved toward Byzantium—as if the West recognized in Russia its eternal enemy, one which has seemingly died only to come back to life again and again. The American-British geostrategy of the Great Game, which for two centuries has aimed to dig a trench between Russia and Western Europe (Germany in particular), is the continuation of the war waged by the medieval West against Byzantium. It is equally striking that the dividing line that Samuel Huntington draws in *The Clash of Civilizations* is substantially identical to what it was a millennium ago. With the current civilizational conflict between the West and Russia, involving profound anthropological issues, history is not repeating itself, but it sure rhymes (as Mark Twain is reputed to have said).

Westerners are not aware of this, but many Russians are. Russians have not forgotten that it was the Latins who, under the pretext of freeing Eastern Christendom from Islam, ultimately destroyed it. They see the hostility of the "collective West" since the 19th century in the light of this age-old duplicity. The message was recently reiterated in a film titled *The Fall of an Empire: The Lesson of Byzantium*, broadcast in 2008 on Russian television.[52] The film attributes the collapse of the Eastern Roman Empire to both corrupt oligarchs and the pernicious actions of the West. The story of Byzantium is presented as a warning to contemporary Russian leaders: they are urged to contain the oligarchs and reinforce their fortifications against the West.

If we bear in mind the spiritual filiation between Constantinople and Moscow, the thousand-year background reveals itself behind the geopolitical conflict which, as I write these lines, is currently concentrated in Ukraine. Our serious revisionism of the standard Western narrative of the Middle Ages allows us to gain a clearer view of this background. Such revisionism, spearheaded by Edward Said's

52 "The Fall of an Empire—The Lesson of Byzantium," produced by Father Tikhon Shevkunov, viewable on YouTube.

seminal essay *Orientalism* (1978), gives us some deeper insight into the forces that move civilizations, and may help us predict in which direction the world is heading. With his broad vision of the forces moving civilizations, Oswald Spengler, though a German, wrote in *Prussianism and Socialism* (1919): "'Russianism' is the promise of a future culture as the evening shadows grow longer and longer over the Western world. The distinctions between Russian and Western spirit cannot be drawn too sharply. As deep a cleavage as there is between the spirit, religion, politics, and economics of England, Germany, America, and France, when compared with Russia these nations suddenly appear as a unified world."[53]

Russia inherited from Byzantium more than its religion. The 19th-century political philosopher Konstantin Leontiev, widely read by Russia's current elite, defined Russia's political tradition as "Byzantinism" (*Byzantinism and Slavdom,* 1875). He refers to what the West pejoratively called "Caesaropapism," but which the Byzantines defined as *symphonia*, or the harmonious collaboration (in the best of times) between the Empire and the Church. In this model, supreme authority in this world belongs to the *basileus*, who is the protector of the Church, while the Patriarch wields spiritual authority and exercises a strong influence on all social classes.

What Leontiev calls political Byzantinism is therefore an enlightened despotism sanctified by the religion of Christ, yet it is also dependent on popular support: "From whatever angle we examine the life and state of Great Russia, we will see that Byzantinism, that is, the Church and the tsar, whether directly or indirectly, penetrate deeply into the very subsoil or our social organism."[54] Russia is never more herself than when it is led by an energetic, awe-inspiring Tsar. Russia has never had a strong aristocratic class comparable to that of Europe or Poland. The Russian boyars took pride not in the seniority

53 Oswald Spengler, *Prussianism and Socialism* (1919), Legend Books, 2023, p. 67.

54 Konstantin Leontiev, *Byzantinism and Slavdom* (1875), Taxiarch Press, 2020, p. 33.

and prestige of their lineage, but in their service to the Tsar. This, too, can be considered a legacy of Byzantium, where merit and public service were more highly valued than blood. The period of the "Tatar Yoke" (1236–1480) left its mark in the fact that Russian Byzantinism has always been more autocratic and less republican than its original model.

Ivan Ilyin (1884–1954) was a disciple of Leontiev, with whom he shared a preference for an authoritarian regime closely combining state and church.[55] Arrested six times by the Bolsheviks, he was finally exiled in 1922 by Lenin, deported on the famous "philosophers' ships" along with 160 other intellectuals. Ilyin is often mentioned for his influence on Vladimir Putin. John Schindler, a former professor at the U.S. Navy War College, wrote in a much-cited 2014 article for *National Review Online*:

> Putinism includes a good amount of Ilyin-inspired Orthodoxy and Russian nationalism working hand-in-glove, what its advocates term *symphonia*, meaning the Byzantine-style unity of state and church, in stark contrast to American notions of separation of church and state. Although the Russian Orthodox Church (ROC) is not the state church, *de jure*, in practice it functions as something close to one, enjoying a privileged position at home and abroad. Putin has explained the central role of the ROC by stating that Russia's 'spiritual shield'—meaning her church-grounded resistance to post-modernism—is as important to her security as her nuclear shield.[56]

We should not underestimate the difficulty of such a project. Despite the colossal sums spent by the Russian state on restoring and building flamboyant churches, mass attendance remains low, while the corrosive influence of Western individualism and consumerism is strong.

55 Ivan Alexandrovich Ilyin, *On Resistance to Evil by Force*, Taxiarch Press, 2018.

56 John Schindler, "Putinism and the Anti-WEIRD coalition," National Review, 19 April 2014.

History will tell us whether the neo-Byzantinism of Putin and his heirs will succeed in reviving a distinctive and lasting civilization.

The rejection of Western democracy is a widely shared principle in this Russian school of political philosophy. Nikolai Berdyaev, a contemporary of Ivan Ilyin and co-passenger of the "philosophers' ships," wrote in *The Philosophy of Inequality* (1918): "Since the creation of the world, it is always the minority which has governed, which governs and which will govern. … The only question is whether it is the better or the worse minority that governs." The government of the best, that is to say "aristocracy" in the proper sense, is "a higher principle of social life, the only utopia worthy of man." For Berdyaev, the triumph of democratism "represents the greatest danger to human progress, to the qualitative elevation of human nature."[57]

Slavism vs. Eurasianism

Byzantinism is only one of the constitutive elements of Russian identity, which also has a strong ethnic element. Slavic ethnicity was emphasized by the intellectual movement known as the "Slavophiles." Among them was Nikolai Danilevsky, whose book *Russia and Europe* (1869) opens with the observation that Russia is fundamentally different from Europe because it has not experienced any of the historical episodes that forged Europe: it was never part of the Roman Empire, and it never experienced feudalism, nor the domination of the papacy; it knew nothing of Latin scholasticism, and it remained untouched by the Renaissance. Some of Danilevsky's contemporaries, such as Pyotr Tchaadaev, concluded from such observations that Russia had some catching up to do and needed to draw more inspiration from Europe, as she had begun to do under Peter the Great (1692–1725). Danilevsky was categorically opposed to these "Occidentalists" (or "Westernizers"), instead advocating that Russia

57 My translation from the French edition, Nicolas Berdiaev, *De l'inégalité*, L'Âge d'homme, 2008, p. 132.

should preserve and develop her original character: "Russia has nothing in common with what is good in Europe, nor with what is bad in it."[58] Influenced by his studies in biology, Danilevsky developed an organic theory of civilizations similar to Spengler's. Each civilization has its distinct nature, which is essentially ethnic. Danilevsky is the founder of pan-Slavism, which aimed at federating all Slavic countries.

Even though his book is a Russian classic in the philosophy of history, his pan-Slavism finds little echo today, because, as Leontiev already pointed out, Slavic countries have followed different paths which cannot converge any longer. Among them, only Serbia, Belarus, and Ukraine are close to Russia. Catholic Poland is the atavistic enemy of Russia. The Czechs, both Catholics and Protestants, have been deeply Germanized, while the Bulgarians are culturally close to the Greeks. Hungary and Romania are closer to Russia, but they are not Slavic.

But above all, Danilevsky's pan-Slavism minimizes the ethnic and cultural imprint of Asia on Great Russia. Berdyaev writes in *The Russian Idea* (1948): "The Russian people is not purely European and it is not purely Asiatic. Russia is a complete section of the world—a colossal East-West. It unites two worlds, and within the Russian soul two principles are always engaged in strife—the Eastern and the Western."[59] This is a recurrent theme in the literature of Russian patriots. Towards the end of his life, Fyodor Dostoyevsky had written that "Russians are as much Asians as Europeans" (*The Diary of a Writer*, January 1881). He made a passing parallel between what America has been for Western Europeans, and what Asia could become for Russians. This parallel is intriguing: if we admit that the spiritual decay of the West is linked by some karmic backlash to the genocide of the Amerindians (who were mainly of Asian origin),

58 Since Danilevsky's works are not translated, I relied on a video conference by Antoine Dresse, "La Russie face à l'Europe," on ego-non.com.

59 Nicolas Berdyaev, *The Russian Idea*, MacMillan, 1948, p. 2.

then a more symbiotic relationship between Russia and Asia prefigures a very different development.

In the early 20th century, a handful of Russian thinkers challenged the negative perception of Turko-Mongol domination (1236–1480) and instead highlighted its positive contribution to the formation of the Russian state. The "Tatar yoke," which began when Alexander Nevsky, Prince of Novgorod, chose to pay tribute to the Mongols in order to repel the Teutonic knights, had the advantage of being accompanied by complete religious freedom, even including the Mongols' protection of churches and monasteries. The alliance with the Golden Horde allowed Nevsky and his descendants to make Moscow the capital of a new kingdom extending east to the Volga. In 1476, Ivan the Great took advantage of infighting within the Golden Horde to free his people from its domination. Yet the new Muscovite Russia was, in many respects, the daughter of the Turko-Mongol Empire. Such a positive reassessment of Asian influence forms the scientific basis of the Eurasianist movement, one of whose pioneers was the linguist Nikolai Trubetzkoy (1890–1938). It was the "Turano-Mongols," Trubetzkoy wrote, who achieved the unification of almost the entire territory of modern Russia under a single state. Moreover, in his words, a "brotherhood and mutual understanding" rooted in "invisible racial consonances" developed between Russians and "Asians."[60]

It is with the same general perspective that the historian George Vernadsky wrote *The Mongols and Russia* in 1953 and the ethnologist Lev Gumilev wrote *Ancient Rus' and the Great Steppe*, published in 1989. Gumilev interprets the reign of Alexander Nevsky as foundational of the inter-ethnic complementarity between the Slavs and the Tatars (the term generally used in Russia for the nomads of the Golden Horde, of which the Mongols were only the initial and the dominant ethnic element). Ultimately, the interaction between

60 Nikolai Sergeevich Trubetzkoy, *The Legacy of Genghis Khan and Other Essays on Russian Identity*, Michigan Slavic Publications, 1991, p. 96.

Russo-Slavs and Tatar-Mongols must be seen "not as the subjugation of Rus' by the Golden Horde," as Western historiography—promoted by the Romanovs of German origin—has described it, but rather as an "ethnic symbiosis," a union between two civilizations for their mutual benefit.[61] Understandably, Gumilev is celebrated in Tatarstan and in Kazakhstan. Kazakh President Nursultan Nazarbayev (1990–2019) was the first post-Soviet leader to call for the creation of a "Eurasian Union," which was inaugurated by Vladimir Putin in 2015. The complementary duality of the Russian ethnic soul is a recurrent theme of its culture that has been celebrated in cinema, for example in films like Akira Kurosawa's *Derzu Uzala* (1975) or Nikita Mikhalkov's *Urga* (1991).

In conclusion, Russia, extending from Saint Petersburg to Vladivostok, is the bridge between Europe and Asia, and therefore the key for the political future of Eurasia. In this respect, Russia is the New Byzantium, and it is also most likely going to be the revenge of Byzantium. The recent rapprochement between Russia and China—largely an unintended result of the West's atavistic Russophobia—is therefore of immense consequence. No one can predict exactly how and when Europe will finally escape the ancient papal curse and forge both its political unity and its sovereignty—for it cannot have one without the other. But two things seem fairly certain: first, Germany is still the center of gravity of Western Europe, for reasons of geography as well as human energy; and second, Europe has no bright future without the friendship of Russia and the good will of China.

61 Mark Bassin, *The Gumilev Mystique: Biopolitics, Eurasianism, and the Construction of Community in Modern Russia*, Cornell UP, 2016, pp. 97–98.

IV

Weird West: Water Thicker than Blood

RADBOD (or Redbad) was the king of Frisia from around 680 until his death in 719. He is considered the last independent ruler of Frisia before Frankish domination. According to a legend first recorded in the *Life* of the missionary Wulfram, Radbod had been persuaded to accept baptism and had already put one foot in the baptismal font when he suddenly had second thoughts and asked Wulfram: "Will I join my ancestors in the hereafter?" Wulfram bluntly told him that such was out of the question, since his ancestors, being not baptized, were all in Hell, whereas Radbod would join the blessed in Heaven. Radbod then retracted his foot and declared that he would rather be with his ancestors. Radbod died a pagan and therefore joined his ancestors. But soon after his death, the Frisians were beaten and baptized, and no more was heard of their national independence.

True or not, this story illustrates the culture shock that Christianity represented for our pagan ancestors. For Radbod, what matters is not where you go after death, but whom you join. The dead are social beings like the living; they are attached to their clan. For Christianity, on the other hand, it is every man for himself. Baptism takes precedence over blood ties. Christian death cancels kinship. There is no nepotism in paradise! Your relatives in the hereafter have no say in where you will end up. By negating the ties of affection and solidarity between the dead and the living, Christianity gradually transformed "solidary death" into "solitary death," in the words of Philippe Ariès.[1]

In a sense, the story of Radbod is now irrelevant, since Christianity has been the religion of our European ancestors for twenty generations. You can theoretically join them as a Christian. Today, most Christians who believe in a "life after death" assume they will meet their loved ones. But this belief does not come from Christianity; rather, it is a natural religious instinct, so to speak, that has persisted *in spite of* Christianity. Fundamentally, the Christian doctrine of salvation (soteriology) stands against the belief that family or clan ties can influence the fate of the individual in the afterlife. Nevertheless, the Christian desacralization of blood ties, even though it failed to eradicate this "pagan" element of natural religion, exerted a huge influence throughout the Middle Ages, leaving an indelible mark even on today's de-Christianized generations.

The "systems of consanguinity and affinity" (Lewis Morgan) or the "elementary structures of kinship" (Claude Lévi-Strauss) are the most essential characteristics of any society. They determine the patterns of relationship between different age groups. And in any traditional society, the dead form an age group; they interact with the living in ways that have a great influence on the social and inner life of the living. The dead keep the living together. By desocializing the dead, the Church has desocialized the living—in order to resocialize them according to new, clan-free rules.

In the first chapter, I argued that the medieval papacy is responsible for Europe's failure to achieve political unity under German leadership. In this chapter, I will argue that the medieval papacy is responsible for the creation of the modern Western individual, that rootless man obsessed by his personal salvation, identity, and self-realization. From the dissolving effect of papacy on the greater political

1 Philippe Ariès, *Western Attitudes toward Death: From the Middle Ages to the Present*, John Hopkins UP, 1974.

level of Empire, the discussion here shifts to its dissolving effect on the smaller ethnic level of the clan and the family. In the first chapter, I did not deny that the "competitive fragmentation of power" (Walter Scheidel) had some positive effects; likewise, here I will not deny that Western individualism has contributed to an exceptional harvest of innovators in all fields of human activity. Obviously, any harmonious society must make room for strong individualities, and societies that don't tend to become ossified in traditions. The issue is about the relationship between the individual and the community. What I will argue is that the pathological — and contagious — stage that Western individualism has reached in modern times is the end-result of a program of de-socialization written by the medieval Roman papacy. To borrow from Joseph Henrich's remarkable book, *The WEIRDest People in the World*: "by undermining intensive kinship, the Church's marriage and family policies gradually released individuals from the responsibilities, obligations, and benefits of their clans and houses."[2] Over many generations, this social engineering has wired our uniquely individualistic psychology.

In Henrich's book we find rich documentation of the causal links between religious history, kinship structures, and individual psychology. Henrich made up the acronym WEIRD to stand for "White, European, Industrialized, Rich, and Democratic," underscoring at the same time that, despite their tendency to think of themselves as the norm, Westerners are the exception, standing in average at one end of the holism/individualism scale: "Unlike much of the world today, and most people who have ever lived, we WEIRD people are highly individualistic, self-obsessed, control-oriented, noncomformist, and analytical. We focus on ourselves — our attributes, accomplishments, and aspirations — over our relationships and social roles. … We see ourselves as unique beings, not as nodes in a social network that

2 Joseph Henrich, *The WEIRDest People on the World: How the West Became Psychologically Peculiar and Particularly Prosperous*, Farrar, Strauss & Giroux, 2020, p. 161.

stretches out through space and back in time." Our psychology is the product of our cultural history, and recent research shows that "you can't separate 'culture' from 'psychology' or 'psychology' from 'biology,' because culture physically rewires our brains and thereby shapes how we think."[3] Indeed, not only *what* we think, but *how* we think and feel about the world and ourselves.

It may be counter-intuitive to blame Christianity for the loss of kinship bonds, since today's practicing Christians are the defenders of family values in the West. The paradox is that Christianity is both revolutionary and conservative. It was revolutionary at the beginning and is now conservative at the end. All established religions are conservative, for such is their main social function: religion is tradition. But Western Christianity's conservatism is about preserving what little kinship structure it didn't destroy in its revolutionary phase: the nuclear family, the final stage before complete social disintegration.[4] Fundamentally, Christian salvation competes with blood kinship.

It is also true that the Church claimed to embody another form of organicity, bringing men and women together in higher brotherhood through the blood and body of Christ. Did the Church succeed? Surely, to some extent. The Church was our mother. But the functions it fulfilled had been fulfilled before Christianity in other ways, and how can we know if the Church fulfilled them better? Who can say that Christians' devotion to the Virgin Mary is more intense than the Mediterranean pagans' devotion to Isis, for example? Judging from Apuleius's *Golden Ass* or from various hymns and prayers that have come down to us, it is doubtful. What is clear is that when the Church, that great organic body, began to disintegrate, when the Christian glue no longer worked, when the Christian God moved away with all his saints, what remained was the rootless individual with nothing to worship but himself. The clan is now decimated,

3 *Ibid.*, pp. 21, 16.

4 David Brooks, "The Nuclear Family was a Mistake," The Atlantic, March 2020.

and the nuclear family has been shrinking into single parenthood. This is the end result of Christianity. More precisely, it is the result of Christian exclusivism: to paraphrase Tacitus, Christianity made a desert around itself and called it faith.

There is a deep mystery here, especially if we think of Christianity as an offshoot of Judaism: if every member of this religion, according to Martin Buber, makes blood "the deepest, most potent stratum of his being," perceives "what confluence of blood has produced him," and "senses in this immortality of the generations a community of blood,"[5] then how and by what Hegelian miracle did such a religion give birth to a salvation cult that declares blood ties irrelevant? And is it not astounding that, having abandoned our own dead, we are now required to participate in the cult of the dead of a people whose identity remains based on blood? I am referring, of course, to the religion of the Holocaust.[6]

Islam, which also derives from Judaism, followed a different path, partly due to the different life patterns of their founders, but also their different social contexts of development. As Thomas Glick writes in *Islamic and Christian Spain in the Early Middle Ages*: "Islam provided a framework which legitimated tribal values and gave them religious significance; Christianity tended to work in the opposite direction, toward the development of inter-personal, rather than inter-group bonds."[7] The 14th-century Arab scholar Ibn Khaldun explained that what made the desert Arabs "so strong and so formidable" was their sense of blood ties: "Affection for one's parents and devotion to those with whom one is united by blood are among the qualities that God has implanted in the human heart. Under the influence of

---

5 Quoted in Geoffrey Cantor and Marc Swetlitz, *Jewish Tradition and the Challenge of Darwinism*, University of Chicago Press, 2006, p. 142.

6 Robert Faurisson, "The secular religion of the Holocaust," 31 July 2008 [www.jailingopinions.com/faurisson-secularreligion.htm].

7 Thomas Glick, *Islamic and Christian Spain in the Early Middle Ages*, Princeton UP, 1979, pp. 141–142.

these feelings, [the Arabs] support one another; they lend each other mutual aid and so make themselves feared by their enemies" (*The Muqaddimah,* Book I).

Here is not the place to explore the differences between the various branches of Abrahamism in any depth. What I will examine, however, is the differences between Eastern and Western Christianity. The corrosive effect of Christianity on kinship structures and ethnic solidarity seems to have had less of an impact in the East. On the national level, the Eastern churches (Orthodox and others) have retained a strong ethnic identity. In the case of the Russian Church, this was in part due to the fact that it was authorized from its foundation to use Slavic rather than Greek. In the West, by contrast, the papacy imposed the uniform use of Latin and combated the autonomist tendencies of national churches. Even today, a Russian Christian attends a Russian Church, placed under the leadership of the Patriarch of Moscow, while a European Catholic attends an international (and ideologically globalist) church whose leader—whether Italian, Polish, Argentine, or American—is sitting in the Vatican.

The same difference is reflected at the clan level. From the 11th century, the Roman Church carried out a series of coordinated assaults on the traditional social organism of the Romano-Germanic populations, an assault that the Greco-Slavic populations did not endure to the same degree. As a result, intensive kinship resisted better in Eastern Europe, especially in South Slavic lands, where, "in the nineteenth century, *zadrugas* [extended families] comprising more than 80 people were observed. This was not the rule, of course, but domestic groups of 20 to 30 members were not uncommon at that time."[8] Slavic Orthodoxy has even preserved a form of ancestor veneration, the keystone of clan cohesion: Serbs celebrate *Krsna Slava*, a baptismal festival during which bread and wine are shared as

8 Michael Mitterauer and Reinhard Sieder, *The European Family: Patriarchy to Partnership from the Middle Ages to the Present,* University of Chicago Press, 1982, p. 29.

offerings to the patron saint of the family, assimilated to the founding ancestor of the clan. No Catholic country has anything comparable.

At the other end of the Christian spectrum, Protestantism is regarded as more individualistic than Catholicism and is arguably responsible for modern liberalism (Max Weber). It is certainly true that modern individualism owes much to Lutheranism and even more to Calvinism. But Protestant individualism could only take root in a sociological and psychological field already plowed by Catholic individualism for dozens of generations.

Before we examine the effects of Roman Catholicism on the social fabric, let us describe the original, pre-Christian nature of that fabric.

Clan-Based Societies and Ancestor Veneration

Whether they were farmers or city-dwellers, our European ancestors lived in clan-based societies. The values cementing such societies are clearly exhibited in the poetry of Homer. Here is how Guillaume Durocher characterizes "Homeric anthropology" in his book *The Ancient Ethnostate*:

> Among the aristocratic ruling class Homer is dealing with, kinship is the basic foundation for identity and solidarity, and therefore of both personal and political action. Strangers are synonymous with uncertainty and potential violence. Kinship in contrast entails inherited resemblance and shared pride in and duties towards one's lineage. Among kin, there is the possibility of security. That security, however, only exists by the strength of the family father, his domestic authority, and his willingness to use violence against hostile aliens. ... For Homer, identity and purpose is found in one's lineage. One acts for the sake of one's ancestors and one's descendants.[9]

Just like Greek society, Roman society was structured around the patrilineal clan or *gens* ("clan" is a Scottish word). So were the Germans

9 Guillaume Durocher, *The Ancient Ethnostate: Biopolitical Thought in Classical Greece*, KDP, 2021, p. 41.

and Britons. Every man was conscious of his own individuality, of course, but the *value* given to the individual was subordinate to the value of the community. We could call it "collectivism" if the term had not taken on a narrowly political meaning. Classical anthropologists call it "holism." Holism is the opposite of individualism, which can then be defined as a value system where the community is subordinate to the individual. Individualism insists on the "rights" of the individual, owed to him by the community, whereas holism insists on the "obligations" or "duties" of the individual toward the community. French philosopher Simone Weil (1909–43), a Hellenist by training, reflected on that opposition. "The Greeks," she writes, "had no conception of rights. They had no words to express it. They were content with the name of justice." The effort to see what is just and act accordingly produces harmony, whereas attitudes based on "I have the right to..." or "you have no right to..." generate a climate of contention.[10]

Marriage was, naturally, the keystone of the social edifice. It was never simply a matter of two persons getting married, but of two lineages contracting a blood alliance by marrying their children — who may or may not have taken part in the decision, but whose best interest parents normally have in any human society. Marriage inside the clan was common, as a way of maintaining the corporate property of the clan land, which comprised the burial ground of the clan ancestors. Marrying in-laws after the death of one's spouse was also common, even expected, for the same reason. However, any civilized state from the city level presupposes a dynamic system of matrimonial alliances between clans; marrying outside the clan then becomes the norm. Although in both Roman and Germanic societies, monogamy was the rule, there was no ban against divorce or second spouses, especially in case of infertility. An alternative heirship strategy was adoption, generally within the clan. This was facilitated by the widespread practice of fosterage, that is, the education of sons by maternal

10 Simone Weil, *Two Moral Essays: Draft for a Statement of Human Obligations, and, Human Personality*, Pendle Hill, 1981, pp. 23–24.

or paternal uncles until adulthood (common in Irish and Briton societies, as illustrated in Arthurian lore).

The social organism had as its backbone the cult of the dead ancestors, which brought communities together, from the family level to the city level. In traditional societies, the living are subordinate to the dead, to whom they owe reverence and loyalty, and from whom they expect protection and guidance. There is actually a wide spectrum of arguments in favor of the theory that human culture evolved from man's effort to maintain social bonds with the dead. It is for their dead that men built their first stone dwellings, notes geographer Pierre Deffontaines. It was to immortalize their dead that they shaped their first images, according to art historian Hans Belting. Tragedy may be a development of funeral rites wherein a shaman, or later an actor wearing a *persona* (mask), made the dead speak. Epic tales probably started as eulogy in honor of the great dead. Myths of the otherworld are intimately linked to the "material metaphors" of burial practices: equipping the dead with some means of transport (boat, horse, chariot, shoes) and providing them with their personal effects is to think of death as a journey.[11]

The theory that culture is man's effort to overcome death (defended by Henri Bergson and Jan Assmann among others)[12] may be unprovable. But the more limited theory that *religion* derives primarily from the cult of the dead finds strong support in ethnology. Weston La Barre made it the subject of his book *The Ghost Dance*, taking as archetype the ritual, trance-inducing dance of the Lakota Sioux

11 Pierre Deffontaines, *Géographie et religions*, 1948; Hans Belting, *Pour une anthropologie des images*, 2004; Frands Herschend, "Material Metaphors — some Late Iron Age and Viking Examples," in Margaret Clunies Ross (ed.), *Old Norse Myths, Literature and Society*, UP of Southern Denmark, 2003, pp. 40–65.

12 Henri Bergson, *The Two Sources of Morality and Religion*, 1932; Jan Assmann, *Death and Salvation in Ancient Egypt*, 2003.

calling out to their ancestors for help.[13] French historian Numa Denis Fustel de Coulanges is the founding figure of this anthropological conception with his book *The Ancient City* published in 1864 and still highly regarded: "This religion of the dead appears to be the oldest that has existed among this race of men. Before men had any notion of Indra or of Zeus, they adored the dead." Among the ancient Greeks and Romans, the family was the primary religious institution. Fustel wrote:

> Generation established a mysterious bond between the infant, who was born to life, and all the gods of the family. Indeed, these gods were his family—they were of his blood. The child, therefore, received at his birth the right to adore them, and to offer them sacrifices; and later, when death should have deified him, he also would be counted, in his turn, among these gods of the family. But we must notice this peculiarity—that the domestic religion was transmitted only from male to male. ... Outside the house, near at hand, in a neighboring field, there is a tomb—the second home of this family. There several generations of ancestors repose together; death has not separated them. They remain grouped in this second existence, and continue to form an indissoluble family. Between the living part and the dead part of the family there is only this distance of a few steps which separates the house from the tomb. On certain days, which are determined for each one by his domestic religion, the living assemble near their ancestors; they offer them the funeral meal, pour out milk and wine to them, lay out cakes and fruits, or burn the flesh of a victim to them. In exchange for these offerings they ask protection; they call these ancestors their gods, and ask them to render the fields fertile, the house prosperous, and their hearts virtuous.[14]

Because the otherworldly happiness of the dead depends on their being remembered by the living, it follows that "every family must perpetuate itself forever. It was necessary to the dead that the

13 Weston La Barre, *The Ghost Dance: The Origins of Religion*, Allen & Unwin, 1972.

14 Numa Fustel de Coulanges, *The Ancient City: A Study of the Religion, Laws, and Institutions of Greece and Rome*, Pentianos Classics, 2017, pp. 38–40.

descendants should not die out. … It was even a duty towards those ancestors whose happiness could last no longer than the family lasted." Another consequence was the abhorrence of adultery, which risked introducing a clandestine stranger into the family cult, so that "the sacred fire became impure; … and there was no more divine happiness for the ancestors." This is why the laws of the ancient world were so severe against adultery. On the other hand, "an adopted son was counted a real son, because, though he had not the ties of blood, he had something better — a community of worship."[15] Because death was conceived as a reunion with the family dead, the hope for a happy afterlife was conditioned on the respect for ancestors and the effort to lead a life that would make them proud. This was symbolized in Roman funeral processions, when the image of the newly deceased was carried toward the family mausoleum, to be met halfway by the images of the dead parents.

Above the clan ancestors, there were the "great dead" honored collectively by the city or wider community, either as founders, benefactors or warriors. They were called "heroes" in ancient Greece, the most famous of whom were celebrated at the Pan-Hellenic festivals and games that were so essential to the Greeks' sense of belonging to a common ethnos. Lewis Farnell defines the Greek hero as "a person whose virtue, influence, or personality was so powerful in his lifetime or through the peculiar circumstances of his death that his spirit after death is regarded as of supernatural power, claiming to be reverenced and propitiated."[16] Heroes are, by definition, exceptional individuals. The heroic principle therefore introduces an element of individualism; legends give the hero a divine parentage (he is a demigod) to signify that he is more than the offspring of his human ancestors; he has a special soul, which explains his immortality and justifies his worship. But the hero is only venerated because he has sacrificed his

15 *Ibid.*, pp. 42, 49.

16 Lewis Richard Farnell, *Greek Hero Cults and Ideas of Immortality*, 1921, p. 343.

individuality to the community, and because the community recognizes itself entirely in him. There is, therefore, a balance between holism and individualism, but the latter is clearly subordinate to the former.

Ancestor worship was central in Greek, Roman, Germanic and Celtic societies before their Christianization. It is, in fact, pretty much universal. What distinguishes the Christian West from the rest of the world is the almost complete loss of this heritage. Even today, it has endured everywhere else, despite the global influence of Western modernity. Anthropologists today prefer to speak of "veneration" rather than "cult" or "worship" of the dead; with some exceptions, the ancestors are not individually deified in any strong sense, they are simply given expressions of respect and gratitude, and they are expected to guide and protect the living—or correct them when they act badly. Not all ancestors are good, but it is better to live in peace with all of them. In exceptional cases, some disreputable dead may be erased from the family memory.

An encyclopedic overview of ancestor worship worldwide is beyond our present scope, but let us mention just a few Asian countries. In Vietnam, every family, rich or poor, has an ancestor altar in their home, no matter if they identify as Buddhists, Christians, or otherwise. Love of ancestors and love of nation are organically linked, because the ancestors built the nation and protected its territorial integrity over the centuries. Ancestor veneration has a long and rich history in Korea, too, and is still an important part of traditional village life. The rituals are practiced throughout the year for ancestors up to the fifth generation. Some Catholics join in these ancestral rites, but evangelical Protestants do not. Many Koreans occasionally engage in shamanism (*musok*), which primarily deals with conflicts between the living and the dead. In Japan, despite the post-WWII undermining of national traditions, most people maintain a degree of veneration toward their dead, even if they claim to have no religion. There were traditionally three levels of ancestor worship, as Nobushige Hozumi explained in *Ancestor-Worship and Japanese Law* (1901): family, clan, and nation. Each family honored their own ancestors, spanning three or four generations, sometimes more. The dead were honored individually on the anniversaries of their death, but also collectively on certain dates, which were occasions for family reunions. Each clan also had their clan-god, generally understood as the founder of the clan, and the protector of its territory. The worship of clan ancestors was the most important until the 19th century, because the original unit of Japanese society was not the family but the clan, each clan being legally represented by its chief. Finally, there was the national cult of the imperial family, which was not a cult of the emperor himself *per se*, but rather the nation's participation in the emperor's own ancestor cult, on the mythic assumption that the emperor's ancestors are the ancestors of the whole nation. In China, despite decades of communist indoctrination, ancestor veneration is still common, based as it is in the ancient tradition of Confucianism, which emphasizes filial piety and respect for ancestors. People participate in ritual offerings to the dead regardless of their other religious affiliation. So strong was ancestor worship in China that the Catholic Church had to make an exception to its usual condemnation: in 1939, a synod retracted the official ban pronounced in 1707, deciding that ancestor veneration was not religious after all and could therefore be tolerated.

In conclusion, ancestor veneration is an essential part of Asian traditions, and although it has declined in large cities, it is still widely practiced. Generally speaking, honoring ancestors is not just a religious custom; it is a moral obligation, because it is an extension of filial piety, which in the East is unanimously considered as the basis of morality: out of filial piety, you join in your parents' filial piety, and so on. The dead are the highest age group on the social hierarchy. They live close by and often visit, although their rights in this world are limited. It goes without saying that filial piety and ancestor veneration have a significant effect on the stability of families: when people feel generationally connected, they feel more responsible for keeping their marriage together as well as for helping their children attain a good marriage. Transmission from past generations to future generations is the primary function of every individual.

If ancestor veneration is so universal, why is it so foreign to us Westerners? Are we fundamentally different? Is our brain, by some evolutionary process, hardwired differently and simply unable to function in this holistic mode? History clearly informs us that this is not the case. Our ancestors venerated the deceased of their family and clan just as much as Asians and the rest of humanity. Why, then, has this tradition disappeared? How have we become worshippers of the self? There might not be a single factor, but there are several that have accumulated over the course of history. Obviously, the Church is not to blame for the latest developments of Western individualism, just as it does not bear responsibility for the fact that the flowers placed on the family grave on All Saint's Day are being replaced by the pumpkins of Halloween (originally a Celtic festival of the dead, but perverted by American culture). I am not concerned here with the latest social phenomena of the latter sort, for they are only the rotten fruits of a civilizational trend that started many centuries ago, with the early attacks of Christianity against the traditional notion of blood as a kind of collective, genealogical soul.

Salvation for Me

Christianity is a salvation religion. By this we mean a way of salvation for the individual, not for the family or the community. Jesus's own emphasis on personal salvation comes with a strong hostility towards blood ties: "Anyone who comes to me without hating father, mother, wife, children, brothers, sisters, yes and his own life too, cannot be my disciple" (Luke 14:26). Quite many of the saints of hagiographic legends applied this command to the letter: they severed their family ties and renounced all worldly responsibility and possession. One of the best-known pieces of literature in the Middle Ages was the *Life of Saint Anthony*, the father of monasticism. Anthony was born of wealthy parents. After hearing Matthew 19:21 ("If you would be perfect, go, sell what you possess and give to the poor, and you shall have treasure in heaven; and come, follow me") at mass, he "went out immediately from the church, and gave the possessions of his forefathers to the villagers." He sold the rest and gave the money to the poor. He committed his sister to a convent, then went into the desert and lived alone for the rest of his life. Quite an egocentric life choice! Such a choice was justified by the belief that salvation is for souls, and that souls are strictly individual. Christianity is a metaphysical individualism. The individual, not the human community, is the image of God, for God himself is an Individual—as opposed to a community of gods. When Dante Alighieri wrote in *De Monarchia* that the more men are united together, the more they are in the image of God, he was not expressing a Christian idea, but a Stoic one.

The point that Christianity is the source of Western individualism was skillfully made by Louis Dumont in his essay "The Christian Genesis of Modern Individualism," originally titled "The Christian Beginnings: From the Outworldly Individual to the Individual-in-the-world." Dumont uses his knowledge of India to identify what most fundamentally distinguishes the modern West from traditional societies. Indian society is holistic, but it allows for some individuals, the *sadhus*, to forsake their social existence for the sake of seeking enlightenment, as long as these individuals do not challenge the social order and its holistic dynamic, thus remaining exceptions that confirm the rule. Christianity, according to Dumont, upsets such a balance by declaring that individual salvation *from* this world is every Christian's calling: "By stages worldly life will thus be contaminated by the outworldly element, until finally … holism will have vanished from ideology, and … the outworldly individual will have become the modern, inworldly individual. This is the historical proof of the extraordinary potency of the initial disposition."[17]

I think Dumont's analysis is correct in general terms, but it lacks some historical context. Two points need clarification. First, Christianity is not the only salvation religion with a universal message: Buddhism, which was actually founded by an Indian *sadhu*, also fits that definition. The emphasis in Buddhism is on individual enlightenment and salvation (the Buddha actually taught the impermanence of the individual self, but popular Buddhism ignores that clause). Yet Buddhist societies did not become individualistic because Buddhism has remained a religion of monks who never aimed at ruling society (except in rare cases such as Tibet). Also, unlike Christianity, Buddhism has no strong claim at exclusivity and does not condemn the private cult of ancestors, which is widely practiced and even encouraged in dominantly Buddhist countries. This helps us understand how it is not so much the Christian doctrine *per se* that made Christian societies individualistic, as it was Christian exclusivism—the jealousy of the Christian God, who demonized every other cult, including ancestor worship—and the dominance of the Church over the intellectual and cultural life of Western societies. Generally speaking, the problem of Christianity is not what it brought, but what it took away.

This brings us to the second qualification of Dumont's thesis: there are different kinds of Christianity, and not all were affected to the same degree by the Christian contempt for kinship and ancestors. Greek Orthodoxy has not raised the "outworldly individual" to the same level of exclusive sainthood as Roman Catholicism has. The Vatican imposes celibacy and chastity on all members of the Church, whereas in Orthodoxy, priests are almost required to be married. Even though monks enjoy a high prestige, and bishops as a rule must be monks (they may have been married, but must be free from family

17 Louis Dumont, *Essays on Individualism: Modern Ideology in Anthropological Perspective*, University of Chicago Press, 1992, pp. 23–59.

obligations), Orthodoxy does not confuse the two functions of priest and monk.

This distinction generally escapes Catholics, but it is crucial and requires further explanation. In the Greek and Roman worlds, priesthood is a social function, entrusted to persons of social standing. The priest represents the community before the gods, he must therefore be a worthy representative of that community. The first priesthood in Roman society was that of the *pater familias*, who was priest in his household. The highest priesthood was the honorary title of *pontifex maximus*, which ended up as the prerogative of the Emperor. That is consistent with the ancient overlap between the functions of king and priest. Unlike the priest, the monk flees the society of men in order to live a life that is as disembodied and desocialized as possible. He forsakes his family ties, even the name he received at birth. He is dead to the world. He seeks a direct relationship with the divine, in maximum solitude and minimal social interaction (monasteries are nothing more than communities of hermits). Ordinary human society disturbs him, prevents him from being alone with his God. Turned inward, he is not of this world and does not wish to influence it. The priest and the monk could not be further apart in their original, essential functions.

In the West, an inversion of this relationship took place in the 11th century: the priest must now belong to this monastic humanity distinct from ordinary, procreating humanity. Not all monks are priests, but all priests must be like monks. In other words, the monastery captured the priesthood. That was in part the result of the alliance between the papacy and the monastic orders — one of the most distinctive aspects of second-millennium Latin Christianity. Before the 10th century, most monasteries followed the same rule of Saint Benedict, but they were poorly interconnected and not under papal supervision. They were usually under the protection of the sovereigns who had granted them land. This changed with the rise of the Abbey of Cluny, the matrix of the Gregorian Reform.[18] Cluny was placed under the exclusive authority of the pope, and expanded into a network of more than a thousand priories throughout Europe. The "Cluniac Church," as it was sometimes called, was "a closely knit monastic society of transregional scope, stretching from Spain to Flanders and from England to Italy. … It was nominally a single large monastery with a single abbot-father at the top."[19] The Cluniac network was superseded in the 12th century by the even more extensive network of Cistercian monasteries. There is nothing comparable in the Orthodox world, which does not even have "monastic orders."

The bond between the monastic orders and the papacy was a crucial factor in the transformation of the Roman Church into a separate society, alien to the world yet claiming sovereignty over the world like the head over its body. The Church became entirely monastic, since all churchmen, and not just monks, were now celibate and chaste for life (in principle). Therefore we can say that the Gregorian Reform was a monastic coup, and that the prohibition on priests raising a family was the real turning point that made Christianity a desocializing and individualizing influence in the West. Monks seized the papacy and forced bishops and priests to abide by their rule. Henceforth, the priesthood is no longer entrusted to family men respected for their social involvement, but to men theoretically pure of all social attachment. The implication is that the monk belongs to a humanity that is not only separate but superior, no longer marginal but commanding. What happens next is that the monk, who has renounced marriage, claims to exercise control over it for others (on which more later).

In *The Discovery of the Individual,* Colin Morris places the rise of the individual's self-consciousness between 1050 and 1200. This is a bit shallow, according to Caroline Walker Bynum: since they are

18 H. E. J. Cowdrey, *The Cluniacs and the Gregorian Reform,* Clarendon, 1970.

19 Michael Mitterauer, *Why Europe?, op. cit.*, pp. 189–190.

based on literary sources, such theories are in reality only theories about the "invention of the autobiography." But what is interesting is that Morris supports his theory exclusively with the writings of monks.[20] What he really shows, therefore, is that the monk probing his own soul is the inventor of the self-contained individual, and that the Roman Church became the source of individualism from the moment it made monks not only into a different kind of humanity, but into a supposedly deeper and superior kind — a chosen people, so to speak.

The contrast with Greek or Russian Orthodoxy is very significant: the Orthodox priest almost has an obligation to marry. He has a wife, children, and even a job. He also has a beard, long if possible, while the Catholic priest must be clean-shaven. That may be a detail, but it is a symbolic one, and public symbols by all means influence the collective mentality. Gregory VII insisted to the clergy of Sardinia that they should "follow the custom of the holy Roman Church" and shave their beards, since it had been "the practice of he whole Western Church from the very beginning"; any Sardinian ecclesiastic who refused to conform would have his property confiscated.[21] The beard is a symbol of virility, quite simply because it is the most visible difference between man and woman. The bearded priest is a patriarch; the beardless priest is like an angel: desexualized, almost non-binary.

This difference is also reflected in the cult of saints. The saints of Western folklore are almost exclusively celibate (those who had wives and children, like Augustine, abandoned them). By contrast, Byzantine saints include laymen who are honored not only for their faith, but also for their life of service to the empire as military leaders, scholars or administrators. Such figures combine worldly authority

20 Caroline Walker Bynum, "Did the Twelfth Century Discover the Individual?," in *Jesus as Mother: Studies in Spirituality of the High Middle Ages*, University of California Press, 1982, pp. 82–109.

21 Robert Bartlett, *The Making of Europe: Conquest, Colonization and Cultural Change (950–1350)*, Penguin Books, 1994, p. 248.

and otherworldly sainthood.[22] Even today, Russian Orthodox churches display icons of kings and national heroes. The worldly great man and the otherworldly saint are not antagonistic figures in Orthodoxy.

The important point to remember is this: even though there is a clerical hierarchy in Greek and Russian Orthodoxy, there is no ontological separation between churchman and layman. The priest is a full member of ordinary humanity. Consequently, the layman is also a full member of the Church. This makes it possible to maintain the idea that the Church is the community of all Christians, united as a single body. Let us examine this point further.

The Organic Church

As a salvation religion, Christianity is by nature an individualizing force. But that force is theoretically counterbalanced by the cohesive attraction of the Church as an organic body. The Church is a supernatural family that is supposed to be superior to the natural solidarities which are the sources of so many ills. We already find this idea in the New Testament: "There is neither Jew nor Greek, there is neither slave nor free, there is neither man nor woman; for you are all one in Christ Jesus" (Galatians 3:28). Through baptism and mass, Christians form a new family, even a new nation (a "new Israel»). The blood of the new Covenant (Matthew 26:28) is a twofold symbol: it is the blood of Christ shed on the cross, and it is the blood of Christ drunk by Christians and running in their veins. The metaphysical individualism of Christianity is therefore compensated by a metaphysical holism: we are engrafted into the sinless lineage of Christ.

If such was the original function of the Church, then the Orthodox are right in accusing the Roman hierarchy of having betrayed it by introducing a strict separation between clerical society and lay society. The former is separated from the latter by its language

22 Sophie Métivier, *Aristocratie et sainteté à Byzance (VIIIe–XIe siècle)*, Société des Bollandistes, 2019.

(Latin) and its way of life (celibacy), which makes it a distinct society. According to Russian theologian Aleksey Khomiakov, as a result of the Gregorian Reform, "the Christian was no longer one of the members of the Church, but one of her subjects. He was no longer part of her decisions. She and he were no longer one. He was outside of her while remaining in her bosom."[23]

Robert Moore's analysis concurs: "the Gregorian programme was nothing less than a project to divide the world, both people and property, into two distinct and autonomous realms, not geographically but socially. In principle and increasingly in practice every community, from Christendom itself to the remotest hamlet, was to contain an independent clerical domain, with its own powers and functions, its own properties and incomes, its own laws, customs and jurisdiction, and its own membership, separated from others by a distinctive manner of life based on the rule of celibacy."[24]

This was made explicit by the Clunisian monk Gratian, the "Father of Canon Law," in the middle of the 12th century: "There are two kinds of Christians," he wrote: the clerics, who are "concerned with the Divine Office and dedicate themselves to meditation and prayer," and who are therefore "the Chosen Ones," while "laymen make up the second kind of Christians." Gratian invokes a fanciful etymology to derive the Latin *clericus* from the Greek *kleros,* which he translates as "chosen."[25]

Catholic priests have exclusive access to the "blood of Christ" (the wine) during communion, while lay Christians are only entitled to the "body of Christ" (the bread). This is highly symbolic, Khomiakov remarks, because the meaning of the Eucharist is "the Church uniting all its members in bodily communion with its Savior."[26] The

---

23 Aleksei Stepanovitch Khomiakoff, *L'Église latine et le protestantisme au point de vue de l'Église d'Orient*, 1872, pp. 38–39.

24 Moore, *The First European Revolution, op. cit.*, p. 11.

25 Mitterauer, *Why Europe, op. cit.*, p. 180.

26 Khomiakoff, *L'Église latine et le protestantisme, op. cit.*, p. 139.

Catholic faithful are not in full communion with their priest. Theirs is a half-communion, experienced as a half-salvation. Communion in both kinds in the Orthodox liturgy makes a big symbolic difference. Russian Orthodox apologists such as Khomiakov argue that the organic unity of the Church as the body of Christ has been better preserved in Orthodoxy than in Catholicism. It is for this reason, they say, that Russians have always defended their Church as the very substance of their collective being, as if saving their Church was more important than saving their own souls.

To strengthen their authority, the Catholic reformers developed a new "canonical" legal system that was to take precedence over civil and customary laws. One of the consequences of the Gregorian Reform, according to Orthodox theologians John Meyendorff and Aristeides Papadakis, was "the transformation of the papacy into the most complex tribunal in Christendom. Legal rather than religious functions were to set the pattern of papal activity for the rest of the central Middle Ages."[27] Significantly, almost every pope in the period 1100–1300 was a specialist in canon law. Papal legalism led to the writing of codified "penitentiaries" in which confessors could find the precise penitence for each kind of sin. Belief itself became a legal matter, and wrong belief punishable by law. To this day, Catholics are required to recite the Nicene Creed at Mass. Orthodoxy is less demanding in that regard; it does not reduce "faith" to "belief" and it admits other ways of access to the Divine besides dogma. It emphasizes liturgy: belief divides, while liturgy unites; belief is personal, ritual is collective. Therefore, the insistence on correct belief—with the criminalization of "disbelief"—has been a factor in the formation of individualism in the West. It has also been, ultimately, a major factor in de-Christianization: what should I do if I can't "believe" that Jesus was born of a virgin, or came out of his tomb physically? Should I lie in front of God and recite the *credo* ("I believe…") anyway? Can

27 John Meyendorff and Aristeides Papadakis, *The Christian East and the Rise of the Papacy*, St. Vladimir's Seminary Press, 1994, p. 211.

I still feel part of the Church if I don't? Orthodoxy has always been more accepting toward those who have a limited capacity to believe the irrational. This explains that all great Russian writers considered themselves Christians and defenders of their Church, even though they were, from the point of view of strict doctrine, heretics. Anticlericalism is not a Russian tradition, because Russians have little reason to feel estranged from their national Church, in which correct belief is not the main criterion of belonging.

The difference in the conceptualization of the Church between Roman Catholicism and Greek or Russian Orthodoxy is linked to a deeper intellectual difference. Orthodox theology was affected neither by Augustinianism nor by Thomism, i.e., Aristotelian scholasticism. Instead, it adhered to the Platonic metaphysics of the Greek Fathers, which gave it greater conceptual flexibility. In Platonic thought, the world of souls is like the world of Ideas, organic and infinitely varied. Every collective being has a collective soul: the conception of the Church as a mystical body is therefore immediately understandable. For Aristotle, on the other hand, only what is material is real; Ideas, therefore, are not real. Aristotle even denies the immortality of the human soul, which for him is only an animal, vital principle. Of course, Christianity reintroduced the soul into its Aristotelianism by postulating that God, being all-powerful, made an exception for the human soul and gave it immortality, but it is a minimal, strictly individual soul. In the scholastic mental universe, the reality of the Church as a collective soul (the City of God) is also recognized, but as another divine exception to Aristotelian metaphysics.

Because Platonism recognizes the real power of ideas, it also recognizes the real power of symbols. In a broad sense, Platonism must be understood "as a divine finger pointing from earth to heaven, from things that are below to things that are above," in the words of Russian theologian Pavel Florensky.[28] Berdyaev also insists on the

28 Pavel Florenski, *The Meaning of Idealism: The Metaphysics of Genus & Countenance*, Sematron Press, 2020, p. 5.

importance of symbolism in the Orthodox tradition, as opposed to the Catholic tradition which, in the 13th century, chose Aristotle over Plato: "Symbolism sees a spiritual reality behind this visible reality. The symbol is a link between two worlds, the mark of another world within this world."[29] From a secular point of view, the difference between the Platonic paradigm and the Aristotelian paradigm may seem to be merely a matter of nuance, but it is rather the case that they are two very different and incompatible mental softwares or operating systems so to speak. This difference is also reflected in sacred art: the symbolism of Orthodox icons contrasts with the realism of Western religious art. There are no bloody crucifixes in Orthodox churches.

In this Platonic conception, the Eucharistic rite of eating the body and drinking the blood of Christ is efficient in itself, as a symbolic gesture. But in the Catholic understanding, since according to Aristotelian theory only what is corporeal is real, the very "substance" of bread and wine must be transformed for the rite to be efficient: this is the justification for the doctrine of transubstantiation, made mandatory at the Fourth Lateran Council (1215). It is strongly criticized by the Orthodox as a magical conception, and it has been a major issue in reform movements ever since Jan Hus. As Keith Thomas argued in *Religion and the Decline of Magic,* with this "magical idea that the mere pronunciation of words in a ritual manner can effect a change in the nature of material objects," the Roman Church encouraged a superstitious mindset.[30]

29 Nicolas Berdyaev, *The Russian Idea,* MacMillan, 1948, p. 229.

30 Keith Thomas, *Religion and the Decline of Magic: Studies in Popular Beliefs in Sixteenth- and Seventeenth-Century England* [1971], Penguin, 1991, pp. 36–37, 51.

The War on the Clan and the Business of Salvation

The Gregorian reformers not only imposed celibacy on priests; at the same time, they took control of the institution of marriage for laymen. French historian Georges Duby has documented this evolution in his seminal book *The Knight, The Lady, and the Priest: The Making of Modern Marriage in Medieval France*: "In northern France in the ninth century, marriage was still something in which priests were not closely involved. There is no mention of nuptial benedictions in the texts, except in the case of queens, where it was still only one element in the ritual of coronation." It was not until the Council of Verona in 1184 that marriage was officially made a sacrament. Duby takes as his starting point the confrontation between Urban II and Philip I. In 1094, during the famous Council of Clermont which started the First Crusade, Urban had excommunicated Philip on the charge of adultery for having repudiated his barren first wife and taken Bertrade of Montfort, previously married to the count of Anjou. The excommunication was part of the popes' theocratic strategy: "The meaning of all the remonstrances, protests, and fulminations," Duby writes, "becomes clear when we restore them to their true context at the heart of the great political question of the age: the fierce struggle of the spiritual power to dominate the temporal." It was a long struggle. Throughout the Middle Ages, the aristocratic value system endured. Its key concept was "*probitas*, a valor of body and soul that produced both prowess and magnanimity. In those days everyone thought this supreme quality was transmitted through the blood." The purpose of marriage, Duby explains, "was to unite a valiant progenitor to a wife in such a manner that his legitimate son, bearer of the blood and name of a valorous ancestor, should be able to bring that ancestor to life again in his own person." The woman participated just as much as the man in the quality of the lineage: "In Carolingian and post-Carolingian Europe people believed that women produced sperm, or at least that both the man and the woman contributed to the act of conception, and that the immediate effect of sexual intercourse was to mingle indissolubly the blood of the two partners."[31] Slowly but surely, this metaphysics of blood and sex was erased by the narrow Christian concept of the soul.

Jack Goody enlightens us on another dimension of the Church's struggle against clan ideology in another important book, *The Development of the Family and Marriage in Europe* (1983), and more recently in *The European Family: An Historico-Anthropological Essay* (2000): "By insinuating itself into the very fabric of domestic life, of heirship and marriage, the Church gained great control over the grass roots of the society itself."[32] The new rules included the following:

- The authority of parents and close kin over the marriage of younger persons was reduced. The Church disapproved of arranged marriages, and allowed spouses to get married without their parents' consent.
- Divorce and remarriage were made nearly impossible, leaving no solution of heirship for infertile marriages. Marriage could be contracted by mutual consent alone, but could not be broken even by mutual consent.
- Strict monogamy was enforced, and the taking of second wives or concubines condemned.

31 Georges Duby, *The Knight, The Lady, and the Priest: The Making of Modern Marriage in Medieval France*, Pantheon Books, 1981, pp. 33–34, 12, 37.

32 Jack Goody, *The Development of the Family and Marriage in Europe*, Cambridge UP, 1983, p. 45.

- Marriage to in-laws after the death of a spouse, common in Europe as in the Middle East, was declared incestuous: in canon law, your husband's brother became like your real brother.
- Marriage to spiritual kin (godfather or godmother) was also tabooed, whether they were blood relatives or not.
- Adoption, widely practiced in the Roman world as a strategy of heirship, became severely limited. Canon law effectively bound all forms of inheritance directly to the genealogical line of descent.
- Most importantly, marriage to blood relatives was prohibited, and the prohibition was gradually extended up to the seventh degree. This essentially tabooed marriage between those who shared one or more of their 128 great-great-great-great-great-grandparents, making marriage virtually impossible in your own village, in theory at least, and in practice providing the Church with a means of leverage on every member of the ruling class.

The gradual enforcement of such laws and ideas transformed society profoundly. The purpose was to replace carnal affections, or what sociologist Ludwig Gumplowicz called the "syngeneic feelings" — the sense of familiarity mostly proportional to genetic proximity[33]—with Christian universal charity, to break up familial, tribal, and national identities so as to unite all Christians into one big loving family, thereby uprooting each person from the lineage of original sin and engrafting them (being "born again") into Christ through baptism.

There was also an economic incentive. As Jack Goody puts it: "Prohibit close marriage, discourage adoption, condemn polygyny, concubinage, divorce and remarriage, and 40 per cent of families will be left with no immediate male heirs."[34] As ownership became privatized, testators were free to bequeath whatever they wished to

33 Ludwig Gumplowicz, *La Lutte des races. Recherches sociologiques*, Guillaumin, 1893.

34 Goody, *The Development*, *op. cit.*, p. 44.

Church institutions, and the alienation of property for the benefit of the Church was greatly facilitated.[35] This strategy was made explicit under the pen of a bishop named Salvianus, who, Goody explains, "refers to adopted children as 'children of perjury,' cheating God (or his church) of what was rightfully his. This statement makes it quite clear why the institution should be banned, in the interests of the Church and of spirituality. The confrontation with past practices is very explicit and had an enormous influence on the future; even if there were a few exceptions later on, the ban was largely complied with throughout Christendom over the centuries."[36]

Naturally, rich people were especially in need of salvation, since it is more difficult for them to go to heaven than for a camel to go through the eye of a needle (Matthew 19:24). They could solve their problem by giving their wealth to the Church. There was no lack of hagiographic models for them to emulate. Consider the exemplary life of saint Paulinus of Nola, a Roman aristocrat who in 394 supposedly decided to follow Jesus' advice and gain "treasures in heaven" for himself by giving away all his family fortune. Few noblemen imitated such radical example. Most preferred to remain rich all their lives, and unburden their soul only at the threshold of death — but not to the point of disinheriting their children completely. In his foundation chart of the Abbey of Cluny, the duke of Aquitaine declared that he made his donation "to provide for my own salvation" and "for the gain of my soul," since "the providence of God has so provided for certain rich men that, by means of their transitory possessions, if they

35 R. Ekelund & co., "How the Church Preempted the Marriage Market," in *Sacred Trust: The Medieval Church as an Economic Firm,* Oxford UP, 1996, pp. 85–112.

36 Jack Goody, *The European Family: An Historico-Anthropological Essay,* Blackwell, 2000, p. 35.

use them well, they may be able to merit everlasting rewards."[37] In other words, blessed are the rich who can buy their place in Heaven.

As more and more lords exchanged their wealth and property for treasures in heaven, the Church became the biggest landowner in Europe. "At the end of the twelfth century," writes Robert Moore, "the churches held perhaps one-third of the cultivated land or northern France, and probably about half as much in southern France and Italy."[38] Unlike every other property, Church land (held by any ecclesiastical institution such as bishoprics or monasteries) was inalienable: at the Council of Lyon of 1274, Gregory IX prohibited donation, sale, exchange (*permutatio*) and perpetual lease (*emphyteusis*) of Church property.[39] Inalienability means that the Church is a corporate body who is not subject to death—precisely what clans were, before property was individualized.

The enforcement of celibacy within the Church contributed to making Church property inalienable, as historian Henry Charles Lea explained in his *Historical Sketch of Sacerdotal Celibacy in the Christian Church* (1867):

> The Church was daily receiving vast accessions of property from the pious zeal of its wealthy members, the death-bed repentance of despairing sinners, and the munificence of emperors and prefects, while the efforts to procure the inalienability of its possessions dates from an early period. Its acquisitions, both real and personal, were of course exposed to much greater risk of dilapidation when the ecclesiastics in charge of its widely scattered riches had families for whose provision a natural parental anxiety might be expected to over-ride the sense of duty in discharging the trust confided to them. The simplest mode of averting the danger might therefore seem to be to relieve the churchman of the cares of paternity, and, by cutting asunder all the ties of the family and kindred, to bind them

37 Ernest F. Henderson, ed., *Select Historical Documents of the Middle Ages*, 1910, pp. 329–333.

38 Moore, *The First European Revolution, op. cit.*, p. 12.

39 Herbert Thurston, "Ecclesiastical Property," in *The Catholic Encyclopedia*, Robert Appleton Company, 1911 [newadvent.com].

> completely and forever to the church and to that alone. This motive … was openly acknowledged in later times, and it no doubt served as an argument of weight in the minds of those who urged and secured the adoption of the canon.[40]

The most zealot among popes and cardinals were not the most exemplary in that regard. Far from being detached from family ties, they had replaced occasional simony with institutional nepotism. For the vast majority of Roman baronial families, write Sandro Carocci and Marco Vendittelli, "the driving force, the determining factor of family greatness must … be rightly sought in the nepotism of a relative elected to the Sacred College, or to the pontifical dignity." Innocent III (1198–1216) built the fortune of the Conti family, and it is to the "brutal nepotism of Boniface VIII (1294–1303)" that the Caetani family owed its meteoric rise. "In the lucrative art of accumulating benefices, the relatives of popes and cardinals naturally excelled."[41]

Death to the Dead!

To the list of Church legislation against ethnic and family ties must be added the condemnation of all manners of ancestor veneration, now assimilated to necromancy or devil-worship. Augustine exerted a strong influence on this issue. Around 422, he composed a treatise "on caring for the dead" which affirmed that traditional funeral rites are useless, and that the manner of dealing with a dead body is of no consequence on the dead man's soul: "The faithful lose nothing by being deprived of burial, just like the unbelievers gain nothing by receiving it" (IX,11). He also made this point in *The City of God* (I,12). This was a logical corollary of the axiom that the realm of the

---

40 Henry Charles Lea, *An Historial Sketch of Sacerdotal Celibary in the Christian Church*, 1867, p. 64–65, quoted by Goody, *The Development of the Family, op. cit.*, p. 81.

41 Sandro Carocci and Marco Vendittelli, "Société et économie," in André Vauchez (dir.), *Rome au Moyen Âge*, Éditions du Cerf, 2021, pp. 127–188.

dead and the realm of the living cannot communicate, and that, consequently, the dead are not even aware of, not to mention concerned by, whatever expressions of love, respect and honor the living give them. The affirmation that burial rites are useless for the dead — even though the living may find them comforting, Augustine conceded — undermined the whole purpose of ancestor veneration, and, in the long run, contributed to the disintegration of kinship structures held together vertically by the confidence that the dead and the living could rely on each other.

However, the people did not give up so easily. In early Latin Christianity, the "pagan" practices of feasting on tombs and feeding the dead are attested by numerous condemnations by Church Fathers, notably Tertullian and Augustine. They are still condemned in the 11th century in Burchard of Worms's *Decretum,* which proves their persistence.[42] The ritualized veneration of ancestors remains strong among the peasantry, but also in aristocratic circles, which had their specific rites and beliefs, as Maurice Keen has shown: "On its own ground, chivalry felt no need of sacerdotal guidance."[43]

In the traditional mentality that the clergy condemned, the living and the dead had rights and duties toward each other. It was important, for example, to avenge any relative who had been killed treacherously. This was not only a natural right; it was "the most sacred of duties — to be pursued even beyond the grave," according to Marc Bloch.[44] The soul of a person who has been killed in unfair conditions and has not been avenged cannot find rest. As I showed in *La Lance qui saigne*, the restless dead demanding or awaiting vengeance is one of the most widespread themes in the vernacular romances of Germanic and Celtic inspiration over the 11th–15th centuries. Chrétien de Troyes's *Conte du Graal*, the seminal romance of Grail

42 Michel Lauwers, *La Mémoire des ancêtres*, Beauchesne, 1997, pp. 74–79.

43 Maurice Hugh Keen, *Chivalry*, Yale UP, 1984, 2005, p. 100.

44 Marc Bloch, *Feudal Society*, vol. I: *The Growth of Ties of Dependence,* Routledge, 1962, p. 125.

literature, is an enigmatic rewriting, with cryptic Christological overtones, of a traditional legend involving a son (Perceval) meeting his dead father (the Fisher King) in the Otherworld (the Grail castle) and healing him by killing his murderer (the Red Knight).[45] It is from a similar medieval Scandinavian legend that Shakespeare borrowed the story of Prince Hamlet, visited by the bleeding ghost of his murdered father who demands vengeance. In feudal society, filial vengeance is an expression of filial piety. The medieval aristocratic ethos is, on this point, hardly different from that found in Greek tragedies, which praise revenge as the very essence of justice.[46] In such a view, justice is not opposed to revenge, but merely strives to moderate it and break the cycles of vendetta. Christianity, of course, banishes vengeance in imitation of Jesus forgiving his tormenters on the cross. Redemptive vengeance is but one aspect of kinship solidarity spanning this world and the next.

Christianity sought to replace, or at least temper, heroic values with the ideal of passive martyrdom. Certain pre-Christian cults associated with tombs were Christianized into cults of saints whose biographies were invented for the purpose. The transformation of the religion of the dead into the cult of the saints was a long and difficult process. Monastic chronicles from the 12th century lament the persistence of "false cults" dedicated to "criminals" and centered on their miraculous blood, sometimes with the guilty participation of the local clergy.[47] If we admit that the cult of the saints was, to some extent, a Christian recycling of the cult of the great dead, we must underscore its radical novelty: first, saints are nobody's ancestors, since chastity is a key element of sainthood; second, as a rule, they are not

45 Laurent Guyénot, *La Lance qui saigne*, Champion, 2010.

46 Anne Pippin Burnett, *Revenge in Attic and Later Tragedy*, University of California Press, 1999.

47 C. S. Watkins, *History and the Supernatural in Medieval England*, Cambridge UP, 2007, pp. 79–80, 108–109.

revered as benefactors of their community, but as "martyrs" (meaning, "witnesses") of the faith.

As with the institution of marriage, the Gregorian Reform was a turning point in the priests' takeover of funerary rites, serving as the occasion for a fierce struggle between the Papal Church and the royal aristocracy. The posthumous fate of Emperor Henry IV's illustrates that struggle. He had always shown a sincere piety toward the dead; his diplomas testify to his concern for the commemoration of the dead who were dear to him, friends and relatives alike. He had built at great expense a mausoleum for his ancestors in the cathedral of Speyer. When he died, his son Henry V had him buried there. Pope Paschal II, invoking the excommunication of Henry IV by his predecessor, had his body exhumed, and it spent the next five years in an unconsecrated chapel. Henry V had to make major concessions to the political ambitions of the papacy to obtain the posthumous lifting of the excommunication of his father, who was then able to join his ancestors.[48] In a sense, this post-mortem episode of Henry IV's struggle against the popes has a greater symbolic value than his humiliation at Canossa. That a pope could prevent an emperor from returning to his ancestors' tomb after his death, effectively making him a lost soul, a wandering ghost, demonstrates the full extent of the power acquired by the papacy since the coronation of Henry IV as King of the Romans forty years earlier.

The clash between the old clan values and the new Christian values ended in favor of the latter, but not without some compromise. Unable to discourage people from caring for their dead, the Church simply imposed its exclusive mediation between the living and the dead. The idea that the living could buy support for their dead from the Church gave rise to the doctrine of Purgatory, a major source of ecclesiastical revenue in which the abbey of Cluny specialized.[49]

48 I. S. Robinson, *Henry IV of Germany 1056–1106*, Cambridge UP, 2008, p. 353.

49 Dominique Iogna-Prat, *Ordonner et exclure. Cluny et la société chrétienne*, Flammarion, 2000, pp. 223–225.

The living could thus alleviate the suffering of their imperfect dead, but the dead, having no money, could do nothing for the living, and whatever signs the living might occasionally receive from them (visions or dreams) were in reality tricks of the devil. Only the saints officially admitted to Heaven (by the bishop, and from the 13th century onwards by the pope alone) could bestow blessings upon the living — but not upon their own descendants, since, being chaste, they had none.

By denying or minimizing the persistency of family ties beyond death, Christianity has deprived them of transcendent value. The individual soul alone is immortal. The holistic conception in which the dead are social beings gave way to an individualist conception that was materialized by an increasingly individualized tomb. In the 13th century there appeared among nobles and rich bourgeois the custom of insuring oneself through buying masses in advance of one's death — a "*post-mortem* fire insurance," as Eamon Duffy calls it.[50]

In the rural folklore collected across Europe in the 19th century, we find many remnants of medieval beliefs in various modes of interaction between the living and the dead, such as the need for the family dead to be ritually welcomed home and fed on special occasions. However, we also observe that the stories relating to such interactions have been transformed as a result of the disapproval of priests and missionaries, so that many supernatural creatures who used to be understood as the dead have lost their identity, surviving in folk tales as supernatural creatures of many sorts — good ones and bad ones, wee ones and giant ones. Names that used to be understood locally as designating special kinds of dead, such as dwarfs, trolls, leprechauns, or "Good Neighbours" — for the dead don't like to be called dead — lost the memory of their past human life, so to speak. But in places where pagan beliefs had survived Christianization in fuller form, folklorists have often been confused by the difficulty of

50 Eamon Duffy, *The Stripping of the Altars: Traditional Religion in England c.1400–c.1580*, Yale UP, 1992, p. 302.

distinguishing between the two categories of beings. W. Y. Evans-Wentz, for example, wrote in *The Fairy Faith in Celtic Countries*: "the striking likeness constantly appearing in our evidence between the ordinary apparitional fairies and the ghosts of the dead show that there is often no essential and sometimes no distinguishable difference between these two orders of beings, nor between the world of the dead and fairyland."[51] There is evidence that folklorists like the Grimm brothers, being less interested in collecting ghost stories than fairy tales, have sometimes transformed the former into the latter.[52] A similar process can already be observed in the retelling of the "Matter of Britain" by medieval poets such as Marie de France. I have provided many examples in my book *La Mort féerique*, based on my doctoral thesis in medieval anthropology.[53] One of the most common themes of folk stories involves young maidens who died before marriage and haunt the living in the form of fairies looking for the love of a mortal man; the origin of their condition is often erased or encrypted in the literate versions. The clearest example of a departed human who is transformed by the narrative tradition into a fairy is Cinderella's fairy godmother: in the oldest version of this international tale, she was none other than the ghost of the dead mother.[54] This case perfectly illustrates how Christianization slowly eroded pagan beliefs in the persistence of social bonds of love and mutual aid between the living and the dead.

Russian Orthodoxy has been more tolerant of this set of beliefs than Roman Catholicism, which is why the cult of the familial dead

---

51 W. Y. Evans-Wentz, *The Fairy Faith in Celtic Countries*, 1911, Citadel Press, 1994, p. 18.

52 Norm Cohen, "introduction" to Gordon Hall Gerould, *The Grateful Dead: The History of a Folk Story* (1908), University of Illinois Press, 2000, pp. xxi–xxii.

53 Laurent Guyénot, *La Mort féerique. Anthropologie du merveilleux (XIIe–XVe siècle)*, Gallimard, 2011.

54 Anna Birgitta Rooth, *The Cinderella Cycle*, Gleerups, 1951, pp. 15–17.

has survived until recent times in barely altered form in rural Russia. George Fedotov wrote in *The Russian Religious Mind*:

> In pagan times all the dead became minor gods whose cult represented the very core of the Slavic religion. … The chief of the ancestors, or the founder of the *rod* [the Russian equivalent of the Roman *gens* or the Celtic *clan*] became a particular patron of the house, who was, and still is called by the general name of 'house spirit' (*Domovoi*). The belief in *Domovoi* was very common among the peasants in the nineteenth century. Every house had its particular house spirit who was thought of as an old dwarf living under the threshold, in the stove, or in the horse stall.[55]

Andrei Siniavsky's classic book on Russian folklore contains a few pages on the enduring belief in the *Domovoi:* "Each izba has its own *Domovoi*," who is "the secret master" of the house, often called "grandfather" because he is "the deified ancestor of the clan, or the founding ancestor of the family."[56]

Atomic Soul and Genetic Sin

As mentioned earlier, the archaic conception of kinship was encapsulated in the idea of blood, understood as the vehicle of physical, moral and spiritual qualities. The blood of ancestors that runs in the veins of their descendants is a sort of genealogical soul. This concept is entirely foreign to Christianity—except in the case of the blood of Christ. The contrast between the Christian individual soul and the ancient holistic idea of blood is key to understanding the paradigm shift brought about by Christianity. Here, as in many other cases, Saint Augustine had an overwhelming influence on the doctrines specific to Western Christianity. Augustine rejected Tertullian's "traducianism," the theory that all souls derive from Adam's through

55 George P. Fedotov, *The Russian Religious Mind: Kievan Christianity, the Tenth to the Thirteenth Centuries*, Harper Torchbooks, 1946, p. 17.

56 André Siniavski, *Ivan le Simple. Paganisme, magie et religion du peuple russe,* Albin Michel, 1990, pp.130–134.

a genealogical process, and instead posited that God creates a new soul for every new body ("creationism"). The soul of each individual therefore owes nothing to his or her ancestors. Thomas Aquinas (1225–74) remained an Augustinian on this issue, unequivocally asserting that every single human soul is directly created by God, while condemning as heretical the belief that it comes from the "seed" of parents. God being equitable, all souls are equal in value and potential. Obviously, there is no difference in kind here between a male soul and a female soul.

Somewhat in contradiction to his theory of the soul, Augustine also asserts that Adam's original sin is transmitted from father to son. Thus, our soul inherits nothing from our parents, except this toxic element, from which only baptism can cure us. This doctrine is found in embryonic form in Saint Paul, who makes the blood of Christ the symbol of a new lineage that extracts the Christian from the lineage of sin (Romans 5:12–21; Ephesians 2:11–13). But it was Augustine who made the doctrine of original sin central to Latin Christianity. According to John Meyendorff, "Augustinian thought had practically no effect on the Byzantine world and the meaning of Adam's sin and its consequences was understood there in a very different way." While Catholicism insists on the necessity—as well as the impossibility—of extirpating man from his state of sin, Orthodoxy emphasizes *theosis*, or "deification": "God became man so that man may become God," in the formula attributed to Athanasius of Alexandria.[57]

The Augustinian theory of the soul does not allow for the concept of psychological heredity, let alone spiritual heredity (if it is possible to distinguish between the two, i.e., to explain how *psyche* differs from *spiritus*). One would search in vain in Catholic theology for some "depth psychology" worthy of the name which would consider transgenerational factors. Such notions could only appear in secular science, and only after a certain degree of de-Christianization.

57 Jean Meyendorff, *Initiation à la théologie byzantine*, Le Cerf, 2005, p. 192.

Psychoanalysis, despite the dubious nature of its scientific claims, and the profoundly disturbing effect of its Oedipus theory (the supposedly universal secret wish of every son to kill his father), has raised some good questions, especially in France with the theory of "ghosts" formulated by Nicolas Abraham and Maria Török in 1978: they define a "ghost" as "a formation of the unconscious that has the particularity of never having been conscious ... and of resulting from the passage, the mode of which remains to be determined, from the unconscious of a parent to the unconscious of a child."[58] These mysterious psychic forces, triggered by traumas or family secrets, can skip a generation or two, and their effects can last for seven generations. Ivan Boszormenyi-Nagy, a pioneer in the field of transgenerational psychology, has documented the "invisible loyalties" that unconsciously connect us with our ancestors and shape our destiny, on the basis of a system of values, debts and merits.[59]

Psychiatry focuses on the pathological, but we obviously don't inherit only the worst parts of our ancestors. This famous quote from Carl Jung's autobiographical interviews provides a fuller perspective:

> When I worked on my family tree, I understood the strange communion of the destiny that unites me to my ancestors. I had the strong feeling that it was under the influence of events and problems that were incomplete and unresolved by my parents, my grandparents, and my other ancestors. I had the impression that there is often in the family an impersonal Karma transmitted from parents to children. I always knew that I had to answer questions already asked by my ancestors or I had to conclude, or continue on the previously unresolved issues.[60]

---

58 Nicolas Abraham et Maria Török, *L'Écorce et le Noyau,* Aubier-Flammarion, 1978, p. 429.

59 Ivan Boszormenyi-Nagy, *Invisible Loyalties: Reciprocity in Intergenerational Family Therapy,* Harper & Row, 1973; also Anne Ancelin Schutzenberger, *The Ancestor Syndrome: Transgenerational Psychotherapy and the Hidden Links in the Family Tree,* Routledge, 1998.

60 Carl Jung, *Memories, Dreams, Reflexions,* Collins & Routledge & Kegan Paul, 1963, p. 221.

Sociology converges toward the same conclusion. Gustave Le Bon writes in *The Psychology of Peoples* (1898):

> The dead, besides being infinitely more numerous than the living, are infinitely more powerful. They reign over the vast domain of the unconscious, that invisible domain which exerts its sway over all the manifestations of the intelligence and of character. A people is guided far more by its dead than by its living members. It is by its dead, and by its dead alone, that a race is founded. Century after century our departed ancestors have fashioned our ideas and sentiments, and in consequence all the motives of our conduct. The generations that have passed away do not bequeath us their physical constitution merely; they also bequeath us their thoughts. The dead are the only undisputed masters of the living. We bear the burden of their mistakes, we reap the reward of their virtues.[61]

Le Bon was not an adept of Kardecist spiritism. Although somewhat eccentric, he was a respected sociologist firmly grounded in the scientific method. But his words are almost incomprehensible to most of our contemporaries. A thousand years of Christian and then secular individualism have ruined our awareness of the genealogical link that connects us to the dead. We are now warned that to think in terms of the "law of blood" is to "think as a Nazi."[62]

With Darwin's theory, biology has come to remind us of the importance of heredity, but has reduced it to the crudest form of materialism. "We are survival machine-robot vehicles blindly programmed to preserve the selfish molecules known as genes," neo-Darwinian high-priest Richard Dawkins tells us in his 1976 best-selling book *The Selfish Gene,* congratulating himself in the preface to the second edition in 1989 that his theory "has become textbook orthodoxy."[63] The "selfish gene" image is misleading: Dawkins does not literally believe that genes are entities driven to replicate themselves by a will of their

61 Gustave Le Bon, *The Psychology of Peoples,* MacMillan, 1898, p. 11.

62 Johann Chapoutot, *The Law of Blood: Thinking and Acting as a Nazi,* Harvard, 2018.

63 Richard Dawkins, *The Selfish Gene,* Oxford UP, 2016, pp. xxix, xix.

own. If they were, they would be like transgenerational souls. In the neo-Darwinian model, genes are not intelligent beings, but simply molecules governed by the deterministic laws of chemistry. And they are the result of a series of chemical accidents selected over millions of years, starting with the first protein capable of self-replication.

In addition to being scientifically obsolete,[64] Darwinism is morally destructive not because it emphasizes the gravity of genealogy and heredity, but because it reduces those principles to random material processes, stripping them of their spiritual dimensions. Ultimately, Dawkins' metaphor is not without value if only we give it spiritual dimension. Genes, he writes, "created us, body and mind; and their preservation is the ultimate reason for our existence." In a spiritualist or Platonic conception of genetics (along the lines of Rupert Sheldrake's theory of morphic resonance, for example[65]), we can reconcile ourselves with the holistic notion that the individual, as a spirit and not just a body, is always a link in a chain of generations. "Blood" is the name that was once given to this principle that connects us vertically to our ancestors and horizontally to our extended family and nation (and "nation," by the way, derives from the Latin *natio*, "birth").

The WEIRD West

In *The WEIRDest people in the World*, Joseph Henrich provides measurable evidence of how, in the West, "the Church's dismantling of intensive kinship in medieval Europe inadvertently pushed Europeans, and later populations on other continents, toward a WEIRDer [more individualistic] psychology." Studies conducted by Henrich's research

---

64 Michael Behe, *Darwin's Black Box: The Biochemical Challenge to Evolution*, Free Press, 2006; Stephen Meyer, *Darwin's Doubt: The Explosive Origin of Animal Life and the Case for Intelligent Design*, HarperOne, 2013.

65 Rupert Sheldrake, *The Presence of the Past: Morphic Resonance and the Habits of Nature*, Icon Books, 2011.

team and others show that "The longer a population was exposed to the Western Church, the weaker its families and WEIRDer its psychological patterns are today." The most significant effect is a shift from "interpersonal" to "impersonal prosociality": "In worlds dominated by impersonal contexts, people depend on anonymous markets, insurance, courts, and other impersonal institutions instead of large relational networks and personal ties. Impersonal markets can thus have dual effects on our social psychology. They simultaneously reduce our interpersonal prosociality within our in-groups and increase our impersonal prosociality with acquaintances and strangers."

The evolution of Western societies toward this impersonal prosociality was driven by multiple factors, some of which are recent and independent of the Church. The transition from an oral society to a written society is one factor: the more we write, the less we speak, and while speech is always interpersonal, writing is much less so. Mechanization is another factor: there is a degree of interpersonal relationship with horses that we do not have with engines. Other factors include urbanization. But long before that, according to Henrich, who builds on the work of the above-cited Jack Goody, the Church had undermined the anthropological defenses that could have helped us resist the dissolving effect of modernity. Comparative studies show that each century of Western Church exposure cuts the rate of cousin marriage by nearly 60 percent, and another study has shown that "People from countries with higher rates of cousin marriage reveal a more holistic thinking style."[66]

Joseph Henrich has the merit of challenging Western ethnocentrism and pointing to the "weirdness" of our value-system. However, although he expresses no sympathy for the Catholic Church, he has a rather positive appraisal of the kind of individualism it has produced. He doesn't dwell on its heavy cost for both the West and the Rest. He argues that the Church, by weakening kinship solidarity, created

66 Henrich, *The WEIRDest People in the World, op. cit.*, pp. 193, 252, 299, 222, 226, 240.

needs and opportunities for new forms of solidarity, cooperation and partnership: "The very idea that a person can act freely, independently of their clans, kindreds, or lineages, to make socially isolated agreements (contracts) presupposes an unusually individualistic world of impersonal exchange. … Overall, the spontaneous formation and proliferation of voluntary organizations capable of self-governance and self-regulation — as illustrated by charter towns, monasteries, guilds, and universities — is one of the hallmarks of European populations in the second millennium."[67]

Loosening family loyalties also led to new concepts of government: "people began to ponder notions of individual rights, personal freedoms, the rule of law, and the protection of private property." These principles are encapsulated in the American Declaration of Independence, which claims as "self-evident, that all men are created equal, that they are endowed by their Creator with certain unalienable rights, that among these are life, liberty, and the pursuit of happiness." Henrich comments: "from the perspective of most human communities, the notion that each person has inherent rights or privileges disconnected from their social relationships or heritage is not self-evident. And from a scientific perspective, no 'rights' have yet been detected hiding in our DNA or elsewhere. This idea sells because it appeals to a particular cultural psychology."[68] To put it more bluntly, this abstract idea is totally disconnected from anthropological reality, and the particular cultural psychology that supports it is dangerously delusional — not to mention the blatant hypocrisy of writing such a profession of faith while depriving Native Americans of their natural rights to their ancestral land, and importing African slaves to support White men's "pursuit of happiness." The United States is founded on a lie that is coming back to haunt it.

67 *Ibid.*, pp. 427, 355.

68 *Ibid.*, pp. 320, 400.

Individualism is the core value of European societies. "Contractualist" theories based on individual freedom began with Thomas Hobbes (*Leviathan*, 1651) and led to Adam Smith (*The Wealth of Nations*, 1776) via Bernard Mandeville (*The Fable of the Bees*, 1714). According to Mandeville and Smith, men contribute best to the public good when they only look after their private interests. Unrestrained selfishness is supposed to guarantee social harmony thanks to the "Invisible Hand" of the market. We are now reaping the fruits of this madness. Shortly after Smith appeared Thomas Malthus, who followed the same train of thought in his *Essay on the Principle of Population* (1798), in which he opposed social welfare laws, arguing that "these laws create the poor whom they assist." Consequently, "if a man cannot feed his children, they must die of hunger." Malthus inspired Herbert Spencer, who in *Progress, its Laws and Causes* (1857) denounced the absurdity of socialist initiatives aimed at protecting weak individuals from the harsh laws of natural selection. Today, Spencer's theory is stigmatized as an abusive misappropriation of Darwin's biological theory, and is called "social Darwinism." In reality, Spencer's book was published two years before Darwin's *On the Origin of Species*. It was Spencer who paved the way for Darwin, and not the other way around. Karl Marx recognized that Darwin had merely projected "his own English society" onto the animal and plant kingdoms. Darwin's theory, he wrote to Engels, is nothing more than "the simple transposition, from the social realm to the living world, of Hobbes's doctrine: *bellum omnium contra omnes* [the war of all against all], and of the thesis of competition dear to bourgeois economists, associated with Malthusian population theory."[69] This complex array of theories constitutes the metaphysics underlying economic liberalism, and its influence extends to politics and international relations. In 1920, in the wake of WWI, the English playwright and polemicist Bernard Shaw warned in the preface to his

69 Marx's letter to Engels in 1862, quoted in André Pichot, *Aux origines des théories raciales, de la Bible à Darwin*, Flammarion, 2008, p. 167.

Back to Methuselah: "Neo-Darwinism [Darwin revisited by August Weismann] in politics has produced a European catastrophe of a magnitude so appalling, and a scope so unpredictable, that as I write these lines in 1920, it is still far from certain whether our civilization will survive it.»

Modern Western individualism, the secularized version of Christian individualism, may have stimulated creativity (although the causality would need to be seriously tested, such as by comparing, for example, liberal Europe and Confucianist China). But it came with a heavy price. The paradox of Western individualism is that it is a collective social construct. Alexander Dugin explains this point with reference to Émile Durkheim's sociological theory that "the contents of individual consciousness are entirely formed on the basis of collective consciousness":

> Thus, the very fact of declaring the individual the highest value and measure of things (liberalism) is a projection of the society, that is, a form of totalitarian influence and ideological induction. The individual is a social concept—without society, human being alone does not know if he is or not an individual, and whether individualism is or not the highest value. The individual learns that he is an individual, a private person only in a society where liberal ideology dominates and performs the function of the environment in operation. … Consequently, liberalism is a totalitarian ideology that insists, through classic methods of totalitarian propaganda, that the individual is the highest instance.[70]

70 Alexander Dugin, "The 'Third Totalitarianism' from the West," Geopolitika.ru/en, 4 July 2018.

Conclusion

Comparing himself to Copernicus, Oswald Spengler criticized the incurable Eurocentrism of Westerners in the first volume of *The Decline of the West,* published in 1918:

> The ground of West Europe is treated as a steady pole, a unique patch chosen on the surface of the sphere for no better reason, it seems, than because we live on it — and great histories of millennial duration and mighty far-away Cultures are made to revolve around this pole in all modesty. It is a quaintly conceived system of sun and planets. We select a single bit of ground as the natural centre of the historical system, and make it the central sun. From it all the events of history receive their real light, from it their importance is judged in *perspective.* But it is in our own West-European conceit alone that this phantom 'world-history,' which a breath of scepticism would dissipate, is acted out.[1]

A full century later, the West's confidence in its inherent superiority is on the decline. The word is out that it was only a fleeting occurrence in world history, and that it is about to end. Recent world-system historians, such as Andre Gunder Frank (*ReORIENT: Global Economy in the Asian Age*, 1998) and Kenneth Pomeranz (*The Great Divergence*, 2001), have set the record straight. Here is how Jack Goldstone summarizes their conclusions in his superb book published in 2008, *Why Europe?: The Rise of the West in World History 1500–1850*:

> In the last dozen years, a group of young economic and social historians has made some new and surprising arguments about World History.

1 Oswald Spengler, *The Decline of the West,* vol. 1, *op. cit.*, pp. 20–21.

> Instead of seeing the rise of the West as a long process of gradual advances in Europe while the rest of the world stood still, they have turned this story around. They argue that societies in Asia and the Middle East were the world leaders in economics; in science and technology; and in shipping, trade, and exploration until about AD 1500. At the time Europe emerged from the Middle Ages and entered its Renaissance, these scholars contend, Europe was well behind many of the advanced civilizations elsewhere in the world and did not catch up with and surpass the leading Asian societies until about AD 1800.[2]

In his masterful work *The Clash of Civilization and the Remaking of World Order*—often misrepresented by the neoconservatives who ignored its warning that "Western intervention in the affairs of other civilizations is probably the single most dangerous source of instability and potential global conflict in a multicivilizational world"—Samuel Huntington reviewed all the major "civilization blocs" and their relationships to one another, and he attempted to predict their development. China is undoubtedly the best prepared for the emerging multipolar world, being the archetypal civilization-state and boasting a huge diaspora strongly connected to the motherland. Since the 1990s, the People's Republic of China has set itself the goal "to become the champion of Chinese culture, the core state civilizational magnet toward which all other Chinese communities would orient themselves, and to resume its historical position, which it lost in the nineteenth century, as the hegemonic power in East Asia." Economically, China's regional ascendancy is already a reality. Huntington wrote:

> 'Greater China' is thus not simply an abstract concept. It is a rapidly growing cultural and economic reality and has begun to become a political one. Chinese were responsible for the dramatic economic development in the 1980s and 1990s: on the mainland, in the Tigers (three out of four of which are Chinese), and in Southeast Asia. The economy of East Asia is increasingly China-centered and Chinese-dominated. Chinese from Hong Kong,

---

2 Jack Goldstone, *Why Europe?, op. cit.*, p. viii.

> Taiwan, and Singapore have supplied much of the capital responsible for the growth of the mainland in the 1990s. Overseas Chinese elsewhere in Southeast Asia dominated the economies of their countries. In the early 1990s, Chinese made up 1 percent of the population of the Philippines but were responsible for 35 percent of the sales of domestically owned firms. In Indonesia in the mid 1980s, Chinese were 2–3 percent of the population, but owned roughly 70 percent of the private domestic capital. Seventeen of the twenty-five largest businesses were Chinese-controlled, and one Chinese conglomerate reportedly accounted for 5 percent of Indonesia's GNP. In the early 1990s Chinese were 10 percent of the population of Thailand but owned nine of the ten largest business groups and were responsible for 50 percent of its GNP. Chinese are about one-third of the population of Malaysia but almost totally dominate the economy. Outside Japan and Korea the East Asian economy is basically a Chinese economy.[3]

The so-called "bamboo network"—the ethnic bond of Chinese worldwide, even after living abroad for several generations—is indeed one of China's great assets. For the Chinese, "blood is thicker than water," and, as Huntington notes, "trust and commitment depend on personal contacts, not contracts or laws and other legal documents."[4] In Joseph Henrich's terminology, the Chinese practice "interpersonal prosociality." They combine a strong civilizational consciousness with a clan-based mindset on the grassroots level.

So far, China is the only superpower that has not been affected by the Mosaic curse. It counts some twelve million Christians (Catholics and Evangelicals) and about twenty million Muslims (among ethnic minorities), but overall it remains molded by Confucianism, which for more than two millennia has provided the Chinese with a metaphysical and ethical framework as well as a system of recruitment for government officials. Confucianism survived the Cultural Revolution, and today, "Confucianism has made a dramatic comeback as the bedrock of imperial Chinese ethics and governance, and

3 Samuel P. Huntington, *The Clash of Civilizations and the Remaking of World Order*, Simon & Schuster, 1996, pp. 312, 168–170.

4 *Ibid.*, p. 71.

other Chinese classics have become the pillars of Beijing's efforts to shore up its intellectual foundation and governance philosophy amid an intensifying ideological competition with the US-led West."[5] Xi Jinping himself often quotes Confucianist classics, and a book has been published with his commentary on his favorite quotes.[6] China has also made Confucius Institutes the main instruments of its cultural diplomacy. These are positive signs.

Confucianism is a "wisdom tradition" rather than a "religion." That's why it has a future: it is rational and non-dogmatic, requiring no faith in a special "revelation" of God or any other supernatural being; it has a cosmic, non-anthropomorphic concept of the divine (Heaven, *Tian,* 天), comparable to the cosmotheism of the Stoics and compatible with the metaphysical implications of the new science (Intelligent Design, for example); and it encourages ancestor veneration as the vertical axis of social order.

This verticality has been eroded in the West by two thousand years of Christianity, with the Christian social order essentially conceived as a horizontal flock of sheep guided by a good shepherd. The Western democratic ideal may be anti-clerical, but it is nonetheless Christian in inspiration. It is based on the assumption that it is possible to create a contractual social order from the pure horizontality of equal individuals. This is a mechanical conception of society that contrasts with the organic conception of Chinese thought, for which the root and model of any social framework is the family. Anglo-American liberalism has added to this contractual model the even more far-fetched assumption that a group of selfish individuals — through their very greed and consumerism — can create harmony, justice, and prosperity for all. Confucianism affirms the exact

---

5 Xinlu Liang, "How Xi Jinping is going back to Confucius to define China's future," *South China Morning Post,* 24 November 2024.

6 Xi Jinping, *How to Read Confucius and Other Chinese Classical Thinkers,* CN Times Books, 2015.

opposite principle: only by prioritizing the public good can individuals realize their full humanity.

The Chinese live, according to their Constitution, in "a socialist state governed by a people's democratic dictatorship," but democracy does not have the same meaning for them. The Chinese state is not democratic by our standards, but it is a republic (the People's Republic of China), and its governance demonstrates, in my view, that a republic works better when it favors meritocracy over democracy. The democratic concept of "popular sovereignty" runs counter to a universal law of human societies, which Italian political scientist Gaetano Mosca formulated in his book *The Ruling Class*, written in 1935: "In all societies, from societies that are very meagerly developed and have barely attained the dawnings of civilization, down to the most advanced and powerful societies, two classes of people appear: a class that rules and a class that is ruled. The first class, always the less numerous, performs all political functions, monopolizes power and enjoys the advantages that power brings, whereas the second, the more numerous class, is directed and controlled by the first..."[7]

A ruling class can be overthrown, either by a foreign conquest, by a *coup d'état*, by a popular revolution, or in more subtle ways that are not always immediately perceptible by the ruled; but any change of regime leads inevitably to the formation of a new ruling class, for "in all forms of government the real and actual power resides in a ruling minority."[8] It follows that democracy—at least for any social community bigger than a Greek city—is a lie, and necessarily ends up being the government of liars.

But republic is a different concept. Democracy is defined by universal suffrage. Republic is defined by the rule of law—the same law for everyone, top to bottom. It was the genius of the Romans to apply this Greek idea on a grand scale. The Empire remained, in

7 Gaetano Mosca, *The Ruling Class*, McGraw-Hill, 1935, p. 50.

8 *Ibid.*, pp. 50, 336.

theory, a Republic, under the banner SPQR (*senatus populusque romanus*, "the Senate and the Roman people"), with the Emperor being only the *princeps senatus* submitted to the same law as others. This was so despite the imperial cult, which, properly understood, was the cult of the emperor's *genius*, more or less equated with Rome's *genius*. Interestingly, Peter Heather compares "public life in the Roman Empire" to "a one-party state, in which loyalty to the system was drilled into you from birth and reinforced with regular opportunities to demonstrate it." As in China's one-party state, "active political participation was very narrowly based": the politically active class probably amounted to "less than 5 per cent of the population."[9] The Eastern Empire was more republican than its Western counterpart, as Anthony Kaldellis has argued, in the sense that the ruling class was not limited to the landowning aristocracy. The Byzantine Empire, according to Christopher Dawson, "was ruled … after the manner of the Chinese, by an official class of *litterati* who prided themselves on their learning and scholarship."[10]

I find such comparisons between Roman and Chinese civilizations thought-provoking. It is a deepening conviction of mine that European civilization is fundamentally Roman (and by Roman I mean Helleno-Roman), and that Christianity has contributed little to the European genius; it has been a superstructure on a preexisting foundation. The European genius—in art, philosophy, science, technology, politics—was the most creative during the Renaissance, which was when Europe rediscovered and redefined itself as Roman. Everything the world admires in European civilization came from the Roman *genius* through the Renaissance. The Helleno-Roman philosophical tradition could give us everything that Confucianism has given to China.

9 Peter Heather, *The Fall of the Roman Empire: A New History*, MacMillan, 2005, pp. 132–133.

10 Christopher Dawson, *The Making of Europe: An Introduction to the History of European Unity*, Meridian, 1956, p. 113.

Had it not been for Constantine the Great and his Christian faith, Socrates might have been to Europeans what Confucius is to the Chinese (both were born 8,000 miles apart, but only 80 years apart). Among the many schools that paid tribute to Socrates, the Stoics had the greatest, albeit the most diffuse, influence on the Romans.[11] Stoicism had the favor of Cicero, and later of Emperor Marcus Aurelius, the last of "the five good emperors" (Machiavelli) whose reign was, according to Gibbon, "possibly the only period in history in which the happiness of a great people was the sole object of government."[12] Stoicism is the Western philosophy that most resembles Confucianism in its general spirit, and it arguably could have sustained the Roman civilization spiritually, ethically, and politically for a thousand more years. It later resurfaced to play a significant role in the Renaissance. Cicero's Stoic treatise *on Duty* (*De Officiis*) was the first classical text to be printed, in 1465. Erasmus published Seneca's work in 1515, and in 1584 Justus Lipsius promoted Stoicism in his essay *On Constancy*, which impressed many thinkers, such as Montaigne (1533–92), and gave rise to what is known as Renaissance Neo-Stoicism.

Like most Greek and Roman philosophers, the Stoics held reason as the highest faculty of the soul, through which man can understand the world and himself. For the Stoics, the Cosmos is rational, and human reason (*logos*) is man's participation in the divine Reason (*Logos*). They could have said, as Hegel would much later: "To him who looks at the world rationally, the world looks rationally back; the two exist in a reciprocal relationship."[13] By reason alone man

11 Anthony A. Long, *Stoic Studies*, Cambridge UP, 1996.

12 Gibbon includes Marcus Aurelius' predecessor Antoninus Pius in that assessment. Quoted in Lisa Hill and Eden Blazejak, *Stoicism and the Western Political Tradition*, Palgrave/Macmillan, 2021.

13 G. W. F. Hegel, *Lectures on the Philosophy of World History*, "Introduction: Reason in History," in Robert Stern, *The Routledge Guidebook to Hegel's Phenomenology of Spirit*, Routledge, 2001, p. 11.

can know good from evil, understand and practice virtue, but the foundation of the good life is the realization of the organic interconnectedness of all things. The Stoics accepted the Socratic equation of wisdom, virtue, and happiness. True happiness is the joy of fulfilling one's purpose in the Cosmos and in human society.

From the premise that God is infinite by definition, the Stoics deduced that nothing can exist outside Him. Consequently, God and the Cosmos are one. The Greek word *kosmos*, which translates as "order" or "harmony," refers, rather than to the universe itself, to the ordering principle underlying the universe. The Stoic concept of the cosmic God is very close to the Confucianist concept of Heaven. The Stoics were monotheists in the sense that they believed in the unicity of God, but they insisted on the immanent presence of God in everything. Most Greek and Roman philosophers saw no incompatibility between the unity of the divine and the plurality of its manifestations or representations as worshipped by the people or the state. They often used the words "God" (*Zeus*), "the god" (*o theos*) or "the gods" (*oi theoi*) interchangeably. In that sense, polytheism was philosophically resolved in an inclusive monotheism.

Stoic cosmotheism, generally called pantheism, is denounced as atheism in disguise by Christian theologians because it rejects the anthropomorphic Christian God in favor of a "cosmomorphic" concept of God. Nevertheless, until the Gregorian Reform, there were still some marginal cosmotheist voices in Christendom. In the 9th century, we find it in the writings of the Irish lay scholar John Scotus Eriugena, who declared: "Everything is in God and God is in everything, and nothing can come from anywhere but Him, for everything is born of Him, through Him and in Him." Scotus proclaimed the sovereignty of reason in man, superior to the authority of Scripture. He was twice condemned by the archbishop of Lyon, but found protection at the court of Charles the Bald. Despite Church censorship, his work was rediscovered at the end of the 12th century by Amaury of Chartres, who taught logic at the University of Paris. After Amaury's death, his followers were hunted down for teaching, as reported by Thomas Aquinas, "that God was the formal principle of all things." According to sources recently collected, the Amauricians believed in "the immanent presence of the Divinity in the whole of Creation, which renders useless the grace conferred by the sacraments."[14] In 1210, fourteen of them, including some priests and deacons, were sentenced to the stake, and ten others to life imprisonment.

We don't know whether Master Eckhart (1260–1328), a Dominican monk teaching at the Sorbonne in the early 14th century, had ever heard of Scotus or Amaury, but he expressed his mystical insights in Stoic-sounding formulas: "The eye with which God looks at me is the eye with which I look at Him; my eye and His eye are identical." His proposition that the human soul is uncreated because it is a particle of God was condemned by Pope John XXII's bull *In agro dominico* in 1329. Eckhart taught in Latin at the Sorbonne, but he preached in German to nuns, who preserved notes of his sermons. As Ernst Benz explains in *The Mystical Sources of German Romantic Philosophy*, the German language had so far been excluded from philosophical and theological discourse, and Eckhart's novel use of it to convey his mystical experiences had a considerable influence on later German thought: thanks to Eckhart, German philosophy arose on a mystical foundation.[15] Eckhart was condemned, but his writings survived to be rediscovered by Franz von Baader, and had a great influence on German idealist philosophers of the late 18th and early 19th centuries (Fichte, Schelling, Hegel). So did another later German mystic, Jakob Boehme (1575–1624), who wrote that "The whole of

14 Marie-Thérèse D'Alverny, "un fragment du procès des Aumauriciens," *Archives d'histoire Doctrinale et Littéraire Du Moyen Age*, vol. 18, 1950, pp. 325–336.

15 Ernst Benz, *The Mystical Sources of German Romantic Philosophy*, Pickwick Publications, 1983, pp. 8–10.

nature is the body or corporeality of God."[16] Boehme was lucky enough to live in one of the most tolerant states of his time.

Giordano Bruno, Boehme's contemporary, did not have that chance. He was condemned to the stake in 1600 after seven years of imprisonment with repeated torture. Bruno went beyond Copernicus' heliocentrism by teaching that the universe had neither center nor circumference. He began his defense before the Congregation of the Holy Office, otherwise known as the Inquisition, with these words: "I teach the infinity of the universe and the action of divine power in its infinity."[17]

Scotus, Amaury, Eckhart, Boehme, and Bruno are some of the mystics and intellectuals that German scholar Sigrid Hunke introduces in her book on "Europe's Other Religion" (*Europas andere Religion*, published in 1969, translated into French but unfortunately not in English), which presents an uplifting apologetics of the "heretical" cosmotheist tradition that exerted so much influence on German philosophy after Kant. Hunke includes in this tradition Spinoza (1632–1677), to whom the term "pantheist" was first applied. The "pantheist controversy," sparked by the posthumous revelation of Lessing's adherence to Spinozism, is the backdrop to Immanuel Kant's *Critique of the Faculty of Judgment*, published in 1790, and contributed in no small way to post-Kantian idealism. Hegel was also much impressed by Spinoza in his young age, writing in one of his early essays, *Faith and Knowledge* (1802), that "Spinoza constitutes such a crucial point for modern philosophy that we might say in effect that there is a choice between Spinozism and no philosophy at all."[18] Hegel represented, in philosophy, the culmination of a heroic German effort to revive Greco-Roman cosmotheism — in other

16 Nicolas Berdiaev, *Études sur Jacob Boehme* (1945), Éditions Localement Transcendantes, 2020, p. 6.

17 Sigrid Hunke, *La Vraie religion de l'Europe. La foi des « hérétiques »*, Livre-Club du Labyrinthe, 1985, pp. 75–83.

18 Pierre Macherey, *Hegel or Spinoza*, University of Minnesota Press, 1979, p. 13.

words, to free the idea of God (or *Geist*) from the chains of Jewish monotheism.

To conclude this book on a hopeful note, let the above serve to point out that Europe has other spiritual resources besides Christianity. It has within its own Helleno-Roman roots an inexhaustible spring of wisdom that is comparable to the Confucian tradition that the Chinese can still tap into. From this perspective, the papal curse was only an aggravation of a more ancient curse cast upon the Roman Empire by Constantine the Great and his heirs, who waged a war to the death not only on the gods and their temples, but on the very spirit that had produced the Greek miracle and the genius of Roman civilization. The process and consequences of Christianization will be the subject of my next book.

Selected Bibliography

Alphandéry, Paul, and Alphonse Dupront. *La Chrétienté et l'idée de croisade*. Paris: Albin Michel, 1995.

Arnold, Jonathan J. *Theoderic and the Roman Imperial Restoration*. Cambridge: Cambridge University Press, 2014.

Arquillière, Henri-Xavier. *L'Augustinisme politique: Essai sur la formation des théories politiques au Moyen Âge*. Paris: Vrin, 1972 [1934].

Ball, Warwick. *Sultans of Rome: The Turkish World Expansion*. Solihull: Olive Branch Press, 2013.

Barber, Malcolm. *The Two Cities: Medieval Europe 1050–1320*. London: Routledge, 1992.

Bartlett, Robert. *The Making of Europe: Conquest, Colonization and Cultural Change, 950–1350*. London: Penguin Books, 1994.

Benoist-Méchin, Jacques. *Frédéric de Hohenstaufen ou le rêve excommunié (1194–1250)*. Paris: Perrin, 2008.

Blin, Arnaud. *1648: La Paix de Westphalie, ou la naissance de l'Europe politique moderne*. Brussels: Éditions Complexe, 2006.

Bloch, Marc. *Feudal Society*. Vol. 1, *The Growth of Ties of Dependence*. London: Routledge, 1962.

Bogdan, Henry. *Histoire de l'Allemagne*. Paris: Tempus/Perrin, 2003 [1999].

Boulle, Pierre. *L'Étrange croisade de l'empereur Frédéric II*. Paris: Flammarion, 1968.

Cantor, Norman. *The Civilization of the Middle Ages*. New York: HarperPerennial, 1994.

Coker, Christopher. *The Rise of the Civilizational State*. Cambridge: Polity Press, 2019.

Cottret, Bernard. *Histoire de l'Angleterre: De Guillaume le Conquérant à nos jours*. Paris: Texto/Tallandier, 2019.

Dawson, Christopher. *Medieval Essays*. Washington, DC: Catholic University of America Press, 1954.

———. *The Making of Europe: An Introduction to the History of European Unity*. New York: Meridian, 1956.

Delaney, Carol. *Columbus and the Quest for Jerusalem*. New York: Free Press, 2012.

Demacopoulos, George. *Colonizing Christianity: Greek and Latin Religious Identity in the Era of the Fourth Crusade*. New York: Fordham University Press, 2019.

Duby, Georges. *The Knight, the Lady, and the Priest: The Making of Modern Marriage in Medieval France*. New York: Pantheon Books, 1981.

Dumont, Louis. *Essays on Individualism: Modern Ideology in Anthropological Perspective*. Chicago: University of Chicago Press, 1992.

Folz, Robert. *The Concept of Empire in Western Europe from the Fifth to the Fourteenth Century*. London: Edward Arnold, 1969.

Fustel de Coulanges, Numa. *The Ancient City: A Study of the Religion, Laws, and Institutions of Greece and Rome*. New York: Pentianos Classics, 2017.

Goldstone, Jack. *Why Europe?: The Rise of the West in World History, 1500–1850*. New York: McGraw-Hill, 2009.

Goody, Jack. *The Development of the Family and Marriage in Europe*. Cambridge: Cambridge University Press, 1983.

———. *The European Family: An Historico-Anthropological Essay*. Oxford: Blackwell, 2000.

Gouguenheim, Sylvain. *Aristote au Mont Saint-Michel: Les racines grecques de l'Europe chrétienne*. Paris: Seuil, 2008.

Guyénot, Laurent. *La Lance qui saigne: Hypertextes et métatextes du "Conte du Graal."* Paris: Champion, 2010.

Hale, John. *The Civilization of Europe in the Renaissance*. London: Fontana Press, 1994.

Harris, Jonathan. *Byzantium and the Crusades*. 2nd ed. London: Bloomsbury Academic, 2014.

Heather, Peter. *Christendom: The Triumph of a Religion*. New York: Knopf, 2023.

———. *The Restoration of Rome: Barbarian Popes and Imperial Pretenders*. Oxford: Oxford University Press, 2014.

Henrich, Joseph. *The WEIRDest People in the World: How the West Became Psychologically Peculiar and Particularly Prosperous*. New York: Farrar, Straus and Giroux, 2020.

Hirschi, Caspar. *The Origins of Nationalism: An Alternative History from Ancient Rome to Early Modern Germany*. Cambridge: Cambridge University Press, 2012.

Housley, Norman. *Contesting the Crusades*. Oxford: Blackwell, 2006.

Hunke, Sigrid. *La Vraie religion de l'Europe: La foi des "hérétiques."* Paris: Livre-Club du Labyrinthe, 1985.

Huntington, Samuel P. *The Clash of Civilizations and the Remaking of World Order*. New York: Simon & Schuster, 1996.

Iorga, Nicolae. *Byzantium after Byzantium*. New York: Histria Books, 2022.

Johnstone, Diana. *Fools' Crusade: Yugoslavia, NATO and Western Delusions*. London: Pluto Press, 2002.

Jones, Eric. *The European Miracle: Environments, Economies and Geopolitics in the History of Europe and Asia*. Cambridge: Cambridge University Press, 2003.

Jouvenel, Bertrand de. *On Power: Its Nature and the History of Its Growth*. Boston: Beacon Press, 1962.

Kaldellis, Anthony. *Byzantium Unbound*. Leeds: ARC Humanities Press, 2019.

———. *Hellenism in Byzantium: The Transformation of Greek Identity and the Reception of the Classical Tradition*. Cambridge: Cambridge University Press, 2007.

———. *Romanland: Ethnicity and Empire in Byzantium*. Cambridge, MA: Belknap Press, 2019.

———. *Streams of Gold, Rivers of Blood: The Rise and Fall of Byzantium, 955 A.D. to the First Crusade*. Oxford: Oxford University Press, 2019.

Kantorowicz, Ernst. *Frederick the Second (1194–1250)*. New York: Frederick Ungar Publishing, 1957 [1931].

Khomiakoff, Aleksei Stepanovitch. *L'Église latine et le protestantisme au point de vue de l'Église d'Orient*. Paris, 1872.

Leontiev, Konstantin. *Byzantinism and Slavdom*. Tacoma, WA: Taxiarch Press, 2020 [1875].

Madariaga, Salvador de. *Portrait of Europe*. Tuscaloosa: University of Alabama Press, 1967 [1952].

McNeill, William H. *The Pursuit of Power: Technology, Armed Forces, and Society since A.D. 1000*. Chicago: University of Chicago Press, 1982.

Meyendorff, John. *Byzantium and the Rise of Russia*. Cambridge: Cambridge University Press, 1981.

Mitterauer, Michael. *Why Europe: The Medieval Origins of Its Special Path*. Chicago: University of Chicago Press, 2010.

Mitterauer, Michael, and Reinhard Sieder. *The European Family: Patriarchy to Partnership from the Middle Ages to the Present*. Chicago: University of Chicago Press, 1982.

Moore, Robert I. *The First European Revolution, c. 970–1215*. Oxford: Basil Blackwell, 2000.

Morris, Ian. *Why the West Rules—for Now: The Patterns of History and What They Reveal About the Future*. New York: Farrar, Straus and Giroux, 2010.

Pirenne, Henri. *Mohammed and Charlemagne*. New York: Dover Publications, 2012. Originally published 1954.

Prawer, Joshua. *The Latin Kingdom of Jerusalem: European Colonialism in the Middle Ages*. London: Weidenfeld & Nicolson, 1972.

Rapp, Francis. *Le Saint Empire romain germanique: D'Otton le Grand à Charles Quint*. Paris: Seuil, 2003.

Riley-Smith, Jonathan. *The First Crusade and the Idea of Crusading*. Philadelphia: University of Pennsylvania Press, 1986.

Riley-Smith, Louise, and Jonathan Riley-Smith, eds. and trans. *The Crusades: Ideas and Reality, 1095–1274*. London: Edward Arnold, 1981.

Robinson, I. S. *The Papacy, 1073–1198: Continuity and Innovation*. Cambridge: Cambridge University Press, 1990.

———. *Henry IV of Germany, 1056–1106*. Cambridge: Cambridge University Press, 2008.

Roquebert, Michel. *Histoire des cathares*. Paris: Perrin/Tempus, 1999.

Runciman, Steven. *A History of the Crusades*. 3 vols. London: Penguin Classics, 2016.

———. *Byzantine Civilisation*. London: Arnold & Co., 1933.

Scheidel, Walter. *Escape from Rome: The Failure of Empire and the Road to Prosperity*. Princeton, NJ: Princeton University Press, 2019.

Schiavone, Aldo. *The Invention of Law in the West*. Cambridge, MA: Harvard University Press, 2012.

Spengler, Oswald. *The Decline of the West*. Vol. 1. London: Legend Books, 2024 [1918].

———. *Prussianism and Socialism*. London: Legend Books, 2023 [1919].

Strayer, Joseph Reese. *On the Medieval Origins of the Modern State*. Princeton, NJ: Princeton University Press, 1973.

Todd, Emmanuel. *La Défaite de l'Occident*. Paris: Gallimard, 2024.

Tout, Thomas Frederick. *The Empire and the Papacy (918–1273)*. London: Rivington, 1921.

Trubetzkoy, Nikolai Sergeevich. *The Legacy of Genghis Khan and Other Essays on Russian Identity*. Ann Arbor: Michigan Slavic Publications, 1991.

Tyerman, Christopher. *God's War: A New History of the Crusades*. London: Penguin, 2006.

Vauchez, André, dir. *Rome au Moyen Âge*. Paris: Éditions du Cerf, 2021.

Vogel, Hans. *How Europe Became American*. London: Arktos, 2024.

Wells, Collin. *Sailing from Byzantium: How a Lost Empire Shaped the World*. New York: Bantam, 2008.

Wickham, Chris. *The Inheritance of Rome: A History of Europe from 400 to 1000*. London: Penguin Books, 2010.

Wilson, Peter H. *Heart of Europe: A History of the Holy Roman Empire*. Cambridge, MA: Belknap Press, 2020.

Wolff, Philippe. *The Awakening of Europe*. London: Penguin, 1968.

OTHER BOOKS PUBLISHED BY ARKTOS

Virginia Abernethy	*Born Abroad*
Sri Dharma Pravartaka Acharya	*The Dharma Manifesto*
Joakim Andersen	*Rising from the Ruins*
Winston C. Banks	*Excessive Immigration*
Stephen Baskerville	*Who Lost America?*
Alfred Baeumler	*Nietzsche: Philosopher and Politician*
Matt Battaglioli	*The Consequences of Equality*
Alain de Benoist	*Beyond Human Rights* *Carl Schmitt Today* *The Ideology of Sameness* *The Indo-Europeans* *Manifesto for a European Renaissance* *On the Brink of the Abyss* *The Problem of Democracy* *Runes and the Origins of Writing* *View from the Right* (vol. 1–3)
Armand Berger	*Tolkien, Europe, and Tradition*
Pawel Bielawski	*European Apostasy*
Arthur Moeller van den Bruck	*Germany's Third Empire*
Kerry Bolton	*The Perversion of Normality* *Revolution from Above* *Yockey: A Fascist Odyssey*
Isac Boman	*Money Power*
Daniel Branco	*The Absolute Philosopher*
Charles William Dailey	*The Serpent Symbol in Tradition*
Antoine Dresse	*Political Realism*
Ricardo Duchesne	*Faustian Man in a Multicultural Age*
Alexander Dugin	*Ethnos and Society* *Ethnosociology* *Eurasian Mission* *The Fourth Political Theory* *The Great Awakening vs the Great Reset* *Last War of the World-Island* *Politica Aeterna* *Political Platonism* *Putin vs Putin* *The Rise of the Fourth Political Theory* *The Trump Revolution* *Templars of the Proletariat* *The Theory of a Multipolar World*
Daria Dugina	*A Theory of Europe*
Edward Dutton	*Race Differences in Ethnocentrism*
Mark Dyal	*Hated and Proud*
Clare Ellis	*The Blackening of Europe* (vol. 1–3)
Koenraad Elst	*Return of the Swastika*
Julius Evola	*The Bow and the Club* *Fascism Viewed from the Right* *A Handbook for Right-Wing Youth* *Metaphysics of Power* *Metaphysics of War* *The Myth of the Blood*

OTHER BOOKS PUBLISHED BY ARKTOS

	Notes on the Third Reich
	Pagan Imperialism
	Recognitions
	A Traditionalist Confronts Fascism
Guillaume Faye	*Against Russophobia*
	Archeofuturism
	Archeofuturism 2.0
	The Colonisation of Europe
	Convergence of Catastrophes
	Ethnic Apocalypse
	The Genocide System
	A Global Coup
	Prelude to War
	Sex and Deviance
	Understanding Islam
	Why We Fight
Daniel S. Forrest	*Suprahumanism*
Andrew Fraser	*Dissident Dispatches*
	Reinventing Aristocracy in the Age of Woke Capital
	The WASP Question
Génération Identitaire	*We are Generation Identity*
Peter Goodchild	*The Taxi Driver from Baghdad*
	The Western Path
Paul Gottfried	*War and Democracy*
Georges Guiscard	*White Privilege*
Petr Hampl	*Breached Enclosure*
Porus Homi Havewala	*The Saga of the Aryan Race*
Richard Houck	*Liberalism Unmasked*
A. J. Illingworth	*Political Justice*
Institut Iliade	*For a European Awakening*
	Guardians of Heritage
Alexander Jacob	*De Naturae Natura*
Jason Reza Jorjani	*Artemis Unveiled*
	Closer Encounters
	Erosophia
	Faustian Futurist
	Iranian Leviathan
	Lovers of Sophia
	Metapolemos
	Novel Folklore
	Philosophy of the Future
	Prometheism
	Promethean Pirate
	Prometheus and Atlas
	Psychotron
	Thanosis
	Uber Man
	World State of Emergency
Henrik Jonasson	*Sigmund*
Edgar Julius Jung	*The Significance of the German Revolution*
Ruuben Kaalep & August Meister	*Rebirth of Europe*
Lance Kennedy	*The Book of the Scribe*
James Kirkpatrick	*Conservatism Inc.*

OTHER BOOKS PUBLISHED BY ARKTOS

Ludwig Klages	*The Biocentric Worldview* *Cosmogonic Reflections* *The Science of Character*
Andrew Korybko	*Hybrid Wars*
Pierre Krebs	*Guillaume Faye: Truths & Tributes* *Fighting for the Essence*
Julien Langella	*Catholic and Identitarian*
Henri Levavasseur	*Identity: The Foundation of the City*
John Bruce Leonard	*The New Prometheans*
Diana Panchenko	*The Inevitable*
Jean-Yves Le Gallou	*The Propaganda Society*
Stephen Pax Leonard	*The Ideology of Failure* *Travels in Cultural Nihilism*
William S. Lind	*Reforging Excalibur* *Retroculture*
Pentti Linkola	*Can Life Prevail?*
Giorgio Locchi	*Definitions*
H. P. Lovecraft	*The Conservative*
Norman Lowell	*Imperium Europa*
Richard Lynn	*Sex Differences in Intelligence* *A Tribute to Helmut Nyborg* (ed.)
John MacLugash	*The Return of the Solar King*
Charles Maurras	*The Future of the Intelligentsia & For a French Awakening*
Graeme Maxton	*The Follies of the Western Mind*
John Harmon McElroy	*Agitprop in America*
Michael O'Meara	*Guillaume Faye and the Battle of Europe* *New Culture, New Right*
Michael Millerman	*Beginning with Heidegger*
Dmitry Moiseev	*The Philosophy of Italian Fascism*
Maurice Muret	*The Greatness of Elites*
Brian Anse Patrick	*The NRA and the Media* *Rise of the Anti-Media* *The Ten Commandments of Propaganda* *Zombology*
Tito Perdue	*The Bent Pyramid* *Journey to a Location* *Lee* *Morning Crafts* *Philip* *The Sweet-Scented Manuscript* *William's House* (vol. 1–4)
John K. Press	*The True West vs the Zombie Apocalypse*
Raido	*A Handbook of Traditional Living* (vol. 1–2)
P R Reddall	*Towards Awakening*
Claire Rae Randall	*The War on Gender*
Steven J. Rosen	*The Agni and the Ecstasy* *The Jedi in the Lotus*
Nicholas Rooney	*Talking to the Wolf*

OTHER BOOKS PUBLISHED BY ARKTOS

Richard Rudgley	*Barbarians* *Essential Substances* *Wildest Dreams*
Ernst von Salomon	*It Cannot Be Stormed* *The Outlaws*
Werner Sombart	*Traders and Heroes*
Piero San Giorgio	*Giuseppe* *Survive the Economic Collapse* *Surviving the Next Catastrophe*
Sri Sri Ravi Shankar	*Celebrating Silence* *Know Your Child* *Management Mantras* *Patanjali Yoga Sutras* *Secrets of Relationships*
Oswald Spengler	*The Decline of the West* *Man and Technics*
Richard Storey	*The Uniqueness of Western Law*
J. R. Sommer	*The Electric Will* *The New Colossus*
Tomislav Sunic	*Against Democracy and Equality* *Homo Americanus* *Postmortem Report* *Titans are in Town*
Askr Svarte	*Gods in the Abyss*
Hans-Jürgen Syberberg	*On the Fortunes and Misfortunes of Art in Post-War Germany*
Abir Taha	*Defining Terrorism* *The Epic of Arya* (2nd ed.) *Nietzsche is Coming God, or the Redemption of the Divine* *Verses of Light*
Jean Thiriart	*Europe: An Empire of 400 Million*
Bal Gangadhar Tilak	*The Arctic Home in the Vedas*
Bostian Marco Turk	*War in the Name of Peace*
Dominique Venner	*Ernst Jünger: A Different European Destiny* *For a Positive Critique* *The Shock of History*
Hans Vogel	*How Europe Became American*
Tim Vorgens	*Legitimate Preference*
Markus Willinger	*A Europe of Nations* *Generation Identity*
Alexander Wolfheze	*Alba Rosa* *Globus Horribilis* *Rupes Nigra*

www.ingramcontent.com/pod-product-compliance
Lightning Source LLC
LaVergne TN
LVHW091130080826
845145LV00008B/2111
* 9 7 8 1 9 1 8 4 1 8 1 7 0 *